# MEMORIES
# of Buenos Aires

A VOLUME IN THE SERIES

**Public History in Historical Perspective**

Edited by Marla R. Miller

# MEMORIES of Buenos Aires

## SIGNS OF STATE TERRORISM IN ARGENTINA

Edited with an Introduction by Max Page

Epilogue by Ilan Stavans

Translated by Karen Robert

*with assistance from Jonathan Soria*

UNIVERSITY OF MASSACHUSETTS PRESS

AMHERST & BOSTON

memoria abierta

Asamblea Permanente por los Derechos Humanos
Centro de Estudios Legales y Sociales
Comisión de Homenaje a las Víctimas de Vesubio y Protobanco
Familiares de Desaparecidos y Detenidos por Razones Políticas
Fundación Memoria Histórica y Social Argentina
Madres de Plaza de Mayo Línea Fundadora

Printed in China
ISBN 978-1-62534-010-8

Originally published as *Memorias en la ciudad: señales del terrorismo de estado en Buenos Aires*, © Memoria Abierta, 2009

SPANISH EDITION

*Production:* Memoria Abierta
*General director of the book:* Patricia Tappatá de Valdez
*Coordinator:* Gonzalo Conte
*Texts:* Pablo Luzuriaga, Natalia Paleo, Soledad Nasif, Jonathan Soria, and Javier Borelli.
*Research and selection of sources:* Julia Rosemberg, Silvina Segundo, and Cecilia Gaitán
*Photographs:* Natalia Paleo, Gonzalo Conte, Soledad Nasif
*Revision of texts:* Bella Friszman e Ilda Iburrusteta de Micucci
*Editorial revision:* Roberto Pittaluga
*Graphic design:* Estudio Punto & Coma (www.puntoycomadg.com.ar)

*Memorias en la ciudad* and translation supported by the Netherlands Embassy in Argentina and by the Argentine Ministry of Foreign Affairs.

Koninkrijk der Nederlanden
Embajada del Reino de los Países Bajos

Ministerio de Relaciones Exteriores y Culto
República Argentina

Publication of this book and other titles in the series Public History in Historical Perspective is supported by the Office of the Dean, College of Humanities and Fine Arts, University of Massachusetts Amherst.

Library of Congress Cataloging-in-Publication Data
Memorias en la ciudad. English
Memories of Buenos Aires : signs of state terrorism in Argentina / edited with an introduction by Max Page ; epilogue by Ilan Stavans ; translated by Karen Robert with assistance by Jonathan Soria.
pages cm. — (Public history in historical perspective)
Includes bibliographical references and index.
ISBN 978-1-62534-010-8 (pbk. : alk. paper)
1. State-sponsored terrorism—Argentina—Buenos Aires—History—20th century.
2. Buenos Aires (Argentina)—Guidebooks.
3. Disappeared persons—Monuments—Argentina—Buenos Aires—Guidebooks.
4. Victims of state-sponsored terrorism—Monuments—Argentina—Buenos Aires—Guidebooks.
5. Memorials—Argentina—Buenos Aires—Guidebooks.
I. Page, Max, editor. II. Memoria Abierta (Organization) III. Title.
HV6322.3.A7M46613 2013
363.3250982'11—dc23

2013018309

British Library Cataloguing-in-Publication Data
A catalogue record for this book is available from the British Library.

**Cover:** Carmen Aguiar de Lapacó, Madre de Plaza de Mayo, in the Parque de la Memoria. September 19, 2008. *Photo: Natalia Paleo.*

# Contents

# Introduction to the English-Language Edition

## The Arc of Memory and the Arc of Justice

MAX PAGE

The former torture centers of Buenos Aires display a rarefied elegance. Old military schools, rusticated neoclassical police stations, Gothic churches, French-inspired mansions, Spanish colonial *estancias:* state terrorism in the 1970s took place in the aged splendor of what is often called the "Paris of South America." At the edge of the Spanish Empire, Buenos Aires was slow to win the role of capital of the new nation (it celebrated its 200th anniversary in 2010) and slow even to consolidate its own boundaries. So too was the system of repression in the 1970s dispersed, based in neighborhoods across the city and nation. The so-called Guerra Sucia or "Dirty War" was no war between equal armies but rather an everyday system of state terror.

A Fulbright Fellowship in 2009 took me to Buenos Aires and into the middle of a long-delayed national reckoning with the state terrorism, variously called the last dictatorship, the "Dirty War," or, in the words of the dictators who ruled between 1976 and 1983, the Process for National Reorganization of 1976 to 1983—the state-sponsored, U.S.-supported, internal war of repression, torture, and murder of those a part of or perceived to be a part of a left-wing revolutionary movement. I visited the Clandestine Detention Centers as well as official and neighborhood memorials to the *desaparecidos*, or disappeared, and interviewed human rights activists, museum officials, memorial designers, and artists obsessed with creatively keeping the legacy of that time in the public eye.

Argentina was the leader of a continent-wide wave of state terrorism: more paranoid about left-wing movements and more committed and organized in its repressive policies than other nations, inspiring and teaching the neighboring countries linked together by Operation Condor, a campaign of terror by right-wing dictatorships against perceived threats from the communist Left. Participant nations in Plan Condor—Argentina, Paraguay, Chile, Uruguay, Bolivia, and Brazil—were aided by the United States. The regime of Carlos Menem, the president of Argentina beginning in 1989, put an end to the persecution of those involved in torture and insisted on closure through erasure. Indeed, he proposed that sites related to the dictatorship, for example, the ESMA detention center, be razed as acts of "national reconciliation." The election of Nestor Kirchner as president in 2003 reopened the debate over the era of state terrorism and how it should be remembered. Kirchner, whose wife, Cristina Fernández de Kirchner, succeeded him as president (he died in October 2010) and was elected to a second term in 2011, was much more sympathetic to the victims and their memories and built political support on the left in part by demanding new accountability of the perpetrators and new respect for the victims and their families.

Today, Argentina is at the vanguard of the struggle over how to preserve sites, remember that time, and honor the victims. Thirty-five years after it was turned into a detention center, the main building at ESMA is slowly being opened to the public, while the debate over the larger site continues, seemingly endlessly. Just a mile east is the vast Parque de la Memoria (Park of Memory), the national memorial to the desaparecidos. And everywhere in Buenos Aires are popular, grassroots memorials and public art installations, flourishing on the sidewalks and walls across the sprawling city. Those memorial interventions into the landscape of the city hold powerful lessons for other nations wrestling with their own painful pasts.

• • •

In a collection of lectures titled *Seven Nights,* the Argentine writer Jorge Luis Borges highlighted a peculiar paradox of someone learning a new language: their ignorance makes these learners especially sensitive to the resonances of each word. Borges wrote that "language is an aesthetic creation. . . . A proof is that when we study a language, when we are obliged to see the words up close, we experience them as beautiful or not. Studying a language, one sees the words with a magnifying glass." Recounting a group of students, himself included, who were learning Anglo-Saxon, he noted that "what always happens, when one studies a language, happened. Each one of the words stood out as though it had been carved, as though it were a talisman." The visitor to a new language, paradoxically, has the capacity to connect to the nuances of a language in ways native speakers have often lost. A neophyte to Spanish, I was able to take note that the word we in English use for something "really deep"—profound—comes from the word meaning deep in the physical sense (*profundus*)—as, in Spanish, a "lago profundo," a deep lake.

I think something similar happens to a visitor to a new city. In our eagerness to learn the ways of the city and connect it to past travels and our home, we are alive to every detail, even as we are oblivious to the many layers of experience that the inhabitant knows deep within herself, which operates almost like instinct. As I explored Buenos Aires, all my senses were in peak form, absorbing and filtering the uniqueness of the city.

But as much as was revealed and as much as can be gleaned from seeing, listening, smelling, so much cannot be known. The great events of the past are narrated in buildings and monuments or in the words of tour guides. But the horrific events are often rendered mute in the landscape of the city, unless they are given a voice. That voice is made through the intentional work of art or craft in the physical environment of the city.

In other words, to explore in the spaces of the city the public memory of that awful time, *porteños* and visitors alike need a guide. Traditional guidebooks I had: four guides to Buenos Aires, soon to be supplemented by additional books acquired on my walks through the city and its glorious bookstores. But what was missing—for me and for human rights activists—was a guide to the memory of the desaparecidos and to the memory of state terrorism, which tore this society apart in the 1970s and 1980s and which to this day remains in the minds of many people the most horrible episode of a century that experienced many coups, assassinations, and ill-conceived wars.

I didn't have the guidebook I needed, until one day late in September 2009, when I met Patricia Tappatá de Valdez, at that time head of Memoria Abierta, the leading human rights organization in Argentina, at a conference it sponsored to celebrate the publication of *Memorias en la Ciudad: Señales del Terrorismo de Estado en Buenos Aires* (Memories in the City: Signs of State Terrorism in Buenos Aires). Dozens of books have been written about this era in South American history, but there has never been anything like *Memorias en la Ciudad.* It immediately caught my attention: it was a beautifully executed history and guide to sites and memorials related to the era of state terrorism. While I was initially drawn to grand public obelisks and fountains, *Memorias en la Ciudad* steered me to neighborhood memorials, such as *baldosas* (street tiles) that mark the homes from which people were forcibly removed, never to be seen again. Where I looked up and saw a magnificent pile worthy of a place along the Champs-Elysées, *Memorias en la Ciudad* revealed a Clandestine Detention Center where hundreds had been incarcerated. There are dozens of such places all across Buenos Aires, as documented in the book. *Memorias en la Ciudad* instantly became my guidebook to the history of that time and to the history of continuing attempts over the past thirty years to remember and interpret that horrific era. The book became, very simply, my guidebook to the city, the book without which I never left home. It essentially remapped Buenos Aires for me and will do the same, I believe, for many other English-speaking visitors and scholars.

One of the most compelling aspects of this book is that it eliminates the line between historic site and memorial site. The book is organized geographically, revealing, neighborhood by neighborhood, the network of places related to the system of repression. But it identifies both the spaces where state terrorism was executed and the communal memorials to that era. The book is therefore a record of three decades of approaches to public history and historic preservation, a history of the events of the dictatorship but also of the echoes of response by citizen activists. We begin in 1977, less than a year after the coup, at the Plaza de Mayo, where the Madres de Plaza de Mayo (the Mothers of the Plaza de Mayo) began what is the longest running act of defiant memory making, marching in circles in front of the presidential palace, the Casa Rosada, their children's diapers tied to their heads like kerchiefs. The book charts the varied memorial responses, all the way up to 2009 and the opening of the national memorial to the disappeared.

This book is, then, not only a map but also a history of memorial efforts, not particular simply to Argentina but to other nations that have contended with their own difficult pasts. Indeed, *Memorias en la Ciudad* is a record of an international trade in memorial ideas over the past three decades. The baldosas, those tiles which mark with great simplicity the homes of those who were disappeared, were inspired by Gunter Demnig's *stolpersteine* ("stumbling blocks"), placed, at first illegally and with little ceremony, in front of the homes where Jews of the Nazi era once lived. And the national memory to the disappeared, with its wall of names, was impossible to conceive without Maya Lin's Vietnam Veterans Memorial in Washington, D.C. Argentina's citizens and artists have taken these ideas and made them their own. They have become exporters of their own unique approaches, such as the ubiquitous graffiti and murals. Buenos Aires is a city in which every wall is considered an artistic canvas or a political chat board. This book is a record of memorials that will be visible for years as well as of those that will disappear tomorrow. Spray-painted images of a man's cap, the symbol of Jorge Julio López, who disappeared after testifying against torturers, appear and then are covered over. Trees lining the Avenida San Juan, planted there to mark the disappeared of that neighborhood, are dying in the inhospitable environment of a busy road. But the baldosas and the national memorial and the hundreds of markers in schools and stores and theaters may remain for decades. By providing a map not only of Argentina's efforts to remember the era of state terrorism, but also of the universal attempts to hold on to the memory of victims and of a state that saw in its own citizens a threat, this book is invaluable.

Argentina is "supremely enigmatic," writes the historian Marguerite Feitlowitz in her magisterial *Lexicon of Terror*. A nation of enormous wealth, high literacy, and enormous scientific and industrial achievement, Argentina has had, through much of the twentieth century, a propensity toward "self-destruction," she writes, in the form of violent coups, the most pronounced symptom of an apparent aversion to democracy. But in its citizens' quest to remember, recall, warn, and demand, Argentina and Buenos Aires are a model of the power of public history. Just as the dictators predicted in the 1970s, Argentina has been the vanguard of the left, if not in the ways the regimes of the 1970s predicted. Argentina's artists and human rights activists, family members of the disappeared, and graffiti muralists have forced their country to confront the era of state terrorism, and in doing so they have inspired a similar process in Chile, Uruguay, Guatemala, and Brazil.

• • •

In a postscript to Whigs and Hunters, his remarkable study of the implementation of the Black Act in eighteenth-century England as an attempt to control the rural poor, the great historian of the working class E. P. Thompson made what appears to be a complete about-face in his argument. After maintaining for over four hundred pages that the law and the courts had conspired to control and punish the poor in Great Britain and that, more universally, the law was a tool enabling the ruling classes to oppress the poor, Thompson sought to rescue the principle of the rule of law for the political left. "The law," he wrote,

> in its forms and traditions, entailed principles of equity and universality which, perforce, had to be extended to all sorts and degrees of men. What had been devised by men of property as a defence against arbitrary power could be turned into service as an apologia for property in the face of the propertyless.
>
> The rule of law itself, imposing of effective inhibitions upon power and the defence of the citizen from power's all-intrusive claims, seems to me to be an unqualified human good. To deny or belittle this good is, in this dangerous century when the resources and pretentions of power continue to enlarge, a desperate error of intellectual abstraction.

I thought of Thompson's emotional plea in May 2011 as I sat behind a glass wall in a dingy courtroom in the basement of a nondescript government building near the new port of Buenos Aires. While traveling with a group of students and faculty, I had read that one of the hearings of the newly launched trials against members of the dictatorship and military would be taking place while we were there. I ventured down past the elegant Plaza San Martin, the English Tower, the decrepit, once-grand train stations to a drab complex of bureaucratic warehouses on the edge of the city's port.

The proceeding was quite boring, as a healthy, democratic judicial system should be. The wheels of justice do not spin—that sounds far too efficient and energetic. Rather, they roll forward, as if in an endless fall, again and again, around and around. In the courtroom people testified, the stenographer recorded, family members listened, the accused sat expressionless. The experience of the trial was, on its face, unexciting, endless, and frustratingly inconclusive.

At the very end of 2009, twenty-six years after the dictatorship, some of the key leaders of the military dictatorship were finally forced to appear before a judge or were brought before the court again after having been pardoned. In the spring of 2012, with the conviction of Jorge Videla, the dictator who led the coup in 1976, as well as of other leaders and military officials who conspired to steal some five hundred children from their imprisoned mothers, there was a sense that closure might be more imminent in Argentina than ever before. None of it is final, and certainly not for the families whose loved ones remain unidentified, simply disappeared. (There is a minority but strongly held view that there can be no closure until those on the left who killed and tortured their enemies are also brought to justice. *Memorias en la Ciudad* is unapologetically focused on acts of state terrorism, not on the crimes of guerrilla groups or individuals.) But the conviction of the most notorious perpetrators was enough for one of the stolen children,

Victoria Montenegro, who learned of her true identity thirty years after being kidnapped, to declare that "with this verdict we are repairing what happened."

The act of repair—"making one whole," as the law frequently declares—is often seen as the work of the courts. In the debates over public history and the difficulty of remembering the difficult pasts of nations and communities, we often separate public memory from procedural justice. Prosecutions, or truth commissions, must do their work to bring the guilty to justice, while artists and community members must remember and recall, bringing healing to a family or community. Artists and activists, we commonly understand, create baldosas and national memorials as a way of recalling the past and coming to terms with it. Porteños are remembering their loved ones and also bearing witness to the evil perpetrated by their political leaders, sometimes with citizens' silent complicity. The work of public art and memorialization is to peer into the past for solace and in order to warn the future.

But *Memorias en la Ciudad* suggests something different. What struck me as I walked the streets of Buenos Aires with this book in hand is how crucial the artistic efforts to expand public memory were in creating the conditions for procedural justice in the present. The post-dicatorship-era political leaders—the democratically elected Raúl Alfonsín and the conservative Menem—worked to move beyond legal justice in order to achieve national reconciliation, Alfonsín fearing another coup and Menem defending his allies. Alfonsín imposed a "full stop" on judicial trials after launching one of the most far-reaching investigations into the era of state terrorism, the National Commission on the Dissappearance of Persons (Nunca Más commission). Menem rescinded many of the convictions, rehabilitated many of the perpetrators, and moved forward with many of the economic policies of the dictatorship, including a disastrous privatization and deregulation plan which brought Argentina to bankruptcy at the beginning of the twenty-first century.

With the judicial system hijacked, it was up to grassroots organizations to keep up the drumbeat for real justice. The memorial interventions in this book were not simply looking backward or far into the future. They were political acts, keeping alive the fact that there would be no closure until the perpetrators, many of whom were living in wealth in Buenos Aires's northern suburbs, had been punished in a court of law. When that day came, there was a sense that the wall had been climbed, and Argentinians could look out to a world beyond these crimes and victims. The punishment of the guilty and the prospect of a new Argentina were made possible by the memorial efforts of grassroots activists over the course of three decades. They redeemed the rule of law and the honor of the nation from those who hysterically and violently, methodically and ideologically murdered thousands.

To this day I keep my courtroom ticket from that day in my wallet. It is nothing but a piece of paper with some xeroxed signature on it, the squiggled mark of a bureaucrat—so very different from the inventive, creative, often brightly colored memorials to the desaparecidos. It is, however, the most important token—call it a memorial—I could bring back from Buenos Aires. The goal of the artists and activists who painted the murals, preserved the detention centers, and designed the memorials goes far beyond punitive justice. They also worked to remember their loved ones and to remind the Argentina of today and of the future of its violent past. In addition, they worked so that the historical record would be set right. But Memoria Abierta, H.I.J.O.S., and the Madres de Plaza de Mayo also hoped and expected to achieve a more traditional form of justice: bringing the perpetrators to face their accusers and be punished for their crimes against society and humanity.

# Introduction

This book offers the reader a set of entry points through which to explore the city of Buenos Aires in a reflective manner, whether as a full-time resident or as a visitor. We are forced to live in a present moment drained of history as we move through our daily trips to work and school, our weekend itineraries, and the routes set by shopping malls and cultural centers, and that same forgetful impulse is rapidly stripping places of their historical and social reality. This book proposes a different kind of urban itinerary. It seeks to reveal the suppressed history buried in every location where the last military dictatorship focused its reign of terror, in order to transform these hidden spaces into outlets for remembrance.

Argentina lived through a period of widespread popular mobilization in the late 1960s and early 1970s, followed by years of extreme violence. Even before the military imposed its system of state terror, the country saw the emergence of the Triple A (Argentine Anticommunist Alliance), a paramilitary group that used spectacular public acts of violence to sow paralyzing fear in Buenos Aires and many other Argentine cities. The bodies of murdered political and trade union leaders appeared in the streets, and a magazine displayed in the city's newsstands even announced killings in advance; yet these crimes went unpunished. The military dictatorship later extended this terror through mass arrests and raids carried out in the streets and in public and private institutions. Most detainees became victims of the sinister practice of disappearance.

Two separate realities thus coexisted in Buenos Aires, a great city that has been widely praised and admired. The city presented a facade of normality or even joyful triumph during the festivities surrounding the World Cup of 1978. Yet this image hid another reality where appalling kidnapping raids against homes and workplaces punctuated the daily rhythms of citizens' lives. This blending of the visible and the invisible sustained the dictatorship's legal and bureaucratic order, as well as its illegal repressive machinery. The ultimate goal was to use any means necessary to eliminate all opposition to the military junta's absolute power.

Though a large segment of the population justified their indifference toward this terror by feigning ignorance, research has proven that information about the repression circulated widely through sometimes-veiled references in the press and through shadowy and terrifying rumors. The depth of the terror could also be detected through telling changes in the behavior of individuals, groups, and institutions. Only recently has a debate emerged about this idea of a society impassive and oblivious to the horrors occurring in its midst. One way to deepen reflection on these issues is to examine the spaces and physical markers that speak to this period in the city's history.

Argentina has now lived through more than thirty years of democracy. Survivors of kidnapping, disappearance, and torture began recording testimonies of their experiences even before the military lost power in 1983. Many statements came to light in 1984 through the investigation of the National Commission on the Disappearance of Persons (CONADEP), and in 1985 during the trial of the military leadership. These advances were stalled, however, by the so-called impunity laws enacted in the late 1980s. First, President Raúl Alfonsín passed the Full Stop and Due Obedience laws to limit the scope of the human rights trials. Then, in 1989, newly elected president Carlos Menem overturned the judicial process when he pardoned and released all those who had been convicted of human rights crimes. Human rights organizations and lawyers have struggled for decades to bring to justice those responsible for the worst human rights violations. Their work has involved painstaking research and an ongoing effort to collect and listen to the stories of witnesses and survivors, testimonies that include descriptions of buildings and other enclosed spaces.

Only later did the idea emerge that these physical places themselves might serve to deepen understanding about the past, or that they could even be put to public use. Several factors helped bring about this realization. Survivors and human rights organizations began to focus their own work on these spaces, and Argentina's political climate also changed. Furthermore, the military and police organizations that controlled the infrastructure left by the dictatorship gradually lost their absolute power, and the political will emerged to wrest control of these spaces and put them to public use. With the passing of time, it also became possible to imagine reclaiming these spaces that had borne witness to such terrible acts of horror.

A changing international context has also fostered these new initiatives to open up sites of memory or create museums connected to these sites, both in Argentina and elsewhere. In particular, a growing international consensus has emerged around the idea that states have an obligation to compensate victims and society at large for damages and sufferings inflicted in the past, whether such compensation takes material or symbolic form. Commemorative spaces and monuments thus fulfill two functions: they pay homage to victims and recognize their dignity, while also sustaining collective memory.

Urban landscapes condense layers upon layers of memories, though these may be blurred by the fast pace of urban life. Buildings, street corners, paving stones, and the names of squares and streets serve their own practical purposes while also indicating absences or attempting to communicate messages from the past. Multiple and diverse elements converge in the space of the city; its streets reveal individual stories, collective projects, and private and public tragedies.

Our aim here is to identify the traces left by state terrorism in the city of Buenos Aires. While some are visible, others can be deciphered only through careful interpretation. In the city's most important political space, the Plaza de Mayo, headscarves painted on the paving stones surrounding the central monument (the Pirámide de Mayo) bear witness to the resistance marches led by the women who came to be known as the Mothers of the Plaza de Mayo (Madres de Plaza de Mayo). Elsewhere, the vestiges of repressive violence can be read in dozens of buildings that functioned as secret detention centers. Finally, the visitor walking through any of the city's neighborhoods may suddenly come across a paving stone marking the place where a victim of disappearance once lived, worked, or was politically active.

Such public markers on streets, public spaces, or buildings associated with particular historical events have usually originated with activists and human rights organizations who have later sought to formalize them and ensure their preservation through government endorsement. Other commemorative spaces and markers pay homage to individual and collective political activism from the past, whether or not their locations bear a direct material link to the historical events in question. Their creators—survivors, fellow political activists, family members, and civil society groups—share a common purpose; they wish to leave a clear and visible public monument to the disappeared that will long outlive their own efforts to keep such memories alive.

Memoria Abierta has developed a detailed survey of Clandestine Detention Centers and other urban spaces linked to state terrorism through its "Topography of Memory" project. Our goal is to support research and public education by focusing on the spatial deployment of state terrorism. Drawing on careful analysis of documents and personal testimony, we have sought to reveal the military's territorial mechanisms of repression through a variety of techniques: illustrations of buildings and their functions, models, animations, and an interactive map.

Our mission is to influence political culture and guard against all forms of authoritarianism by fostering social memory. To this end, we encourage reflection and debate through collaboration with groups, institutions, and the state. We develop educational tools, materials, and traveling exhibitions that reconstruct past events in order to raise awareness and promote critical reflection on the connections between past and present.

Research for this book has drawn on multiple sources about hundreds of separate locations in Buenos Aires, including materials from our own archive, such as journals, bulletins, magazines, and invitations to inaugurations. Other sources used to locate sites include legislative records, official websites of different groups and institutions, and direct communications with organizations that also work in the area of social memory. We photographed each site and, on some occasions, interviewed the people who had helped to designate it or continue to work or study there today.

We have tried to be exhaustive in cataloguing every site in Buenos Aires with a connection to state terrorism, though we know that some omissions remain. Neighborhood associations, government offices, and human rights organizations designate new commemorative sites on almost a weekly or monthly basis. Moreover, the sheer size of the capital city, whose greater metropolitan area contains roughly one-third of the nation's population, makes comprehensive survey virtually impossible. Countless more private and semiprivate commemorative markers undoubtedly bear witness to the years of violence.

The book divides the city of Buenos Aires into nine sectors encompassing the city's forty-eight neighborhoods. Each chapter begins with a title page containing a map of the sector's neighborhoods, principal avenues and streets, transportation links and green spaces, and the exact location of each site. It then lists the different commemorative sites or markers that can be found in these neighborhoods: monuments, sculptures, plaques, paving stones, stencils, and murals. It also enumerates locations bearing commemorative names, including classrooms, grandstands, sports facilities, auditoria, public squares, gardens, cultural centers, and clinics. We have included extra descriptive detail and photographs for certain sites in each sector.

Crucial information was lacking for many of the sites in question. Many commemorative markers point to sites in the city without leaving a record of the events being commemorated or the story of those being honored. Information was sometimes scarce or nonexistent, and people were often unaware of a plaque on the side of a building that may have been hidden from view by plants, signs, or political posters, or may even have been removed during renovations. At times we even found commemorative markers that had been forgotten by the institutions that had created them. The same occurred with sites attached to public banks, administrative buildings, and universities; we faced bureaucratic challenges when trying to photograph these commemorative markers and when their initiators had forgotten or lacked information about their origins.

Once the physical survey was complete, we used archival sources to add more information. Our own collections provided essential sources such as the archives of individual human rights organizations that appear in Memoria Abierta's online catalogue. The Photographic and Audiovisual Archives included photographs and film footage depicting commemorative events and significant moments in the fight for truth and justice. The more than 640 interviews in the Oral Archive allowed us to restore voice and testimony to the stories recounted in this book.

We chose to emphasize people—victims, witnesses, and protagonists—when describing locations and commemorative plaques. Here again the documentary record was essential to achieving accuracy. Our commitment to this investigation only deepened after we consulted the extremely valuable records of the National Commission on the Disappearance of Persons (CONADEP), held in the National Memory Archive. Yet we needed other sources to map out the full strategy and scope of the repression in terms of both its territorial reach and its numbers of victims. We therefore consulted the records of the former federal prosecutor Luis Moreno Ocampo, who played a leading role in the trials against the military junta in 1985. The Luis Moreno Ocampo – Fiscalía (Cámara Federal) collection, organized and digitized by Memoria Abierta, provided corroborating data on many places and events.

Researchers specializing in this area know how difficult it is to consult public archives to deepen stories and confirm specific versions of past events. We would like to remind readers once again that the key accounts of what happened in Argentina have come from victims and their families and more recently from legal investigations. Information from those responsible for planning and executing the repression is virtually nonexistent. While a handful of provincial police archives have been located and declassified, no Armed Forces records have been found.

This book covers a large number of locations: 240 in all. We have included sites designated with a plaque, a sign, or a name and have provided links to related topics or locations in the descriptions. We hope that this cross-referencing contributes to a deepened understanding of the last dictatorship's most important features.

In Buenos Aires, as in the rest of the country, people were kidnapped from their homes or from the street by day or by night. They were taken to Clandestine Detention Centers and illegal temporary holding sites scattered across many neighborhoods. Illegal detentions, tortures, and murders were carried out inside these buildings in the midst of the daily hubbub of city life, right next to workplaces and family homes. They took place inside a house in the heart of the residential neighborhood of Caballito, in the Navy School of Mechanics on one of the city's main thoroughfares, inside an auto repair shop (Orletti), in a centrally located police facility (Coordinación Federal), in a garage (Azopardo) housed in the same building where people have until recently applied for their national identity cards, in a house in the neighborhood of Montserrat, in a building later demolished to make way for a freeway (Club Atlético), and in a former tramway station near Parque Avellaneda (El Olimpo). Other victims of detention and disappearance were held captive inside dozens of police stations, on Navy ships, in private homes, in hospitals, and in public buildings.

The disappeared were kept in some of these sites for years, in others for a matter of hours. Some of the victims were later moved to airplanes that dropped them into the Rio de la Plata. One group was taken to an abandoned area and shot from behind, their corpses later blown apart with dynamite.

We have opted not to distinguish between permanent and temporary detention centers, though it is important to specify each location's function in order to understand the logic and consequences of state terrorism,. A number of human rights organizations and state agencies are currently working to draw up categories to classify the different sites. Yet we have decided to use the valuable testimony of survivors to describe what life was like in all those spaces and the ways in which terror radiated outward from them across the city.

The book's cover bears a photograph of the Rio de la Plata. This river, like the Plaza de Mayo, has been part of our history since the city's founding. In recent years it has become a space for remembering the disappeared, many of whom were thrown into its waters in order to erase all traces of their bodies, their identities, and their political projects. Situated along the river, the Park of Memory contains a huge stone monument inscribed with the names of the detained and disappeared victims whose kidnappings have been reported.

Commemorative events for the missing have proliferated over the last few years. The names of the disappeared are publicly inscribed in many ways: through government resolutions to name streets, trees, and parks; institutional decisions to dedicate classrooms, auditoria, stadiums, sports facilities, and plaques; and popular initiatives to rename public squares or streets, or to dedicate engraved paving stones.

From the founding of our organization we have aimed to use physical spaces—whether those employed by state terror or those created to pay homage to victims—as vehicles for transmitting the past and sharing the conflicting memories they embody. This dynamic process is exemplified in the large number of spaces already identified and the variety of groups and institutions involved in their dedication. Important current political debates and tensions over meaning give shape to memory, inspiring efforts to represent publicly the lives of the people evoked and explore what those lives meant to the recent past.

We set out to "make visible" places considered significant to the development of public memory in Buenos Aires and in the rest of the country. In 2002 Memoria Abierta published a booklet describing some representative sites from the dictatorship period in Buenos Aires. In 2004 we drew up a fuller guided tour linking these and many more sites. We believe that the current volume offers a new step toward the same goal.

Human rights groups and government authorities charged with policies of human rights and memory have recently emphasized the task of studying and recovering sites of repression, and the relevance of such work is no longer called into question. However, simply opening a site offers no guarantee that it will effectively transmit the truth of the past to a public unfamiliar with this history or unaccustomed to the activities of human rights organizations. The site's significance will depend on the organizers' ability to gather multiple memories offered by survivors and researchers and represent these collective memories effectively and faithfully. It will then be up to the public to assimilate the experience into their own personal histories.

Family members of those disappeared and murdered by the last dictatorship assisted in the book's preparation in the hope that the places identified here would not only serve as testaments to horror but also foster the transmission of memory. We wish to recognize the courage and strength they showed by daring to recall and record painful descriptions of the places where their loved ones suffered. They know that this work will help to forge a different future for the citizens of Argentina.

This book was made possible thanks to financial support from the government of the Netherlands, which is carrying out an active human rights policy through its Ministry of Foreign Affairs. Their trust in Memoria Abierta's initiatives and our ongoing dialogue about common concerns stimulated our research and preparation of the manuscript. The support and enthusiasm shown by Ambassador Henk J. W. Soeters and the clarity and perseverance of Jobien Hekking, political secretary from 2005 to 2008, helped us get to where we are today.

At Memoria Abierta we regularly say that memory is a collective effort because it requires us to connect different pieces of a puzzle and tie together different documents, perspectives, and outlooks. The preparation of this book was no exception: it too involved joining scattered and hidden fragments of information. Over the past few months many people have helped by listening to our doubts and challenges, suggesting new avenues of research, providing valuable information, and sharing their own unique knowledge and experience of events as they read over our texts. Though it may sound like a cliché, it must be added that while their comments have enriched this book, they bear no responsibility for any errors it may contain. We thank you so much once again for your commitment and generosity.

*Buenos Aires, July 2009*

# How to Use This Book

## SECTORS AND MAPS

We have decided to organize this book into nine sectors covering the city's different neighborhoods. The main map of the city, which appears inside the front cover, indicates each of these sectors by color as well as by references to all of the sites described. A detail map of each sector appears on the title page of its corresponding chapter.

## SOURCES

Most of the sources used in the research for this book come from the archives of Memoria Abierta. The following abbreviations indicate the specific collections to which each source belongs:

**AO** (Archivo Oral): Oral Archive of Memoria Abierta. Each interview is identified by the letters AO followed by its catalogue number within the Oral Archive.

**FLMO** (Fondo Luis Moreno Ocampo): Luis Moreno Ocampo Collection, which contains the documentation used in the Trial of the Military Juntas.

**AA** (Archivo Audiovisual): Audiovisual Archive.

**FMA** (Fondo Memoria Abierta): Memoria Abierta Collection.

All sources are available for public consultation in the offices of Memoria Abierta.

## ABBREVIATIONS

The following abbreviations appear in the maps and in some of the texts:

**AV:** Avenida (Avenue)

**BV:** Bulevar (Boulevard)

**CDC:** Clandestine Detention Center

**CNEL:** Coronel (Colonel)

**EST:** Estación (Station)

**FCDFS:** Ferrocarril Domingo Faustino Sarmiento (Domingo Faustino Sarmiento Railway)

**FCGBM:** Ferrocarril General Bartolomé Mitre (General Bartolomé Mitre Railway)

**FCGMB:** Ferrocarril General Manuel Belgrano (General Manuel Belgrano Railway)

**FCGU:** Ferrocarril General Urquiza (General Urquiza Railway)

**GRAL:** General

**PTE:** Presidente

**PZA:** Plaza (Square)

**TTE:** Teniente (Lieutenant)

*Words followed by an asterisk in the text are listed in the glossary beginning on page 261.*

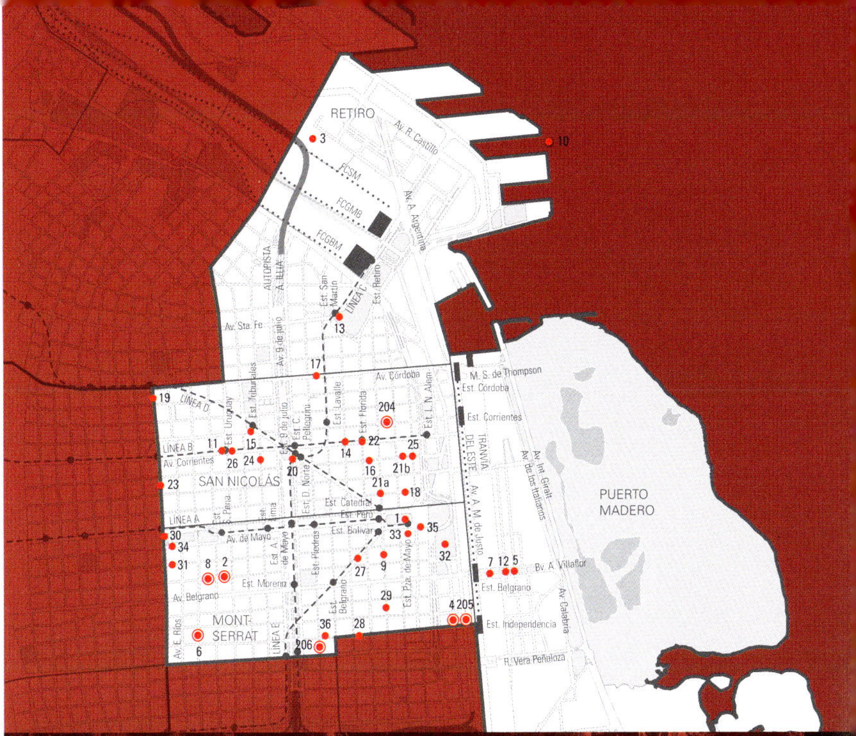

# SECTOR 1

MONTSERRAT, PUERTO MADERO, RETIRO, AND SAN NICOLÁS

# 1. **Plaza de Mayo**

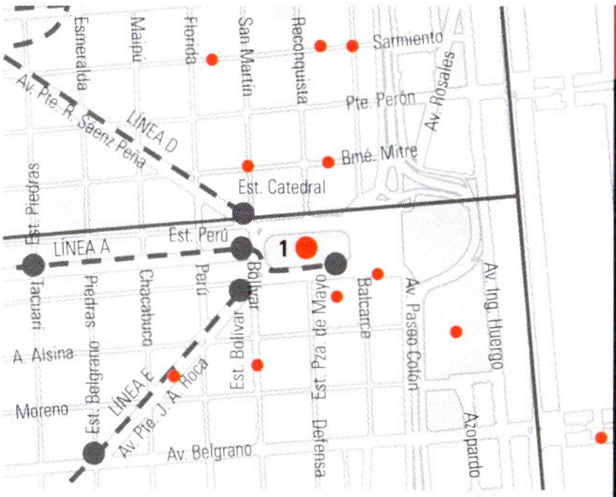


**LOCATION:** BETWEEN AV. RIVADAVIA, HIPÓLITO YRIGOYEN, BOLÍVAR, AND BALCARCE
**TRANSPORTATION:** SUBWAY STATIONS: PLAZA DE MAYO (A LINE), CATEDRAL (D LINE), BOLÍVAR (E LINE), PERÚ (E LINE). BUSES: 6, 7, 9, 10, 17, 22, 24, 26, 28, 29, 45, 50, 59, 64, 67, 70, 74, 86, 91, 98, 105, 111, 126, 152.

The Plaza de Mayo is the public space par excellence in which Argentina's collective memories, conflicts, and disputes all converge. In the midst of the military dictatorship, the mothers of the disappeared defied the dictates of state terrorism and took over this site, restoring it to its function as a spatial metaphor for politics and freedom of expression. Their presence in the square marked the beginning of its recovery as a central space within Argentine democracy and political history.

The families of the disappeared chose to voice their demands from the Plaza de Mayo because of its history and symbolic significance. For more than two centuries this square has been marked by political and social events of distinct qualities and meanings, gradually emerging as a key site for the waging of political disputes where the memories of past struggles have also left their traces. In the twentieth century alone, this Plaza has witnessed multiple and even conflicting political expressions. It was one of the spaces where labor and leftist organizations expressed their dreams of social transformation and celebrated key events such as May 1, or International Workers' Day. In 1916 it welcomed the crowds who cheered on Hipólito Yrigoyen, the first president elected by universal male suffrage in truly free elections. On October 17, 1945, huge crowds of mainly industrial workers marched into this square from the suburbs to show their support for Colonel Juan Domingo Perón, who had been imprisoned by the military. This event became a founding moment in the rise of Peronism, the political movement that profoundly transformed Argentine politics in the middle of the twentieth century.

THE IMAGE OF THE HEADSCARF, SYMBOL OF THE MADRES DE PLAZA DE MAYO, IS PAINTED AROUND THE MAY PYRAMID (PIRÁMIDE DE MAYO).

THE PLAZA DE MAYO, WITH THE CASA ROSADA (GOVERNMENT HOUSE) IN THE BACKGROUND.

The Plaza de Mayo was thus transformed into a kind of witness to these ambiguous expressions of desire for democracy and social justice. Yet precisely because it occupied this privileged place within Argentine political culture, it also became the staging ground for authoritarian policies and attacks on civil rights, often with the approval and backing of broad sectors of society. Thus, in 1930 crowds packed into the Plaza de Mayo to welcome the coup launched by General José Félix Uriburu against the Radical Party government of Hipólito Yrigoyen. And in June 1955 naval aircraft bombarded the seat of government, the Casa Rosada (see "Mayor Bernardo Alberte garden," p. 238), as a prelude to the coup that would put an end to Perón's second presidential term on September 16th of that year.

In the 1960s and 1970s the Plaza became a key space in the deepening political, social, and cultural conflicts that marked Argentine politics. It became much more than a mere backdrop for the crowds who filled it for political demonstrations.

**The coup d'etat of 1976**

The coup of March 24, 1976, brought an end to these years of mass mobilization, when civil society and political organizations had occupied the city's public spaces. The coup brought with it the ratification of the state of siege* in force since November 1974 and the systematic deployment of state terror.

The Plaza de Mayo was completely empty as the new military government broadcast its communiqués at dawn on the morning of the coup. State terror quickly dissolved the social and community bonds that had been formed in the heat of political disputes, restructuring relationships between people around feelings of fear, suspicion, and indifference.

The military quickly went to work to transform the Plaza de Mayo, bringing it in line with its own repressive and demobilizing goals. To redefine it as a leisure space rather than a political forum, they restricted pedestrian access, expanded green spaces, and installed benches and garbage cans around the fountains.

The square was not used again as a meeting place until Argentina won the Soccer World Cup in 1978. As dictator General Videla appeared on the balcony of the Casa Rosada, he received numerous ovations from the crowds that had gathered to celebrate this sporting achievement.

### Plaza de las Madres

Within this climate of legitimization of the military dictatorship, a group of women who would soon be known as the Madres de Plaza de Mayo (Mothers of the Plaza de Mayo) slowly began to take possession of this historic space. Meanwhile, the dictatorship launched a public relations campaign to deflect accusations from the international community regarding disappearances and human rights violations.

As these international criticisms escalated, the government sought to discredit them by arguing that they were part of a supposed "anti-Argentine campaign." It spread slogans such as "Los argentinos somos derechos y humanos" (Argentines are upstanding and humane, with a play on the Spanish words for "human" and "rights"). They also launched publicity operations such as the "Defend your Argentina" campaign, promoted by the pro-government magazine *Para Tí,* which was aimed at a mainly female middle-class readership. Magazines were sold containing free postcards depicting different places in Argentina, and readers were invited to send them to different personalities around the world in order to "respond to the anti-Argentine campaign."

A group of mothers whose children had been detained and disappeared began to organize at this time. They had encountered each other in government offices where they went to demand news of their children, and they decided that the best place to meet was in the Plaza de Mayo.

As Silvia Sigal has noted (2006), the appearance of the Madres overturned an earlier logic that had always measured demonstrations in the Plaza de Mayo by the number of protesters they convened.

María del Rosario de Cerruti, secretary of the Madres de Plaza de Mayo during the association's early years, describes how the women gradually took over the square. Her son was kidnapped on May 10, 1976. The following day she met other Mothers while she was looking for him at the Army Command Unit 1 (see p. 74).

"From that day forward, we started to search in every possible place. . . . We would go to the Ministry of the Interior, we would go to the Command Unit, to the Police Department, but it was no use. Along the way we kept meeting other mothers. . . . In July 1976 we went to the Episcopate. By then there were about forty of us. . . . We started to search everywhere. Two of us would go see one bishop, two would head to a church, two more to a ministry, two to the mental hospital, two to the Devoto prison . . . and so on, searching in more and more places. We would spend the whole day in the streets, completely alone. That was from May to November 1976. Every week we went to the Ministry of the Interior, right next to the Casa Rosada, but only some low-level employees would meet with us. They would promise to show us lists, but they never did. Other Mothers met in the military vicariate, led by Monsignor Grasselli, who was a shameless person. That's when Azucena [Villaflor] first appeared. I first saw her in the Ministry, and she looked very determined. She said, 'We should get a thousand of us together, meet in the Plaza, head into the Casa Rosada, and stay there until they tell us something.'

"One day someone said, 'Let's go to the Plaza de Mayo on the 30th and see how many people show up.' I didn't go that Saturday. I had to clean my house because during the week I was always out and about. Another of the Madres, María Ponce de Bianco [see "Santa Cruz Church," p. 89] promised to drop in later to tell me what had happened. On Saturday she came to my house and said, 'There was nobody there, the Plaza was empty. It's useless to go on Saturday. There'd be no more than twelve or fourteen of us. We have to go on a week day.' We agreed to go on a Friday afternoon. For these occasions, we would usually make up letters. I was usually the one who prepared them. To get them all signed we would meet on the fourth floor of the court of justice, where the Supreme Court is, because there was no one there. We also met in coffee shops" [AO.0437].

Haydée García Gastelú, another member of that first group of Madres, describes the earliest meetings: "By joining together we were able to put together the pieces of information that were denied to us. We had the idea of meeting somewhere, and Azucena [Villaflor] said, 'in the Plaza,' so that we could cross over to the Casa Rosada and draw up our lists of demands. She came from Avellaneda, from a more politicized family. She was used to taking part in political marches, but not the rest of us. We had no political experience. The first time I met her, she was so charged up, so full of dynamism, that if I hadn't bumped into Adela Gard de Antokoletz as well, I think I would have backed out. Because Azucena said, 'We have to do this, we have to go.' And I said something so stupid, because I was just terrified that first day, and I was one of the first to go on that famous Saturday. I asked, 'And who sent you here?' She almost bit my head off, and she was right. It was really the stupidest question anyone could have asked at that moment. She said, 'What do you mean who sent me? We *have* to do this.' And she explained everything to me. She was a very warm and persuasive person, really a special figure. But this all lasted only a few months, because that was in April, and in December they took her away (see "Santa Cruz Church," p. 89).

"This was how the Madres de la Plaza de Mayo took shape. We were flying by the seat of our pants. Once when we went to see Grasselli they started saying we needed to meet, and a date was set to meet in the Plaza de Mayo. It was a Saturday. My husband—I lived in the neighborhood of Caballito—said, 'What are you going to do on a Saturday? Who are you going to meet up with? It's dangerous.' So then I said to him, 'Look, I don't know what we're going to do, but we're going to get together. We have to talk and figure out what we can do.' Actually, our idea was to meet, make a list of demands, and then cross the street to the Casa Rosada to request a meeting with the authorities, with whomever would receive us. My second question to Azucena was, 'Tell me, why did you choose Saturday to do this? Everything is closed.' 'Ah,' she replied, 'by mistake, because we mentioned a date, somebody did, and by mistake it was a Saturday.' So later we changed it. I mean, that was all decided on the fly as well. It was just a mistake to pick Saturday. There was no one there but us and the pigeons. It was a terribly hot day, so the whole Plaza was empty. We each carried nothing but a change purse, not even a handbag because we were afraid they might think we were carrying guns. Each one of us did the same, even though we hadn't arranged it ahead of time. Adela was there with one sister on each arm,

THE MAY PYRAMID (PIRÁMIDE DE MAYO) WITH PHOTOS OF THE DISAPPEARED. DECEMBER 2007.

25 MAYO 1810

carrying just a change purse, and I was there with mine. I had my I.D. card, my house keys to go home afterward, a subway token, and that was it. That was all we took with us, and we were just terrified" [AO.0040].

María del Rosario de Cerruti describes the first meetings they were finally granted: "We were going to head to the Plaza de Mayo in the afternoon of Friday, April 30, but it occurred to one of the Mothers that we shouldn't, because it was *día de brujas* [Walpurgis Day, a European festival associated with witchcraft]. So we agreed to go on Thursday, when the banks would be open, so that there would be more people around. There weren't many of us, maybe fifteen or twenty women, but we didn't march or anything. We just sat on the benches.

"No one agreed to meet with us until mid-July, when we were received by Luis Palacios, the Vice Minister of the Interior, who was later governor of the province of Chaco. He was a military man posing as a kind father figure. He told us that Videla would not meet with us, but the Minister of the Interior, Hargindeguy, would. I went in with Azucena and Beatriz, one of the mothers I had just met. We spent over an hour with him. When he saw Beatriz he said to her, 'But Madam, hasn't your daughter appeared yet?' . . . He took out an agenda and said, 'All these are disappeared, but you know what? The girls who leave the country are in Mexico, working as prostitutes. Would you believe it, Madam? They leave the country saying they are being persecuted.' Azucena called him every name under the sun, and so did Beatriz. She said, 'My daughter isn't a prostitute.' I remember saying to him, 'General Franco was a dictator. He was a dictator his entire life, but he signed every death sentence with his own hand. He carried them all on his own shoulders. You lot haven't signed a single death sentence. You're cowards. And we are not going to leave the Plaza.' Azucena told him, 'We're going to wear our legs out walking in this square.' He said to us, 'Ladies, you cannot be here. We are under a state of siege.' We answered him with threats, saying we wouldn't leave. When we left his office there were more than sixty Mothers in the Plaza, and we were convinced we would not leave until they told us something" [AO].

**The march**

"We didn't want men to come, whether they were sons or husbands," recalls Cerruti, "because the soldiers were much more aggressive with them. The highest-ranking officers never insulted us. They just sent the police to attack us instead of doing it themselves. So they started to call us *las locas* [the madwomen]. We kept going every Thursday, but we would just sit on the benches. They sent the police, who tried to move us out, saying, 'Move on, there's a state of siege. You have to keep moving.' They were the ones who told us to walk. So we started to walk in pairs around the whole square, but it covers more than two hectares. It's very big, so if just a few of us were walking, they wouldn't even see us. We would talk to each other while we walked in pairs, with two more behind and two in front. We would discuss the places we needed to go. And we approached every public figure who entered the country" [AO].

As Nicole Loraux has observed, the marches of the Madres de Plaza de Mayo can be interpreted as a form of political discourse. The women decided to center their march around the Plaza's central pyramid because the full square was too large. Through their actions the Madres forged a new bond with each other, creating a new political community through their common suffering at the hands of the military dictatorship and through their demand for justice. At the same time, the marches represent a form of commemorative exercise that recalls certain funerary rituals in which the footprints of the dead are displayed. The Madres displayed photos and names in place of the missing bodies. Through this practice they exposed the crime of "disappearance" (Martine Déotte, 2000).

MADRES WITH THE BANNER OF IMAGES OF THE DISAPPEARED DURING THE 28TH MARCH OF RESISTANCE.

### The Grandmothers

At the same time that the Mothers were beginning their marches, another group of women was filing a collective writ of habeas corpus* before the courts in the suburban municipality of Morón. On May 15, 1977, they denounced the disappearance of pregnant women and other victims who were taken away with their babies, and they demanded that all adoptions be suspended. This was the beginning of the Abuelas de Plaza de Mayo (Grandmothers of the Plaza de Mayo), who sought to recover children of the disappeared who had been stolen by the dictatorship. They were the mothers of victims of kidnapping and disappearance who knew that their grandchildren had been seized along with their children. Since the recovery of these babies required specific strategies (such as visiting nurseries and juvenile courts and investigating cases of adoption), they decided it would be best to form a separate organization (see "Central Military Hospital," p. 77).

### Paid announcements by the Madres

According to Ramiro de Casasbellas, director of the newspaper *La Opinión* after Jacobo Timerman's arrest, all media outlets received verbal orders on the night of April 22, 1976 that prohibited them from publishing any information about "subversive episodes, discoveries of corpses, kidnappings, disappearances, or the killing of either rebel figures or soldiers, police, or security agents, unless such information had already been reported officially" (Blaustein and Zubieta, 2006).

In these early years, the Madres had to purchase advertisements in newspapers or approach foreign personalities in order to publicize their demands. In October

1977 they presented their first written demand that the government provide information about their children's whereabouts. It was at this time that many Madres themselves were kidnapped. As Maria del Rosario de Cerruti recounts,

"They surrounded us on Rodríguez Peña Street when we took our demands to Congress, loaded us onto five buses, and took us to the police station on Lavalle Street. All kinds of people were already there: journalists, priests, everybody. About twenty guys from the SIDE [Argentina's State Intelligence Agency] came in dressed in civilian clothes, with typewriters to take down our statements. There were a lot of us there, maybe three hundred. They asked us who had sent us, whether it was the Communist Party. We responded disdainfully that we were presenting our demands because each of us had a disappeared son or daughter. . . . They started to let us leave, one by one, in the early hours of the morning, and when we got outside we realized they had emptied the streets over a ten-block radius around the station. We were really scared. . . . That advertisement was published in *La Prensa* in October. We wanted to publish one with the names of the disappeared on December 10, Human Rights Day, but they wouldn't let us, so we had to put our own names. The newspaper *La Nación* agreed to publish it" [AO] (see "Santa Cruz Church," p. 89).

Several people were kidnapped by a Special Task Group* (*Grupo de Tareas*) from the Navy School of Mechanics (see p. 153) between December 8 and 10, 1977, while the group was preparing this second announcement. The victims included several Mothers, family members of the disappeared, and people close to the human rights organizations. María Eugenia Ponce de Bianco, Esther Ballestrino de Careaga, Sister Alice Domon, Raquel Bulit, Patricia Oviedo, Ángel Auad de Genovés, and Gabriel Horacio Horane were kidnapped on December 8 from the Santa Cruz Church. Remo Berardo, Horacio Elbert, and José Julio Fondevilla were abducted on Friday, December 9. On the 10th the same Special Task Group kidnapped Léonie Duquet (a French nun like Alice Domont), and abducted Azucena Villaflor from the town of Sarandí, in the province of Buenos Aires. Azucena had insisted that the announcement go to print even after the kidnappings from the Santa Cruz Church.

**The headscarf**

Aída Bogo de Sarti recalls, "We began to organize ourselves into groups, one for each part of the city: the south, north, west, and east. We held a picnic on the road to the city of La Plata, hidden behind all the foliage. We pretended to be celebrating someone's birthday, and that was when Azucena gave us instructions: 'You will be in charge of this part, you of that one.' I was in charge of the whole southern zone. They all came to Lezama Park. And the other zones, Nora [Cortiñas] and other people were in charge of them. We would gather all the mothers who came to us with their problems, and then we would all go to the Plaza. Whenever Azucena entered a room, it was like magic because of the power she had. She was one of a kind" [AO.0099].

Haydée García Castelú describes how the symbol of the Madres was born: "The headscarves came later. We didn't use them at first. The scarf emerged when we made our first visit to the Basilica of Luján (see "Plaza Madres del Pañuelo Blanco," p. 170) because we kept losing one another. We just couldn't identify each other. Here it was different because we were in the Plaza. We would just walk around it in circles. But as soon as we left the Plaza it was easy to lose each other. I mean we couldn't follow each other. That was how we got the idea. Actually, it was a diaper, not a headscarf. We tied cloth diapers on our heads as a symbolic gesture and as a way of recognizing each other."

27TH MARCH OF RESISTANCE.

María del Rosario de Cerruti describes the Madres' participation in the annual pilgrimage to the Basilica of Luján as well as other mobilizations that took place once the group had grown: "When the priest celebrating Mass came to give us Communion we said: 'For my child who has been detained and disappeared,' and he refused to give it to us. In 1980 they refused to let us into the Plaza. One Thursday at 3:00 in the afternoon they put up barriers and sent in the police. So we started demonstrating at different times of the day to confuse them, so they wouldn't be expecting us. We still weren't using the headscarves while we marched because then they would follow us. We had to be camouflaged. Some time later that year, we went back to marching in the Plaza along with members of the Permanent Assembly [for Human Rights]: Monsignor Nevares and the few politicians who were participating in the Assembly. ([Later President Raúl] Alfonsín wasn't there.) We joined hands, knocked down the barriers, and entered the Plaza. 'They're not going to take us out of here. The Plaza must belong to the Madres.' That was when we started to get tougher. By then there were about two hundred of us."

They formally constituted the nonprofit organization Madres de Plaza de Mayo on August 22, 1979, with a public notary in the provincial city of La Plata. As Enriqueta Maroni recalls, "We kept trying to come up with new ideas to force them to give us information. We made the first banners—I can't remember the year—but we made them in our first offices in Uruguay Street, which we got with funding from a Dutch organization, SAM" [AO.0146].

## Resistance marches

The Madres planned the first resistance march for December 10, 1981, with the goal of occupying the Plaza de Mayo for twenty-four hours. They published the following announcement calling on supporters to join them:

"We summon the people, organizations of workers, students, and professionals, and all religious and political groups, to converge on the Plaza de Mayo on Thursday, December 10, at 3:30 p.m. There we will hold a march, to be called the 'symbol of the Madres' resistance.' We will remain in the Plaza to express our repeated demands for truth and justice and to oppose the obstinate silence that seeks to spread a veil of oblivion over our tragedy."

The next day the Mothers issued the following statement:

"Our Association convened this twenty-four-hour march, covering roughly one hundred kilometers, to challenge of the obstinate silence of the Armed Forces. We demand that the authorities hand over our detained and disappeared family members alive, and we will demonstrate that the sheer strength of the Madres alone can resist the veil of oblivion. As many as 2,500 people participated in the demonstration at its height."

## The Malvinas Islands belong to Argentina, and so do the disappeared

In 1978 a broad cross-section of society gathered in the Plaza to celebrate the World Cup triumph of the Argentine national soccer team. Thousands of people also crowded into the Plaza de Mayo to cheer on April 2, 1982, when General Leopoldo Fortunato Galtieri announced the military occupation of the Malvinas [Falkland] Islands. These islands occupied a special place within Argentine national identity. For decades the British control of this territory had been presented as the last thread to be woven into the fabric of an imagined Argentine national community.

Demonstrators led by the General Confederation of Labor (CGT, or Confederación General del Trabajo) met with brutal repression when they tried to occupy the Plaza on March 30, 1982. Many who had taken part in that demonstration to condemn the dictatorship gathered again on April 2 to celebrate the attempted recovery of the Malvinas. This gathering on April 2 was an opportunity for people, including opponents of the junta, to recover the experience of expressing themselves politically in public since the policies of repression and demobilization had emptied the Plaza in 1976. Not everyone who gathered together that day in 1982 supported the dictatorship. Some of those present in the Plaza opposed the military yet supported the recovery of the islands. For others, this mass gathering in the Plaza represented an opportunity for public resistance, a chance to publicly expose the experience of horror. This is what the Madres did when they displayed the slogan "The Malvinas Belong to Argentina, and so do the Disappeared."

## The Silhouette Protest

The Madres were at the forefront of the many protests that took place once the military began to retreat from power after its humiliating defeat in the Malvinas War, which cost the lives of 649 Argentine soldiers. Protesters at the third resistance march, in September 1983, staged a powerful aesthetic and political action known as the "Siluetazo" (Silhouette Protest) to illustrate the scope of the forced disappearances. Three artists (Rodolfo Aguerreberry, Julio Flores, and Guillermo Kexel) conceived of the initiative, with support from the Madres and Abuelas de la Plaza de Mayo and other human rights organizations. On

GRAFFITI STENCIL NEAR THE PLAZA DE MAYO CONDEMNING THE WORLD CUP OF 1978.

the day of the march, participants traced life-size empty profiles of bodies onto large pieces of paper and hung them on the buildings surrounding the Plaza as a means of representing "the presence of absence" (Longoni and Bruzzone, 2008).

Another goal of the *siluetazo* was to illustrate the physical space occupied by thirty thousand human bodies (which was the estimated number of the victims of disappearance at that time). The march transformed the Plaza into a kind of open-air workshop as participants worked to complete all the silhouettes. This experience was repeated two more times, first in December 1983, when Raúl Alfonsín took office as the first democratically elected president after the dictatorship's fall. The Plaza de Mayo was once again packed with people for that occasion, and demonstrators enacted a *siluetazo* in the Plaza de la República, marching around the obelisk that dominates the Avenida 9 de Julio. Another *siluetazo* took place at the same location in March 1984 to commemorate the eighth anniversary of the military coup.

**The Plaza de Mayo under democratic rule**

The Plaza regained its place as the privileged site of popular demonstrations with the restoration of democratic rule. The Plaza de Mayo's identity had been recast as the Plaza of the Madres both within Argentina and for the outside world.

In mid-1980 divisions began to emerge within the Madres over a variety of issues, some of them long-standing and others associated with the new context of democratic rule. These included differences of opinion over the group's relationship with the constitutional authorities, the exhumation of bodies discovered through investigations into the whereabouts of the disappeared, and the Trial of the Military Juntas*. Members disagreed over the organization's procedures (see "Nunca Más Square and Cultural Center," p. 186).

In 1986 a group of Madres, including several founding members, broke with the leadership of Hebe de Bonafini and formed a separate organization named "Madres de Plaza de Mayo—Línea Fundadora" (Mothers of the Plaza de

Mayo—Founding Line). Some mothers who had recently returned from exile joined them. The members of this new group chose not to elect either a president or a governing board, arguing that the Madres organization under Bonafini's leadership was antidemocratic. They also favored working with other human rights organizations such as the Abuelas (Grandmothers of the Plaza de Mayo) and Familiares (Association of Family Members of the Disappeared). Since then their guiding slogan has been "Remembrance, Truth, and Justice," and they have worked toward these goals with long-term strategic actions.

**Holy Week: "The house is in order"**

In 1986, the government of Raúl Alfonsín enacted the so-called Full Stop Law in response to military pressure. It set a deadline of sixty days for the initiation of criminal proceedings against those accused of crimes against humanity during the period of state terrorism. This law did not satisfy many within the military who continued to face charges, and a group of officers launched an uprising during Easter festivities in 1987. Led by Aldo Rico, they later came to be known as the *carapintadas* (painted faces).

The Armed Forces commanders ignored President Alfonsín's orders to put down the rebellion by insurgents entrenched in the Campo de Mayo army unit. Yet millions of people around the country took to the streets spontaneously to repudiate the military uprising and defend the constitutional government. The Plaza de Mayo became one of the principal meeting sites as the streets remained filled with demonstrators throughout Holy Week.

The biggest demonstration occurred on Sunday, April 19, 1987, when the Plaza was once again packed with people. Raúl Alfonsín asked the hundreds of thousands of demonstrators to wait for him as he went personally to the Campo de Mayo military base to demand the surrender of Colonel Aldo Rico and the *carapintadas*. Hours later he addressed the crowd gathered in the Plaza, announcing that the insurgents had laid down their weapons. He made a statement that later became infamous: "The house is in order. Happy Easter." With these words Alfonsín signaled that the apparent victory of the democratic government supported by the people was in fact a compromise with the military. In exchange for surrender, the president had promised the military that the trials would stop. The Alfonsín government sealed this promise with the so-called Law of Due Obedience* (Ley de Obediencia Debida), which exempted from prosecution most of the military and police personnel who had committed crimes against humanity. Under this law no charges could be laid against those who had followed orders from their superiors. Ultimately, only the junta's leaders were charged and convicted under Alfonsín.

**The nineties**

Soon after coming to power in 1989, Raúl Alfonsín's successor, Carlos Menem, issued a blanket pardon* for crimes committed during the dictatorship and released the generals from prison. The Madres condemned the pardons from the Plaza de Mayo. They kept up their weekly marches in the Plaza and carried out Resistance Marches every December during Menem's period in office.

In 1996 the human rights organizations launched a major publicity campaign to convene a massive demonstration marking the twentieth anniversary of the coup. Huge crowds turned out on March 24, 1996, for the usual march from the Congress to the Plaza de Mayo, including many young people and others who did not normally take part in such actions. They joined with the Madres and other long-standing human rights organizations to demand justice against those responsible for human rights crimes. Those same years saw the emergence of

ANNIVERSARY OF THE MILITARY COUP IN THE PLAZA DE MAYO, MARCH 24, 2007.

the organization known as H.I.J.O.S.* A play on the Spanish word for "children," H.I.J.O.S. stands for Hijos por la Identidad y la Justicia contra el Olvido y el Silencio (Children for Identity and Justice Opposed to Forgetting and Silence).

### December 2001

The last major political events to mark the Plaza de Mayo occurred in 2001, when President Fernando de la Rúa found himself in a profound political and economic crisis just two years into his term of office. Faced with mass demonstrations and supermarket lootings provoked by his economic policies, De La Rúa declared a state of siege and suspended constitutional guarantees on December 19, 2001. This declaration prompted thousands of people from all parts of Buenos Aires to take to the streets and march toward the Plaza de Mayo. That same night saw the resignation of de la Rúa's Minister of Economy Domingo Cavallo, who had been one of the main architects of neoliberal policies in Argentina under Carlos Menem's government.

The demonstrators faced fierce repression in the Plaza de Mayo and in front of the Congress building. On the morning of December 20 mounted police attacked a group of Madres in the Plaza de Mayo right in front of the television cameras, prompting thousands of people to take to the streets again. Thirty-nine people throughout the country died at the hands of the security forces, five of them in the immediate surroundings of the Plaza de Mayo. Fernando de la Rúa resigned as president later that same day.

One area of the Plaza has been closed ever since that day. Barriers had been set up to protect the Government House from demonstrators during Carlos Menem's presidency, and by 2001 they stretched halfway across the square.

## Memory in the Plaza de Mayo

In December 2005 the Plaza hosted a tribute to Azucena Villaflor, founder of the "Madres de Plaza de Mayo." Azucena's remains were discovered, identified by the Argentine Forensic Anthropology Team* (EEAF, Equipo Argentino de Antropología Forense) (see "Santa Cruz Church," p. 89) and returned to her family. Her ashes were scattered next to the central monument, the Pirámide de Mayo. During the ceremony, the government dedicated a plaque in her honor.

During the twenty-sixth Resistance March in December 2006, the Founding Line of the Madres de Plaza de Mayo focused their actions on the case of Jorge Julio López, who had disappeared just three months earlier. Reviving their tactics from the dictatorship years, they demanded that López be found alive. López had suffered his first disappearance during the dictatorship, though he had survived his detention in the Clandestine Detention Centers (CDCs) known as the Pozo de Arana* and Police Station 5* (in La Plata). In 2006 he testified in the trial of Miguel Etchecolatz, the former Chief of Investigations for the police of the Province of Buenos Aires who had overseen more than twenty such detention centers. López disappeared again shortly after testifying. Next to the plaque honoring Azucena Villaflor (see "Azucena Villaflor Boulevard," p. 51) there is a ceramic tile work dedicated to López. It was created by workers from one of Argentina's most successful worker-run factories, formerly known as Zanón, now called the Factory with no Bosses (Fábrica sin Patrones, or FaSinPat). It bears López's face and the words, "We demand from the government that Julio López be found alive NOW" (see "Tribute to Jorge Julio López in Miramar Bar," p. 105).

In March 2005 the Legislature of the City of Buenos Aires declared the space around the Pirámide de Mayo a historic site, recognizing it as the space in which the Madres have been holding their marches every Thursday since 1977 and the symbolic representation of their struggle. White headscarves were painted on the ground to represent these women. Since October 2006 the space has been used by the Association for the Families and Friends of Political Prisoners in Argentina (Asociación y Amigos de los Presos Políticos de la Argentina), an organization that defends those responsible for state terrorism under the military dictatorship. During its activities the Association painted black bands over the white headscarves of the Madres. After the Association circulated a video on the Internet, Carlos Pisoni, human rights director for the city of Buenos Aires, prosecuted its leader, Cecilia Pando, for aggravated damages, inciting criminal acts, and intimidation.

## 2. **Coordinación Federal**

Coordinación Federal, one of the largest Clandestine Detention Centers (CDCs), operated in the building of what is today the Bureau of the Interior and Federal Crimes (Superintendencia de Interior y Delitos Federales). It functioned as a temporary detention center for prisoners being transferred to other CDCs or moved into legal prisons under orders from the National Executive Branch* (Poder Ejecutivo Nacional, or PEN), yet its transitory nature did not preclude the use of torture and murder. The victims of the Fátima Massacre* were transferred from this detention center.

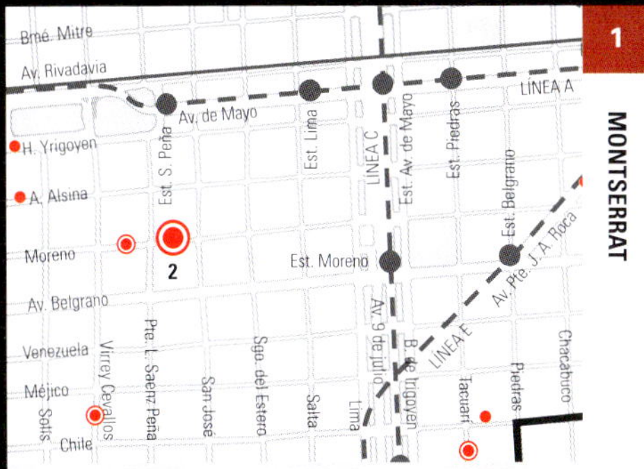


**LOCATION:** MORENO 1417
**TRANSPORTATION:** SUBWAY STATION: SÁENZ PEÑA (A LINE). BUSES: 23, 39, 56, 60, 64, 86, 102, 168.

The Federal Police had used torture as an interrogation technique for many years, particularly inside this facility. From its founding in 1944 under the name Coordinación Federal, this institution had centralized all of the security forces' political activities, functioning as the command center for the persecution of political militants and activists. From then on, repressive actions such as interrogation under torture and even murder were planned through Coordinación Federal.

### **"Political police": The earliest precursors to state terrorism**

The Buenos Aires police have investigated trade union and political activities ever since the beginning of the twentieth century, when Ramón Falcón was the capital city's Chief of Police. Mass immigration and rising social conflict in this period led to greater sophistication in the use of repression. Falcón had presented the Minister of the Interior with a report on anarchist activities just before his 1909 assassination by anarchist Simón Radowitzky.

Some years later Chief of Police Luis Dellepiane created the Public Order Division under the first presidency of Hipólito Yrigoyen (1916–1922). It included three sections: Social Order,

THE BUREAU OF THE INTERIOR AND FEDERAL CRIMES CURRENTLY OPERATES IN THE FORMER CDC.

dedicated to trade union activities and crime; Public Order, charged with political matters; and the Service to the Head of State, which provided security to the president.

The first military coup of the twentieth century took place in 1930. The following year Leopoldo Lugones Jr., the military government's Chief of the Political Order Division, was accused of participating in and directing torture sessions. The electric cattle prod (*picana**) was introduced as a police torture device in the mid-1930s.

## The Federal Police and Peronism

The Federal Police was founded as a national security force after the military coup of 1943. This agency also undertook counterespionage tasks during WWII that fell outside the legal jurisdiction of the Army's Secret Service. Coordinación Federal oversaw these activities, which were redirected against the regime's political opponents after the war.

The Federal Police was divided into four departments in its early years: judicial, security, administration, and investigations. This last department oversaw the Political Police, which was in turn divided into three sections: the Social and Political Order sections, and the Special Section. Torturer Cipriano Lombilla, active in the police since the days of Leopoldo Lugones Jr., was one of the directors of the Special Section during Juan Domingo Perón's presidency. Prisoners held here were kept out of official records, foreshadowing a practice that would become institutionalized under the dictatorship of 1976–1983. Many of the regime's political opponents passed through this facility, including Peronist labor leaders who, like Cipriano Reyes, sought to preserve the autonomy of the labor movement. Reyes was himself tortured inside the Special Section in 1948 (*Clarín,* "Murió Cipriano Reyes, testigo de casi un siglo de historia argentina," August 2, 2001).

A military faction cut short Juan Domingo Perón's second presidential term in a coup that they called the Liberating Revolution. The Navy then took over control of the police and launched a persecution campaign against loyalists of the banned Peronist political party. These years also saw the creation of the Division of Antidemocratic Political Activities (DIPA, or División de Actividades Políticas Antidemocráticas), dedicated to the surveillance and persecution of Communists and Trotskyists.

Agents from Coordinación Federal participated directly in repression or appeared menacingly at political or trade union events, causing the demonstrators to disperse. One notable case involved the murder of Emilio Mariano Jáuregui, former Secretary General of the Journalist's Union, which took place on June 27, 1969, just days after the mass general strike known as the Cordobazo*. A complaint filed soon after the event stated that plainclothes police driving a car without license plates shot Jáuregui dead as he participated in a protest against Nelson Rockefeller's visit to Argentina that had been called by the labor federation known as the CGT de los Argentinos* (Buenos Aires Forum for the Enforcement of Human Rights, 1973: 129).

## The Bureau of Federal Security

In the early 1970s another military government changed the name of Coordinación Federal to the Bureau of Federal Security (Superintendencia de Seguridad Federal) and decreed that only high-ranking military officers could serve as its director.

CELL AREA ON THE THIRD FLOOR.

The Peronist leader Héctor Cámpora won the presidency in March 1973, when the Peronist party known as the Frente Justicialista de Liberación won 49.5 percent of the national vote in anticipation of Juan Domingo Perón's return to politics after eighteen years in exile. Cámpora's new Minister of the Interior, Esteban Righi, strongly condemned the Federal Police and put them on notice that the use of torture would not be tolerated. He also announced the dissolution of the DIPA and ordered the director of the Bureau of Federal Security to burn police records.

Shortly thereafter a former member of Coordinación Federal was put in charge of security measures for General Perón's return from exile. Retired colonel Jorge Osinde was, at the time, Secretary for Sports and Tourism under Minister of Social Welfare José López Rega. On June 20 some three million people marched toward Ezeiza International Airport to welcome Perón. Before the airplane landed, members of the Peronist right wing, led by Osinde and López Rega, opened fire from a platform above the crowd against leftist marchers from the Peronist Revolutionary Tendency* (Tendencia Revolucionaria). The shooting went on for hours and came to be known as the Ezeiza Massacre.

Cámpora resigned the presidency on July 13, 1973, to make way for Perón's return to power. Juan Domingo Perón regained the presidency with 62 percent of the vote and appointed his wife Isabel as Vice President. Perón appointed Alberto Villar Chief of the Federal Police in March 1974. Villar had won notoriety for a number of actions, most notably a violent raid on the headquarters of the Peronist party (Partido Justicialista) during a wake for political prisoners shot dead in the Trelew Massacre* in August 1972. Just before appointing Villar, Perón had named police chief Luis Margaride as his Director of Federal Security. Margaride had led a crackdown on women wearing miniskirts during the regime of General Onganía.

Uruguayan citizen and former Tupamaro* militant Antonio Viana Acosta described his kidnapping by agents of the Department of Federal Security on February 21, 1974:

> "For several days I'd had the feeling I was being followed. I awoke at 3:30 a.m. to the sound of breaking windows and I saw that someone was forcing open my bedroom door. Police captain Juan Ramón Morales aimed a gun at me. Alberto Villar and Luis Margaride were with him. They dragged me to the terrace and laid into me, kicking me for a long time. Since I earned a bit of money by running a small radio repair shop from home, they found some wires and electrocuted me right there. They took me to Coordinación Federal and continued to electrocute me for two weeks" (*Página/12,* August 12, 2007).

Acosta was held captive in Buenos Aires for three months and later sent to Uruguay, where he remained in prison for nearly eight years. His testimony was presented in the judicial investigation into crimes committed by the Triple A* (Argentine Anticommunist Alliance) in 2008.

The Triple A, a far-right paramilitary organization led by José López Rega, had made its first public appearance with the attempted car bombing of Radical Party senator Hipólito Solari Yrigoyen on November 21, 1973. Solari Yrigoyen had received a threat the day before that read, "Beware! The Argentine Anticommunist Alliance (AAA)." López Rega and Villar directed the Triple A's activities. Many Alliance members were recruited to serve in the Department when Cámpora withdrew from power and the Peronist right came to the fore.

Perón promoted Eduardo Almirón and his father-in-law, Juan Ramón Morales at the same time he appointed Villar. (Almirón was extradited from Italy in 2006 as part of the case against the Triple A. He died in April 2009.) Journalist Horacio Verbitsky described their activities: "Deputy Police Commissioner Morales and Deputy Inspector Almirón had been dishonorably discharged from the Federal Police, tried and convicted as thieves, 'Mexicans,' bribe takers, smugglers, drug traffickers, and pimps. In the early 1960s, Morales was chief of the Federal Crimes Brigade of the Federal Police. His gang, working with the gang of Miguel ("Madman") Prieto, were mixed up in all kinds of activities. They were discovered because of the indiscretion of one of their subordinates, and because Deputy Officer Edwin Farquarsohn was caught red-handed. They silenced their accomplices using a technique they would apply a decade later to political activists; the corpses of some of their former associates turned up in garbage dumps and empty lots, their bodies riddled with bullets and their hands tied and burned. Almirón had another notorious incident on his record: his participation in the murder of U.S. Navy Lieutenant Earl Davis in an Olivos nightclub on June 9, 1964" (Verbitsky, 1986).

The Triple A murdered hundreds of political militants and social and political activists between late 1973 and 1975. Their threats forced hundreds more into exile. They operated with such impunity that they were able to kill leading figures within the political, social, and cultural movements that were working for change in Argentina. Some of their most notable victims included Father Carlos Mugica (see p. 25), a leading liberation theology priest; Congressman Rodolfo Ortega Peña; lawyer Alfredo Curuchet, who had represented political prisoners; Atilio López, a former deputy governor of Córdoba and a leader within the militant wing of the Peronist labor movement; Silvio Frondizi, a prominent leftist intellectual (and brother of the former president Arturo Frondizi) as well as his son-in-law Luis Mendiburu; and Julio Troxler, a leading figure in the Peronist Resistance* (see "Julio Troxler Street," p. 240).

On November 1, 1974, the leftist Peronist guerrilla movement known as the Montoneros* killed Alberto Villar with explosives planted on his small yacht. Luis Margaride was promoted from Head of the Department to Chief of Police.

Illegal detentions became more systematic in the months leading up to the coup. Communist Party activist Paula Mahler was kidnapped on June 17, 1975, as she prepared to receive a group of fellow militants who had been held captive in the Department. "I spent three months there. They tortured the prisoners in there every night. At least they let us sleep during the day, because at night it was impossible to sleep because of the screams and the radio at top volume to muffle the cries. Afterward, they presented their torture victims to the judges. This was during the government of Isabelita. The judges must have known what was going on" [AO.0460].

## "The three A's are now the three branches of the Armed Forces"

Writer, journalist, and Montonero militant Rodolfo Walsh asserted in early 1977 that the military junta had taken power on March 24, 1976, not to combat the left- and right-wing armed movements but to expand on the work already begun by the Triple A (see "Corner of San Juan and Entre Rios," p. 96).

In March 1983, just a few months before the military relinquished power, former Federal Police inspector Rodolfo Peregrino presented himself to the Argentine Commission for Human Rights in Madrid and revealed important facts about the structure of the illegal repression. This early testimony was immensely important to the human rights movement, which had been forced until then to rely only on victims' testimonies.

Inspector Peregrino had graduated from the Ramón J. Falcón Police School in 1968 and had worked in the Mounted Police Corps and the General Office of Urban Order (Dirección General de Orden Urbano). During the dictatorship he worked in the Office of the Interior Ministry under Eduardo Hargindeguy. Rodolfo Peregrino Fernández described in detail the functioning of the Bureau of Federal Security and its relationship with the Triple A during the period of state terrorism. Villar's group played a central role in the formation of the Triple A. Many of its members had worked in different facets of political repression. With the military coup in 1976, "a sector of the Argentine Anticommunist Alliance, which was still in operation . . . was for the most part incorporated into the Bureau of Federal Security, taking orders from chief police commissioner Lapuyole, alias "the Frenchman" (El Francés) (Peregrino Fernández, 1983: 20) (see "Automotores Orletti," p. 220).

A wave of detentions swept through the city and surrounding suburbs of Greater Buenos Aires (Gran Buenos Aires) beginning on March 24, 1976, the day of the coup. They were prompted by police intelligence reports issued by institutions including the Bureau of Federal Security. According to Peregrino Fernández, the Bureau's operations were carried out mainly by a Federal Police Task Force that worked directly under the office of the Chief of Police (see "Federal Police Headquarters," p. 40).

## The Clandestine Detention Center after March 24

During the last dictatorship most Bureau of Federal Security detainees were held on the third floor. Survivor Ariel Blaustein was kidnapped in May 1976. He recalls what he saw after he was interrogated on his first day of detention:

"When they were taking me back, I was able to lift my blindfold for a second and I realized I was in a communal cell (*leonera*, or "lion's cage," as they're called in Argentina) with forty other people tossed in there."

The third floor had two *leoneras*, or large communal cells, that could hold dozens of people. Near these large cells there were "tubes," small cells measuring one by two meters. Other prisoners were held on other floors of the building.

Blaustein was kept on the third floor for a week until they legalized his detention and moved him to a regular prison under National Executive order. "I spent the entire week in the dark. . . . I remember that every once in a while they would take us to the bathroom. I had only one freezing cold shower." They later transferred him to the Federal Police Headquarters (see p. 40).

**The bomb in the Bureau of Federal Security**

The Montoneros detonated a bomb on Friday, July 2, 1976 in the Bureau of Federal Security's cafeteria. More than twenty people died and dozens were injured.

This event triggered a series of reprisals. A task force burst into San Patricio Church in Belgrano (see "San Patricio Church and Mártires Palotinos Passage," p. 177) at dawn the following Sunday and murdered five Pallottine priests, leaving a message on one of the walls that read, "For our colleagues blown up in Federal Security." Chief of Police Brigadier General Arturo Corbetta, who had spoken publicly against the illegal repression, was removed from his position after the bombing.

Other acts of reprisal for the Bureau bombing were reported on in the local media. On Saturday, July 3, the newspaper *La Razón* ran the following headline: "Several bodies appeared this morning. Eight were found in a parking lot in San Telmo." On July 4 *La Opinión* announced, "Eight bodies in San Telmo." On July 5 *La Nación* printed the following: "Body discovered next to the Obelisk. Yesterday, at 5:45 a.m., a man's bullet-riddled body was discovered at the intersection of Corrientes and 9 de Julio Avenues. The corpse was found in the Plaza de la República, next to the East face of the Obelisk." On July 8 the *Buenos Aires Herald* reported, "Four bodies near Congress. . . . The four bodies were found yesterday inside a Peugeot car, parked on Rivadavia, between Riobamba and Callao, not far from the entrance to the Chamber of Deputies."

Years later, on May 14, 1985, a former corporal named Armando Víctor who had worked in the Bureau of Federal Security testified in the Trial of the Military Juntas*. When asked whether there had been any reprisals after the bombing, he stated,

"I had left half an hour earlier, because I was working overtime hours in the Faculty of Psychology. I think that night I didn't go in because security barriers had been put up and the Infantry Guard was there. I can't remember if it was the following day, but when I returned to work in the regular prevention service, the Prevention Guard of Federal Security, I found out that some act of revenge had been carried out against the prisoners in the Bureau of Federal Security. They were all removed from where they were detained, taken out of the building, and killed. Their bodies were scattered around the city" [FLMO].

María del Socorro Alonso was abducted on August 11, 1976. After being held in Police Station 24 she was transferred to the Bureau of Federal Security. She stated,

THE PRISONERS WERE BROUGHT IN THROUGH THIS GARAGE.

"I soon realized where we were, because there were bricklayers working, and I knew there had been a bombing in Coordinación Federal in July. They worked there all day, talking to each other, and I heard them say, 'Let's go in through the San José Street entrance.' I knew the area well because it was my own neighborhood. Other detainees who were already there also confirmed this information later on" [AO.0050].

María del Socorro describes one of this Center's unique features: the juxtaposition of legal and illegal realms. The life of the concentration camp, with its practices of torture, coexisted alongside the everyday routines of the public offices:

"When they would drag me to the sessions, we could hear typewriters and normal office conversations on our way to the torture chambers. . . . From the upper floors—Coordinación Federal has nine floors—you could hear the thundering noise of screams and blows. Well, at one point every floor was full. . . . And this place was right downtown. People lived right next door. They took me out of that place in broad daylight."

**The Fátima Massacre***

"Thirty bodies were found in the town of Fátima," announced the daily newspaper *La Nación* on August 21, 1976. That same morning the front page of the daily paper *Clarín* included the following headline: "Thirty bodies discovered in Pilar. Condemnation from the government."

María del Socorro Alonso commented on these events:, "The prisoners massacred in Fátima were removed from Coordinación Federal on August 20. A few days earlier a guard had brought in a newspaper—I think it was *Crónica*, but I'm not sure—that reported the murder of General Actis, who directed the agency in charge of the World Cup in Argentina. The same guard told us he was going to be ordered to hand over several prisoners because of what had happened. . . . this group of prisoners was taken out one or two nights later. There was a lot of commotion in Coordinación. We heard names called, shots fired . . . it was a transfer. And the Fátima Massacre happened soon afterwards" [AO].

Victor Luchina's testimony includes the following information: "Yes sir, there were thirty people. . . . I remember the number because they counted them one by one as they shoved them through the back doors of a truck in the parking lot of Seguridad Federal. It was an open parking lot reserved for the authorities in charge of the facility. It was an army truck. They practically dragged the prisoners down from the floors where they were being kept. I participated in this prisoner transfer because I believed, along with the other people working there, that they were 'drugged.' You could tell by the way they walked, the way they carried themselves, their facial expressions. There wasn't the kind of screaming we usually heard" [FLMO].

From the night of August 19 through the morning of the August 20 thirty detainees in the Bureau of Federal Security were taken to the town of Fátima in the county of Pilar, Buenos Aires province and executed with a gunshot to the head. Their bodies were then destroyed with dynamite.

Residents of the area heard the explosion around 4:30 in the morning. An hour later a group of workers heading to their jobs encountered the victims' remains scattered over a radius of twenty meters. They were found blindfolded and with their hands tied. Five people out of the thirty were identified soon after: Inés Nocetti, Ramón Lorenzo Vélez, Ángel Osvaldo Leiva, Alberto Comas, and Conrado Alsogaray. Another eight were identified in the 1980s by the Argentine Forensic Anthropology Team* (EAAF, Equipo Argentino de Antropología Forense): José Daniel Bronzel, Susana Elena Pedrini de Bronzel, Selma Julia Ocampo, Haydée Rosa Cirullo de Carnaghi, Carmen María Carnaghi (see "Plazoleta (Small Squares) – 25 de Mayo Highway," p. 99), Norma Susana Frontini, Jorge Daniel Argente, and Horacio Oscar García Gastelú. More recently the EEAF identified Juan Carlos Vera, Carlos Raúl Pargas, and Ricardo José Raúl Herrera Carrizo.

On June 24, 2008, H.I.J.O.S.*, the human rights organization representing children of the disappeared, carried out an *escrache* outside Coordinación Federal. In Argentina, the *escrache* is a specific form of protest designed to publicly expose individuals or organizations accused of having participated in state terror. This one took place during the trial of those accused of participating in the Fátima Massacre. In July 2008 the Oral Criminal Court No. 5 sentenced two men to life imprisonment for the crimes of unlawful confinement and homicide committed against the thirty massacre victims. They were Juan Carlos Lapuyole, a retired Federal Police chief inspector (*comisario inspector*) and former director of Intelligence at the Bureau of Federal Security, and Carlos Gallone, retired chief inspector (*comisario inspector*) and former chief of one of the Federal Security Brigades. The Center for Legal and Social Studies (CELS, Centro de Estudios Legales y Sociales) launched the case on behalf of family members of the following victims: Jorge Daniel Argente, Alberto Evaristo Comas, Susana Pedrini de Bronzel, and Horacio Oscar García Gastelú.

## 3. **Chapel of Christ the Laborer – Father Carlos Mujica**



The "shantytown priest" Carlos Mujica Echague made a radical commitment to working with the poor even though he had been born into an upper-class Buenos Aires family. Mujica was born on October 7, 1930. His father Adolfo Mugica was a Conservative party congressman and later Minister of Foreign Affairs in the government of Arturo Frondizi. His mother Carmen Echague was the daughter of landowners. Mujica was murdered by the Triple A* (Argentine Anticommunist Alliance) on May 11, 1974. "We must stand with the people now more than ever," he said before dying.

He began to study law after completing high school. At age twenty-one he abandoned his legal studies and entered the seminary to study for the priesthood. In 1954 he began to take part in mission work conducted by the Parish Church of Santa Rosa de Lima in tenements and poor neighborhoods. He was ordained in 1959 and spent most of his first year as a priest working alongside the Bishop of Resistencia in the Chaco region of the province of Santa Fe. Upon returning to Buenos Aires, he was assigned to tasks in the curia and began teaching theology at the University of Salvador.

In 1966 Father Mugica participated in a rural mission in the province

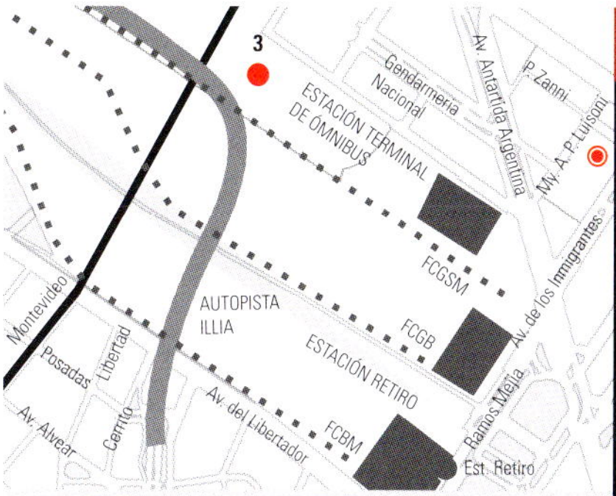


**LOCATION:** BLOCK 30, VILLA DE RETIRO
**TRANSPORTATION:** SUBWAY STATIONS: RETIRO (C LINE). BUSES: 5, 6, 7, 9, 20, 22, 23, 26, 28, 33, 45, 50, 56, 70, 75, 91, 100, 101, 106, 115, 126, 132, 143, 150, 195. TRAIN: RETIRO STATION (MITRE, BELGRANO, AND SAN MARTÍN LINES).

of Santa Fe together with the three men who would go on to found the guerrilla movement known as the Montoneros*: Gustavo Ramus, Fernando Abal Medina, and Mario Firmenich. Two years later he traveled to France, where he deepened his relationship with the priest Rolando Concatti, a leader in the Movement of Priests for the Third World (MSTM, Movimiento de Sacerdotes para el Tercer Mundo). He later traveled to Madrid, where he met Juan Domingo Perón.

CRISTO OBRERO CHAPEL.

PLAQUE HUNG IN 1976 IN REMEMBRANCE OF FATHER CARLOS MUGICA.

CHAPEL ALTAR.

In a 1973 interview Mujica observed that one episode in his life had transformed his ideology. After the fall of Juan Domingo Perón's government in 1955, he said, "I went to work in a tenement as usual. I had to cross a dark alley and suddenly, in the very dim light of a single light bulb, I saw that someone had written in chalk: 'There can be no nation and no God without Perón. Down with the crows [a slang term for priests].' The poor were clearly in mourning, and if they were mourning, I appeared to be on the wrong side."

### Movement of Priests for the Third World

The massive ecumenical gathering known as the Second Vatican Council of 1965 proposed that the church renew itself to better address the needs of the twentieth century. From that moment on, European experiences of "worker-priests" and the "dialogue between Christians and Marxists" were reproduced in Latin America. Many priests followed radical versions of this "option for the poor." One of them was Camilo Torres, a Colombian priest who joined the Colombian guerrilla movement known as the National Liberation Army (ELN, Ejército de Liberación Nacional).

The reforms undertaken in the 1960s by the progressive popes John XXIII and Paul VI were part of this tendency toward change within the Catholic community.

In 1967 Brazilian bishop Hélder Câmara led a group of eighteen bishops from Latin America, Asia, and Africa who drafted a document denouncing the exploitation of impoverished Third World countries by multinational corporations. Two hundred and seventy Argentine priests signed this document in December of that year. The Movement of Priests for the Third World would eventually count 524 full members.

In March 1967 Pope Paul VI promulgated the encyclical *Populorum Progressio,* which denounced the inequalities between rich and poor countries and criticized both capitalism and Soviet collectivism.

The Latin American Episcopal Conference held in Medellín, Colombia, in 1968 underscored the Church's commitment to the poor and the need to address the root causes of poverty. Bishops from several Argentine provinces declared their support for the Third World priests, including Enrique Angelelli from La Rioja (see "Plaza Bishop Enrique Angelelli," p. 138), Alberto Devoto from the city

MURAL IN HOMAGE TO FATHER CARLOS MUGICA.

of Corrientes, Antonio Brasca de Rafaela from Santa Fe, and Jaime de Nevares from Neuquén.

The priests' movement devoted itself to working in impoverished areas between 1968 and 1976 with the support of many laypeople. A number of its members, including Carlos Mugica, aligned themselves with Peronism. Church authorities denounced the movement's declaration in favor of the socialization of economic, political, and cultural power and the abolition of private ownership of the means of production as contrary to the ecclesiastical doctrine of the Episcopate. In 1973 the movement split over political differences, with some priests supporting Peronism and others Marxism.

**Mugica in the shantytown**

Around 1968 Father Mugica collaborated with the pastoral team working in the shantytown known at the time as Barrio de Comunicaciones (today, Villa 31). Father Jorge Goñi's group began to build a chapel which they named the Chapel of Christ the Laborer (Capilla Cristo Obrero).

Juan Domingo Perón returned to Argentina in 1973, nearly twenty years after Peronism had been banned from the political system. Carlos Mugica traveled in the charter plane with Perón. The relationship between the two men intensified from that moment onward.

Fátima Cabrera lived in the shantytown and was a catechist at the time of Perón's visit:

"The chapel bells began ringing to summon us. When we reached the chapel and they told us that Perón had arrived in his car, we couldn't believe it. We had actually just heard on the radio that the General had left his house in Vicente López headed to an unknown destination, but we never imagined he would be coming here to the shanty" [AO 0195].

Perón had traveled to Retiro to meet with Mugica. Afterward, they planned a meeting with other Third World priests.

Mugica endorsed the demands made by a group of local residents who were involved in the national Peronist Shantytown Movement*. An area of six neighborhoods known collectively as the Eva Perón district eventually housed some 50,000 people, most of them port and construction workers. Large numbers of activists, journalists, and political and cultural leaders supported and worked with the movement, including the shantytown leader José Valenzuela. Many of them disappeared during the years of state terrorism, including social worker Lucía Cullen, writer and journalist Rodolfo Walsh (see "Corner of San Juan and Entre Ríos," p. 96), lawyer Héctor Sobel, Marianne Erize Tisseau, Carlos Gustavo Cortiñas, and shantytown activist Alberto Alfaro. Other residents, activists, and supporters of the neighborhood suffered torture, imprisonment, and persecution.

The murder of Alberto Chejolán in March 1974 was one of the first blows to the movement. Chejolán, a local resident and member of the Peronist Shantytown Movement, was killed by police as he took part in a march led by residents of the Barrio de Comunicaciones to oppose the government's plans to raze the shantytowns (see "Club Atlético," p. 129).

Months later Father Mugica was murdered in the doorway of the church of San Francisco Solano in the neighborhood of Villa Luro after delivering Mass on Saturday, May 11, 1974. His presumed killer was Rodolfo Eduardo Almirón (See "Coordinación Federal," p. 17) of the Triple A* (Argentine Anticommunist Alliance).

**Memory in the shantytown**

Several plaques in the entrance to the Chapel of Christ the Laborer (Capilla Cristo Obrero)—the oldest dating to 1976—pay tribute to the "shantytown priest." The neighborhood organizations that have honored him include the Club de Madres Carlos Mugica, the Primero de Mayo shantytown sector, the Amigos del Barrio de Comunicaciones, and the neighborhood associations of Villa Saldía, Laprida, and Comunicaciones. Another plaque was laid in 1999 when Father Mugica's remains were moved to the shantytown from Chacarita cemetery. The Guardians of Mugica *murga* (a group of street dancers and musicians) was founded on that occasion to accompany the procession. A secondary school and a street in the neighborhood of Retiro are also named after him.

Father José "Pichi" Meisegeier continued Father Mugica's pastoral work in the shantytown. Every year a Mass is held in the Chapel of Christ the Laborer on the Sunday following May 11. After Mass, local residents and delegates from Villa 31, along with the Guardians of Mugica, members of the El Campito Cultural Center and of the Father Mugica community kitchen, former catechists, former neighbors, friends, and activists from the shantytown, all gather to celebrate the memory of Father Carlos with traditional games, soccer championships, and *chorizo* barbecues.

# 4. Azopardo Garage



"What is a disappeared person? As long as he remains disappeared, he is an unknown quantity. If he were to reappear, he might be treated in one way. If the disappearance were to be confirmed by death, then he would be treated another way. Yet as long as he is disappeared, there is no certainty. He is unknown, a *disappeared* person. He has no existence; he is neither dead nor alive. He is *disappeared*" [AA].

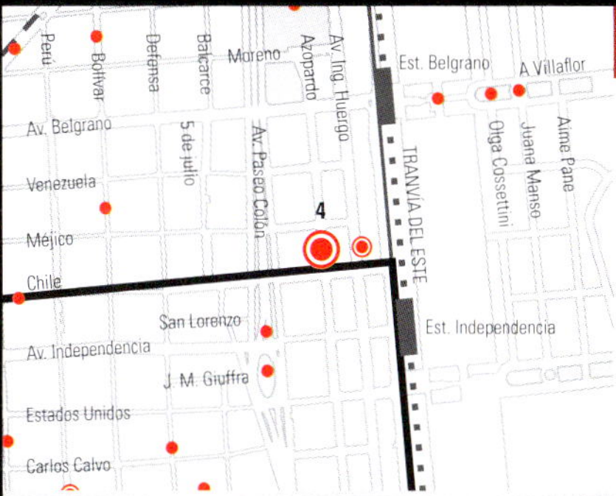


**LOCATION:** AZOPARDO 651
**TRANSPORTATION:** BUSES: 2, 4, 20, 33, 61, 62, 64, 74, 93, 105, 111, 129, 130, 143, 152, 159, 195. TRAMWAY STATION: INDEPENDENCIA.

General Jorge Rafael Videla, leader of the military junta from 1976 to 1981, used these words in a television interview to define the condition of thousands of people who had been detained and disappeared. He made clear that the state terror apparatus sought to erase its victims through the destruction of their identities.

While Videla was thus characterizing the situation of the disappeared, the Mothers of the Plaza de Mayo (see "Plaza de Mayo," p. 3) were demanding that their sons and daughters be released alive. As they marched they carried placards and banners, many of these bearing photographs from their children's national identity cards. While the state denied the existence of the disappeared, the mothers combated that denial with the very photographs this state had used to assign these people an identity. Family members referred indirectly to the dictatorship's repressive practices through the use of these identification portraits; such photographs serve as devices to normalize and enumerate individuals within repressive societies.

A Clandestine Detention Center operated from October 1976 to February 1977 in the building on Azopardo

THE FEDERAL POLICE DOCUMENTATION CENTER CURRENTLY OPERATES IN THE FORMER CLANDESTINE DETENTION CENTER.

Street which until recently served as the Documentation Center of the Argentine Federal Police, where national identification cards and passports were processed. At that time, this building at 651 Azopardo operated as the automotive maintenance shop of the Bureau of Federal Security (see p. 17).

"They kidnapped me along with Patricio Rice, who was a priest at the time. I was working with Carlos Mugica (see "Chapel of Christ the Laborer. Father Carlos Mugica," p. 25). . . . Suddenly a van stopped. There is a neighborhood of police housing at the exit to the Soldati shantytown; the subsidized housing blocks were right across the street. It was a civilian van. A guy got out, started shouting at us, and fired shots at Patricio's feet. . . . Just then another person came out of the police housing complex. They quickly took my handbag and shoved us into the van" [AO.0195].

Fátima Cabrera is a survivor of the Clandestine Detention Center that operated inside the Federal Police facilities known as the Azopardo Garage and Coordinación Federal. After kidnapping her right off the street, the police took her and Patricio Rice to the Villa Soldati police station (see "Police stations as sites of illegal detention," p. 255). They immediately began to interrogate them under torture at the station without processing them:

"'What had we been doing in the shantytown? Who were we with?' And they just got more and more rough. They separated us to ask us questions separately. One of them hit me when I tried to explain something. It started to get really violent. And I just kept asking them to go to my house and let my mother know where I was. And then we found out they were going to move us somewhere else" [AO].

They moved them from the police station to the Azopardo Garage. "When we got there, they took Patricio out first, leaving me in the car a while. The first thing I saw there was a soldier, a conscript. I could hear them asking Patricio very harsh questions. They threw me onto the floor and put a gun to my temple. . . . It was so terrible. And shortly after that they started torturing us. They blindfolded and hooded us."

The first floor of the garage, accessed by a ramp, housed the detention area, the torture room, and the bathroom. They kept the prisoners handcuffed to some hooks hanging from the walls. The security agents would enter the names of the detainees into a register when they arrived, and after the interrogations they would complete the registers with information extracted under torture.

The Special Task Groups* that operated in the Azopardo Garage were made up of Federal Police agents under the command of the First Army Corps.

In December 2008 the Azopardo Garage and Coordinación Federal Commission for Memory and Justice (Comisión Azopardo y Coordinación Federal por Memoria y Justicia), made up of survivors and family members of the victims, dedicated two commemorative paving stones at the site and demanded that the Federal Police be evicted from the building. Nora López Tomé, from the Association of Formerly Detained and Disappeared Persons (Asociación de Ex Detenidos-Desaparecidos) said during the ceremony, "We have to succeed in making this a site of memory because we need to recognize today the identity they stole from us" (*Página 12*, December 17, 2008).

## 5. **Mercedes Benz**

"The Command Unit of Zone 1 wishes to inform the public that on the night of November 2, in the vicinity of the Plaza Constitución, a patrol of loyal forces surprised an activist who was inciting workers to halt their activities and attempting to prevent some factory workers from going to work. He was shot dead, and police are now working to identify him. The forces of law thus fulfilled their mission to ensure the freedom to work" (*La Nación,* November 3, 1977).

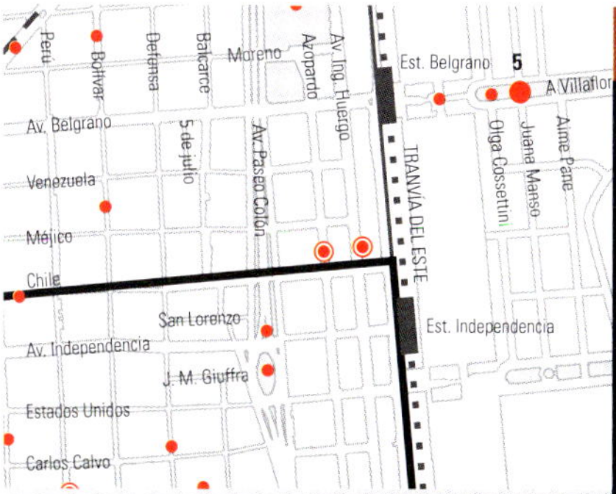


**LOCATION:** BULEVAR AZUCENA VILLAFLOR AND JUANA MANSO
**TRANSPORTATION:** BUSES: 2, 4, 20, 33, 56, 61, 62, 64, 74, 93, 105, 111, 126, 130, 143, 152, 159, 195. TRAMWAY STATION: BELGRANO.

This communiqué published in the newspaper *La Nación* made explicit one of the goals of the repression: the suppression of workers' efforts to organize for better working conditions. The repressive forces appealed to the "right to work" as a justification for the deadly actions taken against workers who intended to strike. The violence employed to dismantle labor activism deepened and broadened as a terror strategy.

Several researchers have noted that attempts to reconstruct the history and operation of state terror since the return to democracy have relied mainly on accounts written by people who had access to the necessary symbolic tools. While organized labor was the sector hardest hit by the dictatorship, workers did not possess the resources to construct an account of their experience, to find an outlet for their testimonies, or to register their experiences in a demand for justice. As noted in the report of the Commission on Disappeared Persons, *Nunca más* (see "Nunca Más Square and Cultural Center," p. 186), most of the disappeared were workers.

Historian Victoria Basualdo has made the following observations with

THE TRIBUTE TO THE DISAPPEARED OF MERCEDES BENZ STANDS ACROSS FROM THE COMPANY'S MAIN OFFICES.

respect to the history of labor during the dictatorship: "New research has just begun to illuminate the relationship between capital and labor in the 1970s and to reveal the close collaboration between the country's largest corporations and the forces of repression. This work is urgent and necessary if we are to understand the nature of the changes that took place [after 1976]" (Basualdo, Victoria, 2005).

During the last military dictatorship seventeen workers from the Mercedes Benz factory were kidnapped; fourteen of them remain disappeared. The Association of Former Mercedes Benz Workers and Family Members of the Disappeared tried to install a plaque in front of the factory in González Catán, but this was impossible. Instead, thanks to a resolution from the Buenos Aires City Council, a plaque commemorating the men was installed across from the company's head office on Azucena Villaflor Boulevard (see p. 51). There is also a space dedicated to their memory in the Paseo de los Derechos Humanos (Human Rights Walk, see p. 235).

Research is currently under way to uncover other cases of kidnappings and disappearances targeting workers. The most notorious cases involve the Ford Motor Company plant located in General Pacheco, in the province of Buenos Aires, which housed a Clandestine Detention Center; the Acindar steel mill in Villa Constitución, in the province of Santa Fe; and the Astarsa shipyards in Tigre, in the province of Buenos Aires (see "Disappeared Port Workers," p. 38).

Founded in Germany in 1880 and active in Argentina since 1951, Mercedes Benz was one of the country's twenty most productive companies by the 1970s. The Argentine military was one of its biggest clients. Adolf Eichmann, a leading architect of the Nazi "final solution" in Eastern Europe, worked as an electrician at Mercedes Benz when he first settled in Argentina after the war. In 1960 Mossad intelligence agents kidnapped him and returned him to Israel to stand trial.

**The union bureaucracy**

Many union leaders joined in the complicity between the economic establishment and the state terror apparatus. The autoworkers' union (SMATA, Sindicato de Mecánicos y Afines del Transporte Automotor) signed an agreement with automakers in July 1975 that dedicated one percent of the sale value of each automobile to a special fund to finance the "eradication of negative elements," giving the union a direct role in the repression.

In October 1975 workers at Mercedes Benz demonstrated against the delegates chosen by the union. Former Mercedes Benz worker Hugo Crosatto describes how they challenged the union bureaucracy:

"What happened at Mercedes Benz can be divided into two periods: before and after the strike of October 1975. It was one of the country's last big labor conflicts. After that, a nine-member commission was formed to represent the workers. It won recognition from management as well. But this commission was never able to do its work because the coup happened almost immediately. In October 1975 the conflict heated up when representatives of the company, SMATA, and the plant workers got together to negotiate our contract. Our five representatives were threatened at gunpoint by SMATA and thrown out of the meeting. This really pissed people off. . . . On October 8 we held a spontaneous workers' assembly. We stated that we wanted to resolve these issues, and we wanted elections. We convened an assembly the next day and named a nine-member commission that was to be recognized by the union. I was one of the nine.

THE PLAQUE WAS DEDICATED IN 2005.

"That day union officials came to tell us that SMATA was not going to recognize our commission and would not lead our struggle until we put a stop to our actions. We reiterated that we wanted to be represented by our own commission until the union called for elections, and we asked them to go away and reconsider our proposal. They never came back, and we continued our strike. Things got worse when the company sent out 117 telegrams of dismissal. We went to the factory that day, but many of us were barred from entering. We called on all the workers to leave the factory. . . . We held a meeting outside and invented the slogan 'Mamadera, mamadera, mamadera, los 4,000 adentro, los 4,000 afuera' (a rhyme that called on the 4,000 workers to stick together, either inside or outside the factory).

"That's when the struggle began on the outside with the strike, and all the Mercedes Benz plants found themselves without workers. We went to the National Congress to speak with the politicians; we wanted to inform them of our goals. But everyone we spoke to just passed the buck. . . . SMATA took out an advertisement accusing us of being subversives and lackeys of the armed movements. To make such a statement at that moment was like saying to the Triple A* [Argentine Anticommunist Alliance], 'Here's a blank check; go do whatever you want with those guys' " (see Coordinación Federal, p. 17).

"We used our strike funds to respond to SMATA with our own advertisement in *Clarín*. We organized a demonstration afterwards at the Ministry of Labor. Carlos Ruckauf was there, but he refused to meet with us. . . . Next, we demonstrated at the head offices of Mercedes Benz on Libertador Street. By then it was October 30, and we'd been out for twenty-two days. At that point the company accepted all our demands: quarterly bonuses and the reinstatement of all the workers who had been fired. It recognized the new internal commission and did not carry out any reprisals for what had happened" [AO.0510].

### The kidnapping of Heinrich Metz

In the midst of the negotiations between the internal commission and the directors of Mercedes Benz, the guerrilla group known as the Montoneros* kidnapped Heinrich Metz, the factory's production manager, on October 24, 1975. Hugo Crosatto describes how they found out about the kidnapping:

"What they did was completely disconnected from our struggle. Neither the internal commission nor the group of activists was directly involved in the kidnapping. . . . The next day some people from the Montoneros met with us on the street to tell us about it. We had an argument because, even though we were sympathetic to these organizations, this action in particular seemed wrong to us because we were right in the middle of a struggle that we were close to winning. We were getting mixed up in a situation not of our own making. One of the Montoneros told us that when they picked up [kidnapped] the German, they found a list in his briefcase with the names of Mercedes Benz workers. They warned us to be careful. . . . Metz was held captive during the negotiations and released in November. But for us it was an isolated event; we were never involved in it at all. The company recognized that a figure like Metz provoked a lot of resentment, and they replaced him as with retired racing star Juan Manuel Fangio, a celebrity no one was going to criticize. But in the interim they appointed a former secret service agent named William Mozetti. He led the negotiations with the Montoneros over Metz's kidnapping. He was a valuable and experienced asset for the repressive forces. . . . He had participated in the German bombings during the Second World War. . . . Mercedes Benz was full of Nazis" [AO].

Raúl Magario belonged to the Montoneros and spent time in prison for his role in the Metz kidnapping. He appears in the documentary film *Milagros no hay* (There are no miracles), directed by journalist Gaby Weber and based on her book *Los desaparecidos de Mercedes Benz* (The Disappeared of Mercedes Benz). In his interview in the film Magario explains that the Montonero national leadership had ordered the businessman's kidnapping without communicating with the factory's internal union commission. The Montoneros also demanded money from the company after the workers were reinstated. The Mercedes Benz head office in Germany claims they paid seven million dollars in ransom, while the Argentine office cites a figure of four million. The Montoneros claim it was only two million dollars.

**Disappeared workers**

Seventeen workers were kidnapped from the Mercedes Benz factory between late 1976 and the end of 1977. Alberto Arenas, Oscar Bauman Alvarez, Héctor Belmonte, Carlos Cienciala, Fernando del Contte, Alberto Gigena, Miguel Grieco, Charles del Carmen Grossi, Jorge Leichner, Juan José Mosquera, Diego Núñez, Esteban Reimer, Víctor Hugo Ventura, and José Vizzini remain disappeared to this day. The three survivors include Héctor Aníbal Ratto, Juan Martín, and Alfredo Martín, who was plant supervisor at the time of his detention in December 1976.

Several pieces of evidence point to the company's complicity in the arrest, kidnapping, and disappearance of the factory's union delegates and workers. A number of workers were kidnapped from their homes, others from their workplaces. Héctor Ratto, who testified in the Truth Trials*, was kidnapped in August 1977 from the factory in González Catán. The company's production manager, Juan Rolando Tasselkraut, approached Ratto as he was returning from a union assembly. He told him that plainclothes agents were looking for him. As Ratto waited for them in Tasselkraut's office, he overheard Tasselkraut inform the agents of the home address of Diego Núñez, who was disappeared that same day. Ratto was held captive in the Clandestine Detention Center inside Campo de Mayo military base and in the Ramos Mejia police station. He was released in March 1979.

Juan Martín was kidnapped from his workplace. He was tortured inside the San Justo police station, which was directed at the time by Rubén Lavallén, later contracted by Mercedes Benz as chief of security. Lavallén was convicted years later for the appropriation of a young child named Paula Logares, who was kidnapped in Montevideo, Uruguay, along with her parents (see "Central Military Hospital," p. 77). Juan Martín survived his disappearance thanks to pressure from a large workers' mobilization outside the La Tablada military base that demanded his release.

Pablo Cueva, director of legal affairs for Mercedes Benz, acknowledged during the Truth Trials that he had provided the security forces with a list of the names and addresses of the members of the factory's internal union commission.

María Luján Reimer, wife of Mercedes Benz worker Esteban Reimer, had organized community meals (*ollas populares*) along with other women outside the company's offices during the strike in 1975. On January 4, 1977, her husband and a fellow worker named Hugo Ventura were called to a meeting at company headquarters. María Luján recalls that they had taken a list of demands with them; when her husband returned that night she was surprised when he told her that the company had agreed to all of them. At 1:00 a.m. nine men broke into their home and took Esteban Reimer away. Hugo Ventura was kidnapped that same night. The soldiers first looked for Ventura in the house next door, which was the address he had provided to Mercedes Benz.

The military coup presented the company with a perfect opportunity to rid itself of the factory's internal union commission, which was outside the control of the labor bureaucracy headed by José Rodríguez, General Secretary of the autoworkers' union (SMATA) from 1973 to 2009. Moreover, production manager Juan Rolando Tasselkraut acknowledged in his testimony at the Truth Trials that Mercedes Benz benefited from a boost in productivity after the disappearances of the plant's union leadership.

Apart from supplying the security forces with the names and addresses of union activists, Mercedes Benz appears to have also been complicit in the military's theft of babies from political prisoners. This widespread practice included the occasional kidnapping of young children along with their parents. More commonly, female prisoners who were pregnant at the time of their disappearance were kept alive until they gave birth. Their babies were then handed over to military personnel or to civilians who sympathized with the military's goals. To cite one example mentioned above, the company hired Rubén Lavallén as head of security in 1978, the same year that Lavallén appropriated as his own daughter a young child named Paula Logares, who had been kidnapped along with her parents, Mónica Grispon and Claudio Logares. Mercedes Benz also donated advanced neonatology equipment to the clandestine maternity ward inside the military hospital of the Campo de Mayo military base, one of the largest Clandestine Detention Centers in the country (see "Central Military Hospital," p. 77). These details, along with other documentary evidence, point to an ongoing and coordinated relationship between the company and the repressive forces. Yet further research is needed to clarify the company's precise role in the theft of babies during the dictatorship.

# 6. **Virrey Cevallos**

**LOCATION:** VIRREY CEVALLOS 630
**TRANSPORTATION:** SUBWAY STATIONS: INDEPENDENCIA (E & C LINES). BUSES: 2, 6, 12, 98, 111, 129, 130, 143, 152, 195.

Miriam Lewin was nineteen years old when the Air Force Intelligence Services kidnapped her as she was leaving the factory where she worked in Lomas del Mirador. She was disappeared and detained in the Clandestine Detention Center that operated in a private house at 628 Virrey Cevallos Street, in the neighborhood of Monserrat.

Lewin had become involved in an anarchist movement in the early 1970s, when she was still in high school. She later joined the Peronist University Youth Movement* (JUP, Juventud Universitaria Peronista) and the Montoneros*. She was first taken to Police Station 44 (see "Police stations as sites of illegal detention," p. 255):

"For some reason they moved me to another room after the first torture session. There I was tied to one of those bed frames with metal strips that form a grid. . . . I never knew who had tortured me. I spent quite a long time in that place. At one point . . . they took me to Virrey Cevallos 628. They took me up to a room that was in a kind of mezzanine, in a courtyard with very high walls. There were two cells on that floor, and they locked me up in one of them. The cell was completely covered in hardboard, which is a kind of brown material filled with small holes" [AO.0065].

The house on Virrey Cevallos had two floors. Kidnapping victims were brought in through a garage; to the left was the torture room, followed by a courtyard with stairs leading up to a mezzanine floor with the two cells. According to survivors, agents of the Federal Police and Army also worked at this site. Lewin spent ten and a half months in isolation.

It is not known for certain how many kidnapped people were held at Virrey Cevallos. The only testimony besides Miriam Lewin's was by Osvaldo López, who was kidnapped from his home in San Miguel, in the province of Buenos Aires. He managed to escape sometime later (see "Automotores Orletti," p. 220, and "House in Franklin Street," p. 226).

Lewin describes what life was like in the center: "Once they secretly took me into the kitchen on the first floor to make me wash the dishes, without letting the commanding officers know. Some of the plates bore

PLAQUE HUNG ON THE FAÇADE OF THE FORMER CLANDESTINE DETENTION CENTER.

THE FORMER CLANDESTINE DETENTION CENTER ON VIRREY CEVALLOS, RECOVERED IN 2004.

Air Force insignia. Very few kidnapped people were held there during the time spent there. There was a room off the patio where they tortured people. They brought people there to torture them all the time, but they didn't keep them here. They took them away after, I guess to the Seré Mansion*. I could hear he screams of people being tortured; I suspect it wasn't just me [who could hear] but all the neighbors too. When they would take me down to the bathroom I could see the little windows of the building next door; they weren't too bothered about covering up the noises. They would turn on Radio Rivadavia, but at times the screams could be heard very clearly. . . . When they took me out of here, they moved me to the ESMA [Navy School of Mechanics]" [AO].

Lewin was transferred to the Navy School of Mechanics (see p. 153). She was released in early 1979 under a "regime of supervised release" and worked at he Ministry of Social Welfare. Some time later she was able to obtain a passport and go into exile. She later returned to Argentina and testified in the Trial of the Military Juntas* in 1985*; in 1988 she was able to identify the Clandestine Detention Center on Virrey Cevallos Street. In 2001 Lewin and other survivors published the book *Ese infierno* (That hell), a collection of accounts by five female survivors of ESMA. In it, Lewin also describes her imprisonment at Virrey Cevallos.

The San Cristóbal Neighborhood Association Against Impunity organized to recover this site, and in 2004 the Legislature of the City of Buenos Aires passed he law to expropriate the property and declared it of public significance

# 7. Disappeared Port Workers



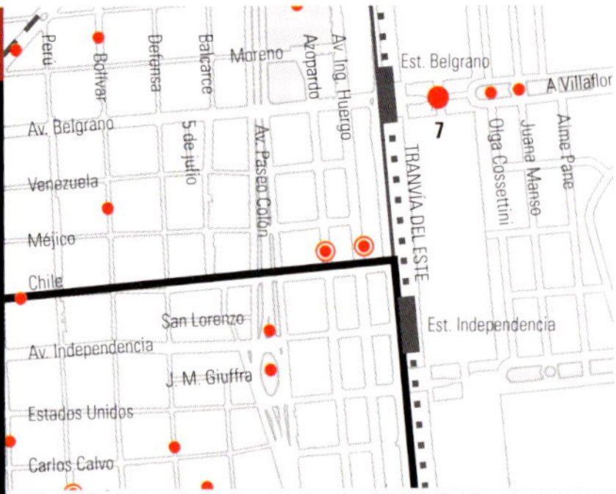


**LOCATION:** BV. AZUCENA VILLAFLOR AND JUANA MANSO
**TRANSPORTATION:** BUSES: 2, 4, 20, 22, 33, 56, 61, 62, 64, 74, 93, 105, 111, 126, 129, 130, 143, 152, 159, 195. TRAMWAY STATION: BELGRANO.

INAUGURATION CEREMONY FOR THE SCULPTURE, NOVEMBER 17, 2005.

A plaque was dedicated on April 30, 2004 in the small square at the intersection of Azucena Villaflor Boulevard (see "Plaza de Mayo," p. 3) and Juana Manso Street to honor disappeared workers from the Port of Buenos.

A monument was erected the following year on the site of a former workers' canteen to commemorate disappeared dockworkers from the union of the Port of Buenos Aires. Artist Omar Gasparini created the sculpture using old iron bars and pieces from boats and cranes. That same day a plaque was dedicated in honor of Eduardo de Pedro, José Manuel Moreno, Francisco Pana, Rubén Correa, and Osvaldo Camarotti, employees of the General Port Administration (AGP, Administración General de Puertos), kidnapped in 1977 and 1978 because of their trade union activities.

## Trade unionists

Odila Casella was kidnapped along with her husband Eduardo de Pedro at three o'clock in the morning on June 29, 1977. In her testimony she recalls, "It was something we had been sensing was going to happen because they had been following us for a week. . . . From the moment they took us out of the house, I never saw him again." Odila was later released.

"Eduardo was already working in the port in 1974," continues Odila, "and a new union movement had formed there to challenge the one that was in place. He was one of the sector delegates; and it was precisely the delegates representing the different sectors within this new union movement in the port who were disappeared. . . . The first one to disappear had been fired a year earlier; he was a sector delegate and he was going to be the union's general secretary. He disappeared in February 1977. . . . When the military authorities

PLAQUE LOCATED NEXT TO THE MONUMENT.

intervened in the port administration, a fellow union member came to live in our house for a year. He is now disappeared. . . . One of the other men was taken directly from his workplace in the New Port (Puerto Nuevo)" [AO].

The *Nunca más* report indicated that 30.2 percent of the cases of disappeared persons brought to the National Commission on the Disappearance of Persons* (CONADEP, Comisión Nacional sobre la Desaparición de Personas) were blue-collar workers; another 17.9 percent were white-collar employees. These figures followed from the military's "Continued Offensive Against Subversion." This decree's "Mission" section ordered that "the Military shall take action selectively in industrial establishments and State corporations . . . to prevent and neutralize labor conflicts provoked or exploited by subversive forces, in order to prevent mass unrest and uprisings and to contribute to the effective operation of the country's productive apparatus" (CONADEP, 1984).

This plan accounts for the disappearance of delegates from the union of Buenos Aires port workers and was also applied against other labor organizations such as the autoworkers' union, SMATA (Sindicato de Mecánicos y Afines del Transporte Automotor); the Confederation of Education Workers of the Argentine Republic, or CTERA (see "Disappeared teachers," p. 204); and the electrical workers' union, Luz y Fuerza. Workers were disappeared from industrial establishments like the Ford factory in General Pacheco (see "Mercedes Benz," p. 31), the Mestrina Shipyards in the northern part of the province of Buenos Aires, and the Astarsa Shipyards in San Fernando. The dictatorship singled out the union movement's most militant sectors; disappearances of labor activists continued from 1976 through 1978. Most of these shop-floor union activists remain disappeared today.

# 8. **Federal Police Headquarters**

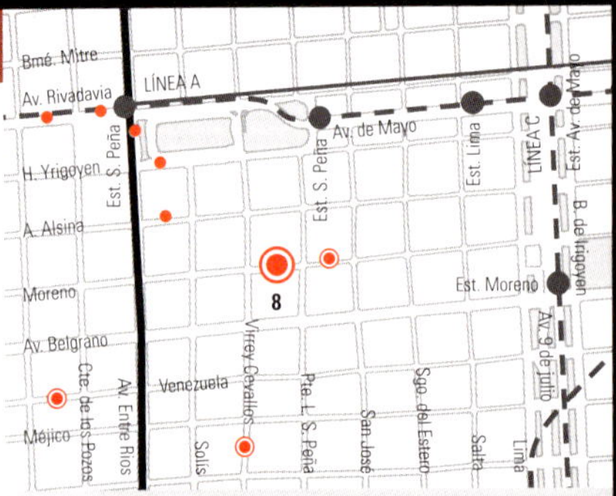


**LOCATION:** MORENO 1550
**TRANSPORTATION:** SUBWAY STATION: SÁENZ PEÑA (A LINE). BUSES: 2, 4, 20, 22, 33, 56, 61, 62, 74, 93, 105, 111, 126, 129, 130, 142, 143, 159.

The municipal office located in the Federal Police Headquarters operated as a secret detention site during the dictatorship, just one block away from the Clandestine Detention Center known as Coordinación Federal (see p. 17).

Peronist militant Horacio González was detained here "immediately after the coup" [AO.0379]. The Montonero* guerrillas had killed several police officers and higher officials in the previous days. González, who had recently lost his job, was looking at the want ads near his home when a police officer who had arrested him four years earlier recognized him and arrested him again on the grounds that it was suspicious to find him in that location.

González was held illegally for three or four months at the Federal Police Headquarters. Describing the office of his arresting officer, he recalls, "This man had pictures of [nineteenth-century military strongman] Juan Manuel de Rosas alongside pornographic photographs." The officer disagreed with the dictatorship's methods of repression, and he tried to help González by falsely reporting that González had been carrying a weapon at the time of his arrest, in order to have him tried by a war tribunal. Though he might face a twenty-year prison sentence, his life would not be in danger.

Gónzalez, current director of the National Library, was transferred weekly to the Patricios First Regiment headquarters (see p. 74), where he faced interrogation and verbal attacks by the military tribunal. Ultimately, however, the tribunal declared that it lacked the legal authority to try his case.

During his time in captivity González saw prisoners brought in from other Clandestine Detention Centers in very bad shape from beatings. Political prisoners were held along with common prisoners in a large, overcrowded cell that was called the henhouse (*gallinero*). González learned about other Clandestine Detention Centers during this period of detention.

General Cesáreo Ángel Cardozo was named Chief of Police five days after the coup on March 31, 1976. Three months later the Montoneros* killed him by detonating a bomb under his bed. He was replaced by Arturo Amador Corbetta, a general and lawyer who had publicly declared himself a "legalist," someone who believed that the military should exercise power within the existing legal framework.

Corbetta lasted only ten days in his post. On July 2, 1976, another bomb exploded, this time in the Bureau of Federal Security, killing twenty-seven police officers. The police called for a bloody reprisal. Two officers appeared in the police chief's office with a list of eighteen political prisoners who should be executed. Corbetta fired the two men and filed his own resignation.

Although a blood pact bound the members of the security forces, some individuals rejected the methods of illegal repression. According to the *Nunca más* report written by the National Commission on the Disappearance of Persons* (CONADEP, Comisión Nacional sobre la Desaparición de Personas) (see "Nunca Más Square and Cultural Center," p. 186), "Brutal punishment awaited any member of the Armed and Security Forces who demonstrated ambivalence toward the methods used to detain and eliminate people. Passing on information to family members about the whereabouts, fate, or physical condition of anyone detained and disappeared was punishable by death. It was even forbidden for soldiers in the ranks to share information about the operations they had carried out. Any gesture of humanity toward an individual prisoner was rigorously punished." (CONADEP, 1984).

Ariel Blaustein was held at Coordinación Federal before being transferred to the Federal Police Headquarters. He recalls that he heard the bomb explode at Coordinación Federal while he was there. He encountered more humane treatment at the Police Headquarters: "I became just another regular guy. There were lots of prisoners together in a large block, so you could move and walk around; you weren't blindfolded or handcuffed. We could talk to each other and discuss things. We even played the guitar while they were holding a wake for Cardozo in the central patio of the Police Headquarters. It was crazy. . . . We didn't even know they were holding a wake until they told us to shut up. You had a social life; it was completely different. Prisoners would come and go. They would come in from Chaco, from Sierra Chica, they would go on to Devoto [see p. 199]. A great many were given the option to go into exile. Uruguayans and Chileans would pass through, as would others on their way to Peru. Some had accepted exile and were heading to Mexico. We talked about politics all the time because the guards weren't like regular prison guards. They were 'softer' cops, less professional" [AO].

Blaustein recalls that during the three months he was held captive, people would arrive from different Clandestine Detention Centers in very bad shape. A large number were experienced political activists from the north of the country. He was detained alongside Carlos Slepoy, who went on to work as a lawyer with the Argentine Association for Human Rights (AAPDH, Asociación Argentina pro Derechos Humanos) in Madrid. In his testimony at the Truth Trials*, Slepoy told the Federal Court that he had been detained for political reasons before the coup. During an interrogation session at the Navy School of Mechanics (ESMA), the interrogators warned him that "if he was a subversive he would end up in the river." After being held prisoner at Coordinación Federal, he was transferred to the Federal Police Headquarters: "We were in some kind of large hall where they kept throwing in blindfolded people. Many had bloody noses from the tight blindfold that kept them from seeing anything," he observed. He also reported that his wife Andrea Benitez was kidnapped while leaving the building after visiting him (Permanent Assembly for Human Rights 2001).

Rodolfo Daer was a delegate from the construction workers' union. He was detained along with his girlfriend on June 19, 1976, by a group of plainclothes men carrying Itaka guns. "They forced me into a bottle green Ford Falcon," recalls Daer [AO.0427]. When the car stopped "they took me to a large room. There were lots of people lying there; one man had his hands tied behind his back. One was missing a leg. There was water on the floor. They threw me a blanket and then they took me out of there and put me in a cell. Then I started to hear Elsa's screams." They were torturing his girlfriend. A police officer told him, "Start talking, because she's telling us everything." Then they took him to another room, where they sat him down and painted his lips and eyes with the lipstick they had taken from Elsa's purse. "They were laughing their heads off at me," said Daer.

Next, they took him to the torture room. They asked him for names, telephone numbers, and addresses. He spent thirty to forty hours in captivity before being released: "As they were putting me into the trunk of the Falcon, I saw the entrance to the Buenos Aires Police Headquarters through my blindfold." This is how Daer, who went on to lead the General Confederation of Labor (CGT, Central General de Trabajadores) in 1996 and then became head of the Union of Food Industry Workers, recognized where he had been detained. He heard the sound of weapons being loaded when they took him out of the car, and he thought they were about to execute him. Yet it was just a simulation; they had decided to let him go.

## 9. **Buenos Aires National School**

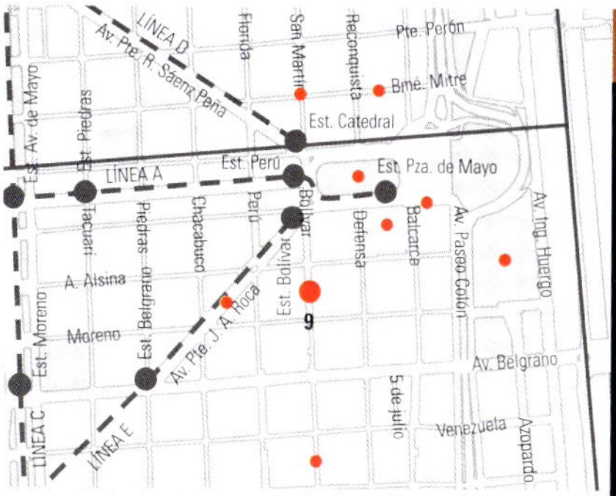


**LOCATION:** BOLÍVAR 263
**TRANSPORTATION:** SUBWAY STATIONS: PLAZA DE MAYO (A LINE), BOLÍVAR (E LINE), CATEDRAL (D LINE). BUSES: 2, 4, 20, 22, 24, 33, 56, 61, 62, 64, 74, 93, 105, 111, 126, 130, 143, 152, 159, 195.

Eduardo Blaustein went to school on August 23, 1974, as he did every day. He was sixteen years old and in his fourth year of high school at the Buenos Aires National School. He saw a dead body for the first time in his life that day. It was the body of one of his fellow students, Eduardo Bekerman. "I remember how frightened I was by the idea of seeing a dead body. I had never been to a funeral, and I had always been quite a wimp about death and horror films" [AO.0242]. Bekerman, who was president of the Union of Secondary School Students* (UES, Unión de Estudiantes Secundarios), had been murdered by the Triple A* (Argentine Anticommunist Alliance) the day before, on the second anniversary of the Trelew Massacre*. School principal Raúl Aragón, who had been appointed after the presidential election of Héctor Cámpora in 1973, suspended classes and offered the school as the venue for Bekerman's wake. According to student union records, Eduardo Bekerman was one of 106 students of the Buenos Aires National School who were victims of state terrorism.

The Buenos Aires National School is a traditional institution founded in 1863 by Argentine president Bartolomé Mitre. It was annexed to the University of Buenos Aires in 1911 as a preparatory school. This unique status has contributed to the school's historic prestige and given it greater autonomy with respect to academic programing. Many leading figures in Argentine politics studied here, contributing to the school's mystique as a "training ground for the ruling classes." The climate inside the institution always reflected the nation's political mood, varying from an atmosphere of rigid discipline to one of greater freedom and politicization.

PLAQUE DEDICATED IN 1997 WITH THE NAMES OF NINETY-EIGHT VICTIMS OF ILLEGAL REPRESSION.

Many young people in Argentina became involved with labor organizing and student politics during the 1960s and 1970s, a period of revolutionary movements in politics, arts, and culture. An activist culture developed around certain issues and key figures.

One of these was the ideal of political commitment. "To commit oneself to reality" meant to "do something" to bring an end to injustice in the world through social, labor, or political activism. Participants in these types of organizations spoke in terms of "commitment to the poor," "commitment to their fellow activists," or "commitment to the (revolutionary) cause."

Paula Mahler, who graduated from the Buenos Aires National School in 1972, recalls, "Political activism meant a commitment to a collective sense of identity, like a social group or family. It gave you a sense of belonging. At that time, young people of different backgrounds who went to a school as politicized as the National School became activists because of the social context in which they were living." [AO.0460].

Eduardo Blaustein describes his own high school experiences as follows: "Everyone inevitably got caught up in what was going on. . . . And if you already had some kind of political background, it was impossible not to get carried away by all the issues of the time: Vietnam, the Beatles, rock and roll, the events of 1968 in France. . . . The number of political activists exploded between 1973 and 1974. That's where the idea came from that the school had four hundred political militants. What we now refer to as the 'quiet majority'—those people who preferred to remain conservative and 'mind their own business'—were actually a minority" [AO].

### Spring at the Buenos Aires National School

Novelist Martín Caparrós graduated from the Buenos Aires National School in 1973. He describes the appointment of Raúl Aragón as school principal that year in his novel *No velas a tus muertos* (You don't honor your dead) (1986): "When it came time to name a new school principal, they came and asked *us* our opinion. And later during the ceremony when he took office, we were the ones setting the rhythm with our drums and everything. And that was an official ceremony. The school principal was taking office and we were the masters, we were in control of everything."

Aragón lasted just over a year as head of the school. Yet though it was brief, his tenure is remembered as having been one of the most democratic periods in the school's history. Students felt they were being listened to and even included in the school's administration, perhaps more than ever before in the institution's history. National Reconstruction Workshops were held during this period. These were forums for debate over such issues as the school's governance structure, admissions procedures, regime of discipline, forms of evaluation, and even curriculum. Over three hundred students, fifty teachers, and thirty staff took part. Many reform proposals were put forward and later implemented: the entrance exam was replaced by a less "elitist" lottery system; the traditional uniforms were eliminated; and the small shelters that had previously been used as sentry boxes to keep watch on the students' activities in the galleries were reassigned to the school's different political groups. The institution's traditional atmosphere of silence and solemnity gave way to one of continuous discussion and student participation.

Principal Aragón defended the students' political participation as long as it did not affect their academic performance, and the student movement within the school in turn supported his leadership. Nonetheless, the principal's situation grew increasingly precarious as the national government of Juan Perón began to distance itself from its left wing, which had backed Aragón's appointment. After

BRONZE PLAQUE DEDICATED IN 1985.

MONOLITH IN MEMORY OF THE NOCHE DE LOS LÁPICES.

Perón's death in July 1974, the students held a meeting and decided to stage a peaceful occupation of the school to defend the principal and oppose the advance of the right. During the occupation, which lasted for more than a month, students guaranteed the continuation of classes, organized various activities, and slept in the school in shifts to "watch over it." However, in September of that year, Aragón was dismissed when the government of Isabel Martínez de Perón intervened in the University of Buenos Aires's administration. With the arrival of spring in Buenos Aires, the school's own "spring" came to a close.

**The period of state terrorism at the school**

As students returned to classes in October 1974, they encountered a message written on the blackboard opposite the main entrance of the Buenos Aires National School: "Assemblies of any kind are prohibited." The school had been closed since Aragón's dismissal a month earlier, and this was the students' first contact with the school's new principal, Mario Garda. Both he and his successor, Antonio Muñoz, were forced to resign following constant clashes with the students, who mounted an organized resistance to the ban on political activism. The students enjoyed the support of many parents, who protested against the arbitrary policies enacted against their children.

Eduardo Aníbal Rómulo Maniglia took office as the new principal on September 5, 1975. Shortly thereafter, he wrote an internal memo describing his perspective on the school's situation: "To summarize, the Buenos Aires National School represented an explosive reflection of the chaos affecting the entire country, which saw stateless Marxism attempting to seize political control. When the current principal, Rómulo Maniglia, took office, he began a process of gradual recovery by quickly suppressing disturbances within the school and eliminating their instigators, be they students, staff, teachers, or administrators" (Garaño and Pertot, 2003).

The changes at the school were unmistakable after Aragón's departure. The entire staff of school monitors was dismissed, and their replacements were assigned intelligence tasks. Many teachers and teaching assistants were fired. Maniglia reimposed uniforms and strict discipline, as well as the old rules of personal cleanliness and presentation. The administration placed controls on students' movements within the school and used more punishments and expulsions to discipline those who broke the rules.

The new climate at the school provoked many students to drop out. From 1975 to 1980 the school lost 935 students. Some were dismissed for academic reasons but most because of accumulated absences and punishments or expulsions. In the two years after Aragón's departure, 531 students lost their regular status at the school.

The gloomy atmosphere inside the Buenos Aires National School was an extreme example of the broader repression against the student movement. According to official statistics compiled by the National Commission on the Disappearance of Persons* (CONADEP), 21 percent of the disappeared were students, and 10.61 percent were between the ages of sixteen and twenty.

**Empty desks**

"When they kidnapped Mirta, her absence was obvious, because all the seats in the classroom were taken except one: Mirta was missing. One girl who was her close friend spent the entire day in tears" (Garaño and Pertot, 2003). This testimony comes from a twelfth-grade student from the same class as Mirta Lovazzano, who was an activist in the Union of Secondary School Students (UES). It also appears in the book *The Other Juvenilia: Militancy and Repression at the Buenos Aires National School, 1971–1986* (*La otra juvenilia: Militancia y represión en el Colegio Nacional de Buenos Aires [1971–1986]*), written by Santiago Garaño and Werner Pertot. These two graduates of the school "grew tired of hearing over and over again the names of former students who were national heroes," when the institution had never made any effort to remember the names of its disappeared.

With the return to democracy, family members and friends focused their efforts on discovering the truth about what had happened to the disappeared and fighting for justice against those who were responsible. In time, they organized tributes and remembrance ceremonies to preserve the memory of what had happened. The school's student union supported these efforts; its Human Rights Commission initiated investigations into what had happened during those years. As a result of these joint initiatives, the first commemorative plaque paying tribute to the disappeared was dedicated in the central patio of the school in 1985. It took the institution another eleven years to add its own official recognition.

In 1996 acting principal Enrique Groisman allowed the school's main auditorium to be used for the "Bridge for Remembrance" ceremony organized by the Madres de Plaza de Mayo, the Foundation for Argentine Historical and Social Memory, the school's student union, and a group of former students. The first list of disappeared was drawn up at this time. A bronze plaque was finally installed in November 1997. Designed by the artist Pablo García Reinoso, it bears the names of ninety-eight victims of state terrorism who had been identified by that point. A smaller plaque placed next to it reads as follows: "Given the nature of illegal repression, this list may be incomplete. Any further information may be directed to the school's Student Union." The students and, through them, the entire civil society bear the responsibility for preserving memory.

# 10. **Prison Ships: *Bahía Aguirre* and *33 Orientales***

During the last dictatorship several ships were used as prisons and as Clandestine Detention Centers (CDCs). Testimonies exist relating to the following ships: the *Muratore,* the *Ciudad de la Plata,* the *Bahía Aguirre,* and the *33 Orientales.* The last two were located in the port of Buenos Aires. Owing to their special circumstances, information about these Clandestine Detention Centers is scarce.

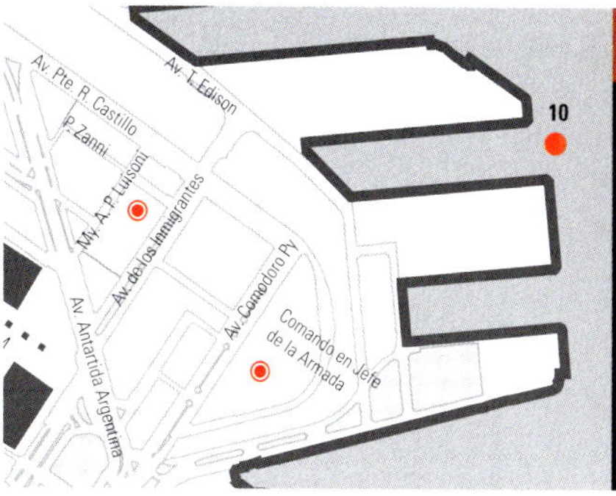




### *Bahía Aguirre*

This merchant ship was built in a Canadian shipyard and incorporated into the Naval Transport Service of the Argentine Navy in 1950. It was taken out of service in 1981 and scrapped by the Acindar steel company.

On March 30, 1976, three plainclothes men arrested an employee of the National Atomic Energy Commission and identified themselves as personnel from Coordinación Federal (see p. 17). They claimed to be doing a "background check," according to the employee's testimony to the National Commission on the Disappearance of Persons* (CONADEP) (see "Nunca Más Square and Cultural Center," p. 186). The man was taken first to Police Station 35 (see "Police stations as sites of illegal detention," p. 255), where he was beaten and then forced into a Navy truck containing seven other people. They traveled along Avenida Libertador for roughly twenty minutes and then arrived at the port, where they were taken aboard the *Bahía Aguirre.* They were blindfolded, hooded, and tied to the berths by their wrists. The detainees were tortured. This man, who later testified before the CONADEP, was then driven to Devoto Prison (see p. 199) in a Federal Police car and on to Prison Unit No. 9 in the city of La Plata. His declaration reveals that the *Bahía Aguirre* also held women detainees, who were naked and covered in blood. He was released on October 8, 1976.

### *33 Orientales*

This merchant ship was specially built in Cádiz, Spain, to navigate along the Río de la Plata. With luxurious facilities including a large bar, swimming pool, en suite cabins, and first-class and tourist-class dining halls, it traveled between Buenos Aires and Montevideo and could even reach Rio de Janeiro.

Between 1976 and 1977 the ship stopped carrying passengers and was turned into a prison ship. Several union and political leaders were held captive in it. One man who later declared before the CONADEP claimed he had been detained and disappeared on board this ship. He had gone there to inquire about his son's disappearance. They arrested him on the spot, detained him for forty-five days on the ship, and then moved him to Police Station 18. He was illegally detained there for a month and then transferred to Devoto prison. They later moved him to Unit 9 in La Plata and then back to Devoto, until they eventually released him and he went into exile.

The *33 Orientales* returned to passenger service in 1978. It was used for cruises to Brazil until being moored and sold at auction in 1979. After changing owners several times, in June 2006 it was sold as scrap in India.

# 11. **Héctor Germán Oesterheld**

**LOCATION:** AV. CORRIENTES AND URUGUAY, URUGUAY SUBWAY STATION
**TRANSPORTATION:** SUBWAY STATION: URUGUAY (B LINE). BUSES: 5, 6, 7, 23, 24, 26, 29, 39, 50, 102, 146, 155.

In 1991 a scene from the famous Argentine science fiction comic *El eternauta* was re-created to decorate the Uruguay subway station on the city's B line. A large ceramic mural along the station's platform wall depicts scenes by two of the comic's illustrators, Alberto Breccia and Solano López.

In 1957 Héctor Germán Oesterheld wrote the story line for *El eternauta*, one of the most widely read comics in Argentina. It tells the story of an alien invasion of Buenos Aires from the perspective of a character named Juan Salvo, a middle-class man who runs a small company that manufactures electrical transformers. Salvo is shocked when a deadly snowfall of radioactive flakes begins to fall one day while he is home with friends playing a popular Argentine card game called *truco*. He seals his home to guard against the radiation and then embarks on an adventure with family and friends. Along the way, they encounter other groups of survivors who are trying to resist the invasion of the "Others" (*Ellos*). At one point Salvo becomes lost in a time warp. An old man he meets dubs him the Eternaut, the eternal time traveler.

Oesterheld founded the Frontera publishing house, which introduced such characters as the test pilot Bull Rocket and two comic strips illustrated by Hugo Pratt: *Sergeant Kirk* and *Ernie Pike,* whose main character was a World War II news correspondent. Working with illustrator Solano López, Oesterheld also published several chapters of *El eternauta* in the magazine *Hora Cero*.

URUGUAY STATION ON THE B SUBWAY LINE.

Oesterheld was born in Buenos Aires on July 23, 1919, and graduated with a degree in geology. His career mirrored that of journalist Rodolfo Walsh (see "Corner of San Juan and Entre Ríos," p. 96). Both of these men began their careers working in what some critics have called minor genres. Walsh, who wrote works of investigative journalism such as *Operación masacre* (1957), began his career writing detective stories, just as Oesterheld was writing comic strips. Yet both men were marked by the political radicalism that affected an entire generation of intellectuals in the 1960s, and they brought their creative work in line with their political activism. Both *Operación massacre* and *El eternauta* were repeatedly rewritten to reflect changing political events.

Oesterheld's story of alien invasion, first published in 1957, reappeared in 1969 with illustrations by Breccia. The changes made in this second edition showed how international events had shaped Oesterheld's views of imperialism. His politicization stemmed from events such as Che Guevara's death in Bolivia and the worker-student uprising in 1969 known as the Cordobazo*, which left an indelible mark on Argentine history. The modified story line tied the alien invasion to the problem of imperialism. When Juan Salvo turns on the radio for news of the invasion, he learns about the complicity of foreign powers. One of his fellow card players makes the following observation: "We're like the Aztecs or the Incas fighting against the Europeans. . . . The enemy invaders come from another solar system, and somehow they have convinced the United States, Russia, and the other economic powers that the world must be shared with them. To protect themselves from attack, these large powers have handed over South America."

Both Oesterheld and Walsh committed themselves to armed struggle by working for the press service of the Montonero* guerrilla movement. Evidence of this choice can be found in the modifications made to their creative work. Walsh worked with Jorge Cedrón and Julio Troxler to produce a film version of *Operación masacre* that highlighted the views of the main protagonists and presented an argument in favor of armed struggle. Oesterheld wrote a new story of alien invasion, *La guerra de los Antartes* (The war of the Antartes) as a follow-up to *El eternauta*. In this story, the aliens once again agree to share their technology with the world's economic powers in exchange for the right to occupy South America.

In 1968 Jorge Álvarez Publishers contracted Oesterheld to create graphic biographies of several historical figures from Latin America. He completed one about Che Guevara and was planning another about Eva Perón when the military government banned the work and seized the originals before they could be delivered to the printer.

By 1969 Oesterheld and his four daughters had become activists in the Peronist movement; they later joined the Montonero armed movement. In 1970 he began publishing *La guerra de los Antartes* in the magazine *2001*, but he soon had to stop. He began to publish it again in February 1974 in the daily *Noticias*, but publication stopped once again when the newspaper was shut down later that year. He also wrote *América Latina, 450 años de guerra* (Latin America, 450 years of war) for the Peronist Youth* magazine *El descamisado* (no. 10, July 24, 1973). In 1976 Oesterheld went underground* and wrote the sequel to *El eternauta*, collaborating again with illustrator Solano López.

Oesterheld's daughters Beatriz and Diana were kidnapped in 1976, Estela and Marina in 1977. All four remain disappeared. Diana was disappeared along with her partner, Raúl Araldi. Their son Fernando was taken as well but was later recovered by the family. Diana was eight months pregnant and is believed to have given birth in the Campo de Mayo* military base, where she was detained.

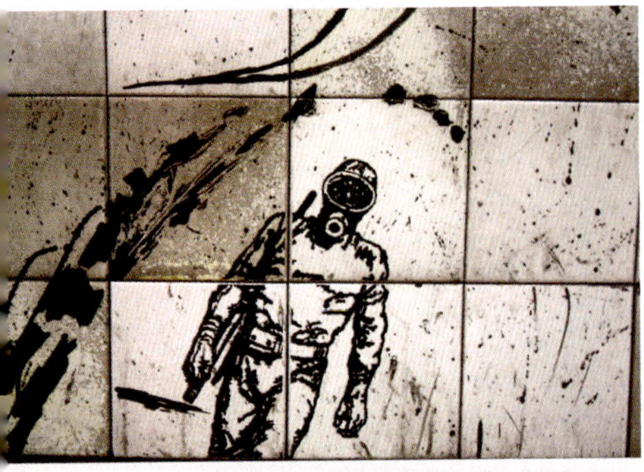

EL ETERNAUTA.

JUAN SALVO IN THE ILLUSTRATION BY ALBERTO BRECCIA.

Estela was kidnapped along with her partner, Raúl Motola, who remains disappeared. Their three-year-old son Martín was recovered and raised by his maternal grandmother. Marina was also pregnant at the time of her kidnapping. Fernando, Martín, and his wife, Elsa, continue to search for Héctor Oesterheld's other two grandchildren.

Héctor was kidnapped in the city of La Plata on April 27, 1977. According to survivors' testimony, he was held in a series of Clandestine Detention Centers: Campo de Mayo*, El Vesubio*, and another known as the Sheraton*. The story of *El eternauta* is viewed today as a foreshadowing of Oesterheld's own story.

In 1997 a small plaza in Puerto Madero was dedicated in Héctor Oesterheld's name, following an initiative that won universal approval from Buenos Aires City Council. The plaque, which was later stolen, bore a quotation from the prologue of *El eternauta:* "The only true hero is the collective hero, never the solitary hero who stands alone." When this plaque was stolen, an ad hoc group prepared a replacement; it too was removed. Today, the plaza located at Avenida de los Italianos and Azucena Villaflor carries no sign bearing Oesterheld's name.

## 12. **Azucena Villaflor Boulevard**

In 1995 the Urban Nomenclature Commission chose a selection of important women to honor with street names in Puerto Madero. One boulevard today bears the name of Azucena Villaflor in honor of her commitment and dedication. A plaque was also dedicated in her memory near the Old Puerto Madero Corporation building in October 2001.

**LOCATION:** BETWEEN AV. INGENIERO HUERGO AND AV. DE LOS ITALIANOS, PUERTO MADERO.

## 13. **Tribute to Representatives of Different Religious Faiths**

On March 24, 2006, thirty years after the military coup, a plaque was dedicated to representatives of different religious faiths. The unveiling was organized jointly by the Secretariat of Worship of the Ministry of Foreign Affairs, the Argentine Human Rights Secretariat, and the Government of the City of Buenos Aires. A priest, a rabbi, a Muslim dignitary, and a Protestant minister all participated.

**LOCATION:** CORNER OF AV. SANTA FE AND AV. MAIPU, PLAZA SAN MARTIN, RETIRO

## 14. **República Building**

Two plaques dedicated by FOETRA (the Federation of Telephone Workers and Employees of the Argentine Republic) pay tribute to the disappeared union members Elizabeth Franco and Silvestre Andreani. Elizabeth was twenty-nine years old when she was kidnapped on July 23, 1977, near what was then the Abasto Market. A paving stone was place in Plaza Almagro in her memory. Silvestre was thirty-two years old when he was kidnapped on April 11, 1977, in a parking lot near his workplace.

**LOCATION:** CORNER OF AV. CORRIENTES AND MAIPU, SAN NICOLAS

## 15. **Plaza Lavalle**

The Buenos Aires Lawyers' Association dedicated two plaques in front of the city's central courthouse (Palacio de Tribunales) on March 24, 1996. One pays tribute to the more than 150 lawyers who were detained and disappeared. The other commemorates 15 legal employees who were disappeared. "Affirming the ideals of justice and keeping social memory alive, we say, *Nunca más* [Never again]."

LOCATION: CORNER OF LAVALLE AND TALCAHUANO, SAN NICOLAS.

## 16. Tribute to Disappeared Bank Employees

In the building of the former Banco Avellaneda, which functions today as the headquarters of SEDRONAR (Secretariat for the Prevention of Drug Addiction and the Fight against Drug Trafficking), a plaque was dedicated in honor of Alicia Mateos, Roberto Lázzara, and Nancy Ibáñez, all disappeared union delegates from the bank. A fourth employee, Eduardo Dimas Berrozpe (currently Press and Broadcasting Secretary of the Banking Association) survived when he managed to escape by hiding in an armored van.

**LOCATION:** SARMIENTO 546, SAN NICOLAS.

## 17. Tarnopolsky Family

The Tarnopolsky Family Documentation and Memory Archive was inaugurated in July 2001 in the SeTCIP (Secretariat for Technology, Science, and Productive Innovation). Hugo Tarnopolsky, an industrial chemist and member of the Chamber of the Chemical Industry, and his wife, Blanca, an educational psychologist, were kidnapped along with their fifteen-year-old daughter, Betina, their son Sergio, and their daughter-in-law Laura de Luca. Daniel, the couple's third child, survived because he did not sleep at home that day.

**LOCATION:** AV. CORDOBA 831, SAN NICOLAS.

## 18. Employees of the Banco Nación

A plaque was unveiled in a ceremony on March 20, 2006, to commemorate the twelve employees of the Banco Nación who were detained and disappeared. Two photo exhibits were also inaugurated. One depicts the activities of the employees and the other, called *De la identidad* (On identity), recounts the stories of the more than eighty kidnapped children who have been recovered by the Abuelas de Plaza de Mayo (Grandmothers of the Plaza de Mayo, see pp. 3 and 78).

**LOCATION:** BARTOLOME MITRE 326, SAN NICOLAS.

## 19. La Rioja House

In a ceremony in the Casa de la Rioja on August 19, 2007, two plaques were unveiled to pay tribute to the disappeared from the province of La Rioja and to Monsignor Enrique Angelelli (see p. 138). Both were placed in the reception hall that bears his name. Among those who took part were representatives of the Mothers of the Plaza de Mayo and Grandmothers of the Plaza de Mayo as well as the governor of La Rioja, Luis Beder Herrera.

**LOCATION:** AV. CALLAO 745, SAN NICOLAS.

## 20. Health Workers from the City of Buenos Aires

Thirty years after the military coup a ceremony took place in the Health Secretariat of the City of Buenos Aires. Hundreds of people attended, including authorities from the Secretariat and directors of several of the city's hospitals and health centers. Dr. Donato Spaccavento, Health Secretary at the time, unveiled the plaque.

**LOCATION:** CARLOS PELLEGRINI 313, SAN NICOLAS.

## 21a. Employees of the Banco Provincia

A ceremony at the headquarters of the Banco Provincia on March 23, 2006, paid tribute to the 27 bank employees who were disappeared. It included an exhibit of photos and newspaper clippings, as well as paper cutouts of handprints bearing photos of the disappeared, and an earlier request to the bank's administrators was reiterated: that they remove portraits of bank directors active under the dictatorship from the gallery dedicated to past bank presidents.

**LOCATION:** CORNER OF BARTOLOME MITRE AND SAN MARTIN, SAN NICOLAS

## 21b. Banco Provincia Exhibition Center

The Dr. Arturo Jauretche Historical Archive and Museum of the Banco de la Provincia de Buenos Aires displays official documentation relating to the bank's history since its founding. One area is dedicated to disappeared bank employees and to more recent campaigns organized by employees. This permanent exhibit is open Monday to Friday, 10 a.m. to 6 p.m.

**LOCATION:** SARMIENTO 362, SAN NICOLAS

## 22. Tribute to Disappeared Uruguayans

On May 20, 2006, a paving stone was dedicated to mark the thirtieth anniversary of the kidnapping and murder of Uruguayan citizens Zelmar Michelini, Héctor Gutiérrez Ruiz, Rosario Barredo, and William Withelaw. It was placed at the Hotel Liberty, the site of Michelini's kidnapping. A March of Silence was organized on the same day in Uruguay to remember those who had been detained and disappeared.

**LOCATION:** CORNER OF AV. CORRIENTES AND FLORIDA, SAN NICOLAS.

## 23. **Juan Arano – Luis Cervera Novo – Ricardo Gómez – Carmen Román**

On May 20, 1977, a commando unit that was watching the Communist Party headquarters in the capital kidnapped seven party activists as they were leaving the building. Three of them were later released. Juan, Luis, Ricardo, and Carmen remain disappeared. The kidnappings were part of a joint operation between Chile's National Intelligence Directorate (DINA) and the Argentine Army to prevent the transfer of funds to the Chilean Communist Party.

**LOCATION:** AV. CALLAO 274, SAN NICOLAS

## 24. **Martín Bercovich – Eduardo Merajver**

Martín and Eduardo were cousins. They were kidnapped by a gang of men and held captive in the headquarters of Coordinación Federal on May 12–13, 1976. Both men distributed the underground newspaper known as *El Combatiente,* published by the PRT-ERP* political movement. Family members, friends, and the Commission of Neighborhoods for Memory and Justice placed a paving stone paying tribute to them at the site of their disappearance.

**LOCATION:** LIBERTAD 378, SAN NICOLAS

## 25. **Employees of the Ministry of Justice**

A ceremony took place on May 27, 2008, on the mezzanine of the Ministry of Justice headquarters, to pay tribute to detained and disappeared employees. Participants included Ministry employees and representatives from the Argentine Workers' Federation (CTA) and from human rights organizations. A plaque was dedicated during the event.

**LOCATION:** SARMIENTO 329, SAN NICOLAS

## 26. **Miguel Francisco "Chufo" Villarreal Villegas**

On July 8, 1978, "Chufo" realized that a Special Task Group* was waiting for him in a café on the corner of Corrientes and Uruguay Streets. He entered the B subway line and swallowed a cyanide pill before they could kidnap him. A paving stone was placed in his honor on the same corner on August 24, 2008, in the presence of his children and friends.

**LOCATION:** CORNER OF AV. CORRIENTES AND URUGUAY, SAN NICOLAS

## 27. INDEC Employees

A plaque dedicated on December 7, 1988, in the former headquarters of INDEC (National Institute of Statistics and Censuses) honors Carlos Noriega, Raúl Miranda, and Hugo Bivi. It was later moved to the current headquarters. On March 25, 2008, the internal board of the ATE (Government Employees Association) union delegation at INDEC paid tribute to Carlos Cortiñas, a disappeared employee. Nora Cortiñas, of the Founding Line of Mothers of the Plaza de Mayo (see p. 3), participated in the ceremony.

**LOCATION:** AV. JULIO A. ROCA 615, MONTSERRAT

## 28. Francisco Isauro Arancibia – Marina Vilte – Eduardo Requena

In the headquarters of the Confederation of Education Workers of the Argentine Republic (CTERA), a plaque pays tribute to Isauro, murdered in the Tucumán offices; to Marina and Eduardo, members of the National Executive Board; and to disappeared teachers and students. The auditorium, which holds a display of photos and a brief biography of each, was named after Isauro (see p. 204).

**LOCATION:** CHILE 654, MONTSERRAT

## 29. TELAM Employees

Two plaques pay tribute, respectively, to Alejandro Almeida and Célica Gómez in the central hall of the TELAM (National News Agency) building. Speakers at the dedication ceremony included Martín Granovsky, director of TELAM, Taty Almeida, the mother of Alejandro and a founding member of the Mothers of the Plaza de Mayo; and Néstor Gómez, Célica's brother.

**LOCATION:** BOLIVAR 531, MONTSERRAT

## 30. Tribute to Disappeared Members of Congress

In the conference room of the Salón de Pasos Perdidos (Hall of lost steps) in the National Congress building, a plaque was unveiled on March 23, 2006, bearing the names of members of Congress who were detained and disappeared. Congress employees took part in the ceremony.

**LOCATION:** CORNER OF AV. RIVADAVIA AND AV. ENTRE RIOS, MONTSERRAT

## 31. Plaque in the Argentine Actors' Association

In 1997 the Association's Human Rights Commission dedicated a plaque to remember disappeared colleagues and to resist oblivion and indifference. In 2003 another plaque with the names of twenty-one disappeared actors was installed. Adjacent to it, a display of photographs recalls the lives of the victims and reconnects them to friends and family. The film *Podrán cortar todas las flores* (They may cut all the flowers) was shown during the ceremony.

**LOCATION:** ALSINA 1762, MONTSERRAT

## 32. Ministry of Defense

A white plaque was placed on the ground floor of the Ministry thirty years after the coup. Nilda Garré, who was at the time Minister of Defense, passed Resolution 1309-06, which called for similar remembrance plaques to be placed in military establishments where Clandestine Detention Centers operated between 1976 and 1983. "Never again must we face a military coup or an experience of state terrorism. There must always be respect for the National Constitution. Truth and Justice."

**LOCATION:** AZOPARDO 250, MONTSERRAT

## 33. AFIP Employees

The Employees' Association of the Internal Revenue Service paid tribute on May 19, 2005, to activists and employees of tax institutions who had been detained and disappeared. A plaque bears their names in the central hall of the AFIP (Federal Administration of Public Revenue), opposite the Plaza de Mayo.

**LOCATION:** HIPOLITO YRIGOYEN 370, MONTSERRAT

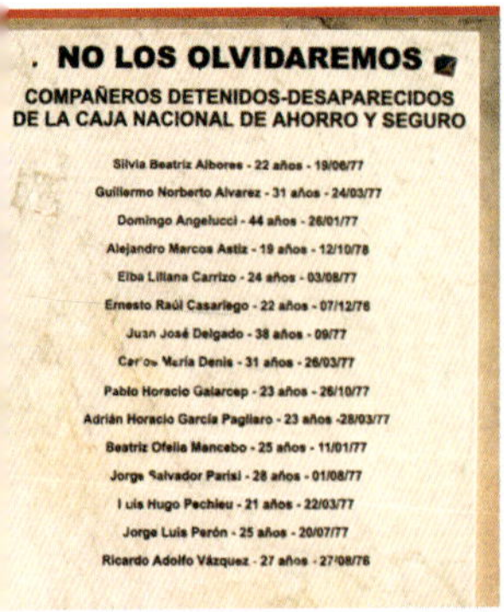


## 34. Employees of the Former National Savings and Insurance Bank

To pay tribute to the fifteen employees and union delegates of the bank who were detained and disappeared, a plaque was placed in the Plaza de los Dos Congresos on bank employees' day, November 6, 2007.

**LOCATION:** ON HIPOLITO IRIGOYEN STREET, BETWEEN SOLIS AND AV. ENTRE RIOS, MONTSERRAT

## 35. **Employees of the Ministry of Economy**

The plaque dedicated on March 31, 2006, reads in part as follows: "As a tribute to the disappeared who worked in the Ministry of Economy and Production and in repudiation of the economic plan imposed by the dictatorship." Present at the ceremony were then-Minister of Economy Felisa Miceli, members of the federal cabinet, and Ministry of Economy employees.

**LOCATION:** HIPOLITO IRIGOYEN 250, MONTSERRAT

## 36. **Susana Pedrini – José Bronzel – Cecilia Podolsky**

On July 13, 1976, José was kidnapped together with his wife, Susana, and his mother, Cecilia. All three were murdered in the Fátima Massacre* of August 20, 1976. Susana was two and a half months pregnant. The bodies of José and Susana were recovered and identified in November 2000. Cecilia remains disappeared.

**LOCATION:** CORNER OF CHILE AND PIEDRAS, MONTSERRAT

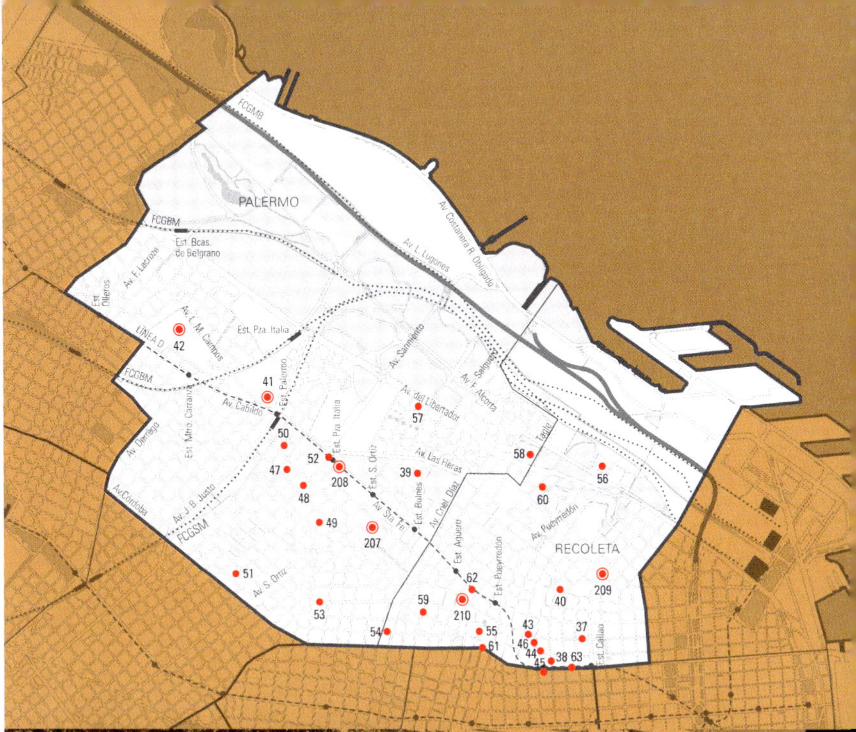

# SECTOR 2

PALERMO AND RECOLETA

# 37. **Carlos Pellegrini Advanced School of Commerce**

Over a thousand people crowded into the patio of the school during an unveiling ceremony that revealed a plaque bearing the names of the thirty-four students and two teachers detained and disappeared during the last dictatorship.

This event took place On September 17, 1998, in the Carlos Pellegrini Advanced School of Commerce (Escuela Superior de Comercio Carlos Pellegrini), one of the public high schools that operates under the direction of the University of Buenos Aires (see "Buenos Aires National School," p. 43). An earlier memorial with seven names had been dedicated in 1986. Sometime later a committee of school alumni undertook an investigation to complete the list.

An exhibit was opened on the second floor of the school during the 1998 unveiling ceremony that narrated the victims' life stories. The school's principal Leonardo Abraham Gak gave a speech during the ceremony. The unveiling took place one day after the anniversary of *La Noche de los lápices* (Night of the pencils), an army operation led by General Ramón Camps on September 16, 1976, that involved the kidnapping and disappearance of a group of high school students from the city of La Plata. These activists from the Union of Secondary School Students* (UES, Unión de Estudiantes Secundarios) had been organizing around a number of issues, including subsidized bus fares for students.

The film *Flores de septiembre* (September flowers), directed by Pablo Osores, Roberto Testa, and Nicolás Wainszelbaum, was produced in collaboration with Memoria Abierta. In this film Roberto Escribal, principal of Carlos Pellegrini School from the beginning of the post-dictatorship period until 1991, recalls, "Ten days after I was appointed, a Federal Police officer came and asked me, as if it were the most natural thing in the world,

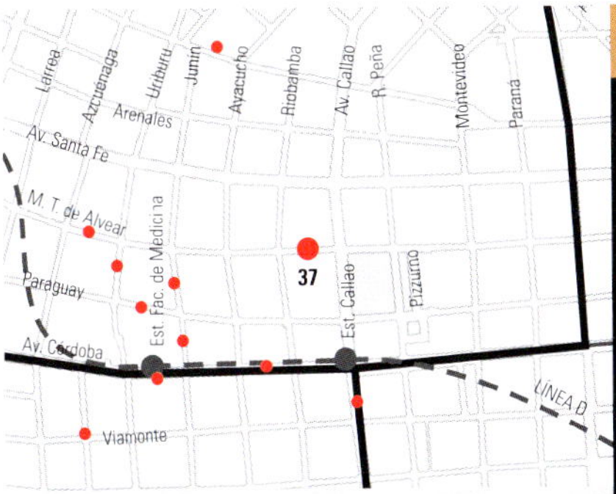


**LOCATION:** MARCELO T. DE ALVEAR 1851
**TRANSPORTATION:** BUSES: 12, 29, 37, 39, 60, 75, 99, 101, 106, 109, 111, 124, 132, 140, 150, 152. SUBWAY STATION: CALLAO (D LINE).

CARLOS PELLEGRINI ADVANCED SCHOOL OF COMMERCE.

for the names of the kids who were on the Student Union. I asked him how he dared to ask me such a thing, and he responded that it was the norm, and that he was just following routine procedures" [AA].

## Cultural and educational policies under state terrorism

Carlos Mora, who was a teacher during the dictatorship, describes the documents that the military government distributed to the schools: "Teachers were given lists of texts that were not just discouraged, but outright banned for use in the schools. . . . So, as teachers, we just focused on the routine aspects of our jobs: giving classes and trying to stay out of trouble. Documents were circulated in many of the public schools instructing us on how to identify subversives and how to interact with them in the school environment. We were told to pay attention to students' questions. If we noticed 'dissociative' thoughts, as they were called at the time, we were to inform the school principal."

Under the direction of Juan José Catalán, the Ministry of Education published a leaflet during the dictatorship titled "Subversion in the Education Sector (We Must Know Our Enemy)" (*Subversión en el ámbito educativo [conozcamos a nuestro enemigo]*). It was obligatory reading for all teachers. An internal Armed Forces document signed by Guillermo Suárez Mason (see "Patricios First Infantry Regiment," p. 74) described the steps to be taken by the repressive forces in the "annihilation of subversion." A special section focused on "Psychological Action," with details on the "targets" that had come under military scrutiny: television channels, radio stations, publishing houses, and various cultural media, including plays, films, books, and newspapers.

The pamphlet "Subversion in the Education Sector" included the following instructions relating to institutions of secondary and postsecondary education:

"a. Subversive activities aim to develop in students a personality that is hostile to society, to authority figures, and to all the fundamental principles and institutions that sustain them: spiritual, religious, and moral values, the Armed Forces, the organization of economic and family life, etc. This aggression aims to achieve a collective psychological transference that will ultimately transform the basic concepts of our society into completely different concepts. We are thus witnessing a strange evolution of ideas (that are alien to our country), one that transforms some students into enemies of the social order in which they currently live in peace, and makes them friends of those agents responsible for the disturbances that arouse their fanatical support for this other ideology so alien to our national identity."

This document aimed to involve educators in a massive political exercise of censorship and denunciation. The dictatorship infiltrated intelligence agents into schools, universities, and a variety of cultural arenas in order to "detect subversives." They drew up "black lists" of students, teachers, artists, writers, and intellectuals, along with lists of films, books, and publishing houses that went against the supposed "essence" of the nation's identity. In 1978 a handbook titled *Terrorism in Argentina* was distributed in schools and universities with the same purpose. Produced by the military government, it presented a collection of newspaper clippings and other documents produced by the armed political movements before the military coup.

"Subversion in the Education Sector (We Must Know our Enemy)" went on to state, "The subversive activities described here are carried out both objectively and subjectively from the early years of secondary school. They advance in a gradual manner, becoming more pronounced as the student gets older. The methods employed include the following:

STENCIL IN THE SCHOOL'S COURTYARD.

THE FIRST MEMORIAL, DEDICATED IN MARCH 1986.

1. Marxist teaching staff take advantage of the privacy of the classroom to teach subjects following a Marxist ideological approach.

2. Non-Marxist staff who are aware of the destructive actions of certain Marxist teachers, monitors, or students do nothing to stop them. Their inaction stems from complacency, fear, or the attitude common in our society of 'mind your own business' [*no te metás*]."

As this document made clear, the repression within the education sector was directed not only at so-called subversive elements but also anyone who did not collaborate with the regime. The phrase "mind your own business" is particularly noteworthy in this context. This expression captured the attitude of many citizens faced with the crimes of state terror. It was used regularly along with other expressions directed at the victims of disappearance, such as "they must have done something" or "there's got to be a reason." Anyone who did not openly collaborate with the regime or who did not share the military's ideas about family values, tradition, or property (which were the traditional preserve of antidemocratic sectors of Argentine society) could be considered an "enemy" or an evil force to be "extirpated" or "annihilated." This amounted to an attempt to justify the forced disappearance of people. In the words of General Ramón Camps, "We do not kill people. We kill subversive elements." In his capacity as the military's Chief of Police in the Province of Buenos Aires, Camps was responsible for the kidnapping of high school students during the Night of the Pencils (*Página/12,* "La hora de la indignación," September 4, 2004).

**A climate of effervescence**

Former Pellegini student Alejandro Cataruzza offers this description of the school in the film *Flores de septiembre:* "I entered the school in 1971 [during the dictatorship of 1966–1973], with a strict uniform and almost military discipline. There was a very different relationship between the students and the school authorities. I seem to remember the school as being very distant, except for the relationships I had with my schoolmates. It was a hostile institution that made no effort to communicate with us. . . . The boys considered the

Montoneros* heroes because they could put their lives on the line for what they believed in. They resisted unjust power structures through a method that had been imposed on them: armed struggle. . . . After [the return to democracy in] 1973, we became much more actively involved in the school. We began to debate the curriculum, and a huge percentage of students got involved, even if they didn't go on from there to join in any other forms of political action. We really seemed determined to have a say in things" [AA].

In fact, thousands of young people from around the country, mindful of the social injustices they saw around them, started to challenge the authorities and work toward radical social change.

José Luis Calvo, who had also entered the school before 1973, recalls, "It was in ninth grade that I began to realize that our generation had grown up under dictatorships. Then we started to see that we had not been living in any kind of a normal political order and that whatever had been imposed on us could be deposed. . . . The school's courtyard was where we stood in line. It was like a military parade ground attached to a barracks. They didn't allow ninth-grade students to leave the second floor. . . . For us, taking over the school courtyard was a real achievement. On November 17 [1973], Perón was returning to the country, and for us it was like a growing spiral of political participation. We felt like it was now or never. . . . We were totally convinced that we were going to change the world, that Argentina was on the brink of a revolution" [AA].

Thousands of students took part in revolutionary organizations. One group of students from the Pellegrini joined the Union of Secondary School Students (UES). This student organization had formed in the 1950s during the second presidency of Juan Domingo Perón and had dissolved after his overthrow in 1955. It had regrouped in the 1970s with links to the Montonero guerrilla movement. Several testimonials from *Flores en septiembre* help to reconstruct the climate in which many young people lived during those years from the return to democracy on May 25, 1973, to the beginning of the last military dictatorship in March 1976.

Gustavo Froján remembers the changes that accompanied the return of democracy: "In 1973, with [the electoral win of the Peronist candidate Hector] Cámpora, the entire administrative structure changed. There was a change of regime from a dictatorship to a democracy. And the changes within the university stirred up the entire activist and student protest movement. And the university dragged the Pellegrini and the Buenos Aires National School with it. It was like a wave that came from the older grades, and for those of us who were thirteen or fourteen it took longer to arrive, but it arrived" [AA].

Alejandra Naftal similarly recalls, "In 1973 there was a lot more freedom with respect to the school uniform, with being able to walk around the school. We started to have dances, marches, assemblies, and we began to discuss politics. The Student Union began then, too, and we had to elect representatives and meet with the vice principals" [AA].

According to Betty Ruiz, the wider conflicts in the country resonated within the school: "At that time, change was occurring within the school to overturn everything that had previously been enforced: the discipline, the limits to student participation. But this change was sustained by what was going on outside. There was a reciprocal relationship between events outside and inside the school. In that sense, the school operated as a place of experimentation, a kind of laboratory experiment for what was happening in the rest of the country" [AA].

THE SCHOOL'S COURTYARD WITH GRAFFITI PAINTED BY STUDENTS.

PLAQUE HUNG IN THE SCHOOL'S COURTYARD IN 1998.

Naftal describes the students' understanding of the actions undertaken by the guerrilla movements: "The thinking within the UES [Union of Secondary School Students] came straight from the Montoneros. All the UES members aspired to join that organization, although this did not always happen. The students eagerly awaited and celebrated news of Montonero actions" [AA].

Former students from the Pellegrini recall that persecution and repression returned during Perón's last presidency and intensified after his death, when his wife, María Estela Martínez de Perón, took office. According to Froján, "You have to take the year 1975 into account because the persecution of young people didn't begin with Videla. It started in 1974 and got much worse in 1975. That year, a whole new team of monitors entered the school. They were strange men with short hair and military faces. Some of them even carried guns" [AA]. According to Alejandra Naftal, "The worst year was 1975, because it was chaos. We had the Triple A* [Argentine Anticommunist Alliance] in the school" [AA]. Betty Ruiz remembers the ritual on the last day of classes in 1975, known as the "vuelta olímpica" (celebration lap around the school): "The *vuelta olímpica* that year was really violent. We pelted the school monitors with eggs. . . . It ended up with us huddled in a corner of the school's courtyard surrounded by the Army, and they fired a couple of shots" [AA].

Alejandro Cataruzza describes the ceremony that accompanied the unveiling of the plaque dedicated to the memory of disappeared students from the Carlos Pellegrini Commercial School: "We wanted to show that any one of us could have been one of them. Furthermore, because nothing is ever certain in a country like Argentina, we wanted to show that even today, anyone could become one of them." The plaque's surface is mirrored so that whoever reads the names can see his or her reflection.

# 38. **Plaza Houssay**

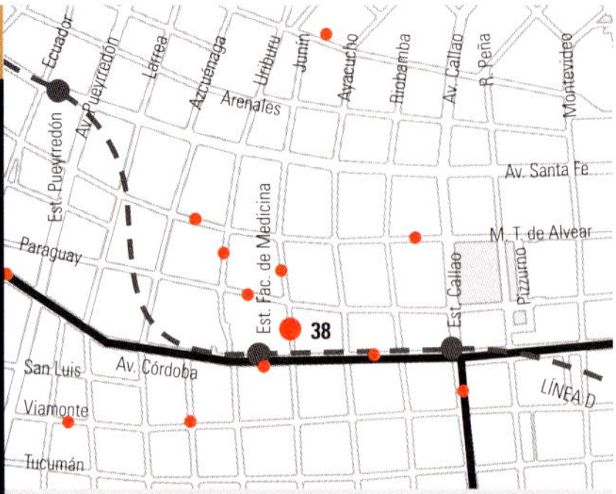


**LOCATION:** BETWEEN AV. CÓRDOBA, PTE URIBURU, PARAGUAY AND JUNÍN
**TRANSPORTATION:** BUSES: 12, 29, 39, 60, 61, 68, 75, 95, 99, 101, 106, 111, 132, 140, 152, 194. SUBWAY STATION: FACULTAD DE MEDICINA (D LINE).

A memorial set up in Plaza Houssay in December 2007 pays tribute to the students, teachers, and staff of the University of Buenos Aires (UBA) and to the staff of the José de San Martín Clinical Hospital who were victims of detention and disappearance during the last military dictatorship. The Clinical Hospital and the faculties of Economics, Medicine, Pharmacy and Biochemistry, Dentistry, and Social Sciences of the UBA all surround this square.

From 1877 to 1975, when its demolition began, the Clinical Hospital stood on the site of the current Plaza Houssay. The facilities were then moved to a new location in the next block, on the corner of Avenida Córdoba and José E. Uriburu Street. The Plaza, named after Bernardo A. Houssay, winner of the Nobel Prize in Medicine, was inaugurated in July 1980. The final project differed from the original plan, which had envisaged the site as the hospital's square and parking lot. The only building to be preserved from that block was the chapel from the central courtyard of the old Clinical Hospital.

### Dictatorship and urbanism

The effects of the last military dictatorship's policies can also be seen in some of the changes made to public spaces. The urban design projects developed in those years displayed an aesthetic of rupture and rigidity. Projects embodied fragmentation, dissociation, and a reformulation of the city's relationship to its inhabitants. For example, the Urban Freeway plan divided the city, prompting the forced displacement of an economically marginalized segment of the population toward the outskirts. This expulsion took shape in the shantytown eradication plan carried

MEMORIAL IN THE PLAZA BERNARDO HOUSSAY.

PLAZA HOUSSAY, WITH THE FACULTY OF ECONOMICS IN THE BACKGROUND.

out by the Municipal Housing Commission (see "Club Atlético," p. 129). Other design interventions included paved squares like the Plaza Houssay, which were created in vacant lots or on the sites of older neighborhood squares. These revealed aspects of the dominant ideology, though sometimes only unconsciously. Urban space has always been a stage for the expression of social conflicts, and the state has often sought to design space as a medium of control and discipline. It has done so by structuring not only the space itself, but also its modes of use, thereby regulating social practices and the manner in which people have inhabited urban space.

Plaza Houssay was designed and built as a "transitory space" emptied of its function as a site for human encounters and socializing. Below the level of the sidewalk, the main material used is concrete. Isolated green areas are enclosed in concrete borders, and access to the Plaza is restricted and defined by cement blocks, ramps, and stairways.

**Transmission and the resignification of space**

The plaza took on new characteristics with the return to democracy after 1983. The university students transformed some of its original properties once they were free to use it for social purposes. It became a place for meetings, many of them organized by students from the surrounding university faculties. It also hosted an annual sculpture competition from 1988 to mid-1990. Public art played a key role in transforming the square. The walls that had earlier marked its boundaries became backdrops for political action, as they were decorated with graffiti and a large mural bearing the names of disappeared students. Sellers once again used the Plaza's informal entryways for their craft stalls and secondhand book stands, thereby reclaiming the space as a marketplace. Since the 1990s the Plaza has witnessed several massive demonstrations in defense of publicly funded university education and in favor of increases in education spending.

The university sector was hit particularly hard by state terrorism. According to the *Nunca más* (Never again) report, students made up 21 percent of those detained and disappeared, while teachers accounted for another 5.7 percent. Those years saw the forced closures of university faculties, faculty and student unions, and any forum dedicated to political debate relating to the defense of public education or to the demands of academics. At the same time, hundreds of university professors were driven out of the university or into exile.

In 2007 the municipal government of Buenos Aires established a memorial that, according to its accompanying text, "seeks to recover the graffiti that were drawn at different times and in different parts of the Plaza to remember the disappeared." The city used this opportunity to make changes to the design of the plaza, which had first been inaugurated in 1980 under the military's appointed mayor, Osvaldo Cacciatore. Local authorities stated that these design reforms aimed to restore the plaza's qualities as a public meeting space rather than just a transitory space. Flowerbeds were removed to make it easier for people to walk around. Lampposts, garbage cans, and benches were replaced; new species of trees were planted; and two fountains were installed.

Daniel Tarnopolsky argues that this type of physical transformation is important to the process of reclaiming spaces, remembering, and leaving traces of the past. Yet the state also plays a crucial role in transmitting memory across generations: "This is what monuments are all about. I was surprised to find a monument I didn't even know existed. Several months ago I was walking across the Plaza Houssay in front of the Faculty of Medicine. Suddenly I saw something really beautiful from afar, a sort of floating sculpture. It was sunny, and the sculpture's glass and metal reflected the sunlight. I approached to see what it was, and then I realized it was a monument to the memory of disappeared university students. I was amazed because I had no idea this monument existed. And so I started to look at the names, because it bears the names of the many university students who were kidnapped. And I found the names of my father, my mother, my sister-in-law, and my brother. . . . So I thought: 'This is just incredible.' I mean, these things occur whether or not the victims and family members are consulted. It was really moving because this monument now forms part of the public sphere. It's no longer just a private matter, it belongs to the Nation. I mean, private individuals and institutions have the right to act in the name of the disappeared, and thankfully they do so. The square itself might be ugly, but this monument is really beautiful."

## 39. *The Applause* (*El aplauso*): Sculpture Dedicated to Disappeared Actors

Mariana Gabor's sculpture *The Applause* (*El aplauso*) was inaugurated above the entrance to the headquarters of the Antonio Cunill Cabanellas Department of Dramatic Arts to remember the actors disappeared by the last military dictatorship. In 2003 the Student Affairs Secretariat and the office of the Dean of the Department of Dramatic Arts at the National University Institute of the Arts (IUNA, Instituto Universitario Nacional de Artes) installed the sculpture along with plaques bearing the names of seventeen disappeared actors who had been identified through an earlier investigation. The floor of the building's foyer displays a text written by the actor Tato Pavlovsky, and one of the walls bears the following words written by the artist herself: "These actors are heading out to speak in the face of the violent imposition of silence. They advance, high above us. They are waiting for eye contact , for answers, for movement. They are waiting for life."

For Víctor Bruno, an actor, teacher, and Dean of the Institute, "this tribute signifies remembering the past and living the present to the fullest, both of which will help us to better project the future. In this instance, it is irrelevant whether or not one shares the ideas of each and every one of the disappeared. We are talking about state terrorism here. That is why we suggested an artistic performance. This is not going to stand as a requiem, but as a song to celebrate life" (*Página/12,* June 29, 2003).

All of the illegitimate governments imposed by the Armed Forces repressed cultural expression and censored artistic productions that were oppositional or even simply unconventional. As a result, many academics, intellectuals, artists, and cultural figures were persecuted, murdered, disappeared, imprisoned, or forced into exile.

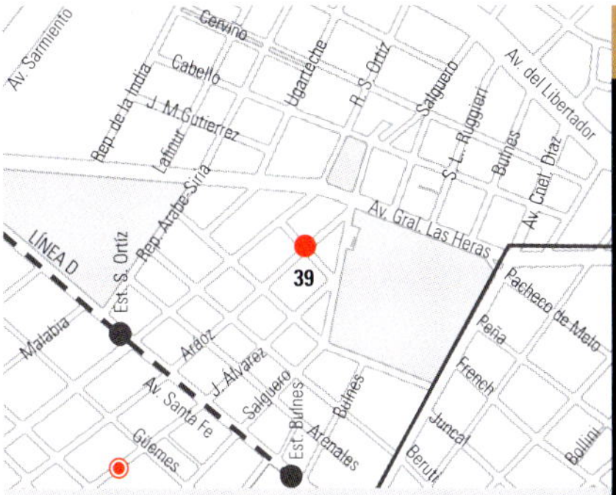


**LOCATION:** FRENCH 3617
**TRANSPORTATION:** BUSES: 10, 15, 37, 41, 57, 59, 60, 93, 95, 108, 110, 118, 128, 141, 160, 188.
SUBWAY STATION: SCALABRINI ORTÍZ (D LINE).

THE NATIONAL UNIVERSITY INSTITUTE OF THE ARTS.

THE NAMES OF DISAPPEARED ACTORS.

**Open Theater (Teatro Abierto)**

In 1981 over two hundred writers, directors, actors, and theater staff (many of them blacklisted) came together at the Open Theatre (Teatro Abierto), a landmark of cultural resistance to the military dictatorship. Victor Bruno was among them:

"The Teatro Abierto experience was initiated by a group of authors . . . including, for example, Osvaldo Dragún, Roberto Cossa, who were joined by a large group of fellow theater artists. The objective was to see how theater could react in the face of dictatorship. The work was all voluntary. People would just start writing in order to act or direct. . . . Each cast included important figures and others who were not so well known. . . . Not everyone was open to the idea, but many people were" [AO.0445].

Teatro Abierto began when a group of writers decided to prove that there was indeed such a thing as Argentine theater by introducing important and relevant works to the public. Some figures within the cultural establishment had called this existence into doubt, and official theaters did not perform any works by Argentine authors. When the director of the Teatro San Martín was asked in 1980 why there were no plays by Argentine authors on the program, he responded, "What authors? There are no Argentine authors." The final straw came when the course in Contemporary Argentine Theater was removed from the curriculum of the National School of Dramatic Arts. Still, Teatro Abierto was created not only to address this specific problem but also to build a cultural movement to oppose the dictatorship.

The initiative began when a group of playwrights were invited to create a series of short, one-act plays. The Picadero Theater was chosen as the venue, and season tickets were sold in advance to cover the costs of production. The Open Theater Movement (Movimiento Teatro Abierto) was inaugurated on July 28, 1981. Public reaction was overwhelming. The large crowds who attended the performances proved that Teatro Abierto had filled a cultural void.

On August 6, one week into the season, unidentified arsonists planted incendiary bombs in the theater. The Picadero was destroyed by fire. The right-wing journalist Bernardo Neustadt, a key voice of legitimation for the dictatorship, made the following ironic comment about this event on his radio program: "What a shame! An illusion has been burned down."

"They wanted to stop the first Teatro Abierto, and that's when they set fire to the Picadero Theater, located in the dead end on Rauch Street. So we went out on a march, a mass rally. We approached different theaters, and we began to put on short, reasonably priced performances at 6 p.m. The idea was just to cover costs. With that fire," recalls Bruno, "they didn't only fail to stop us, they actually made us stronger" [AO].

Performances began again just one week after the fire, this time in the Tabarís Theater. During the week that performances were suspended, people showed their solidarity by lining up in front of the main doors of the burned-out Picadero Theater just before the normal show time. Over the next two months the group offered three daily performances. Some 25,000 people attended the theater, and around 150 actors took part. This performance cycle continued until 1986.

This project used creative cultural forms to resist the dictatorship. Its influence extended to other artistic media, with similar initiatives being undertaken in other fields, both in the capital and in several provinces of the interior. These included Danza Abierta (Open dance), Música Siempre (Music forever), Libro Abierto (Open book), Poesía Abierta (Open poetry), and Folclore Abierto (Open folklore). Teatro Abierto was an aesthetic social movement that made a major artistic contribution to the democratization of culture.

# 40. **Plaque in the SICA**



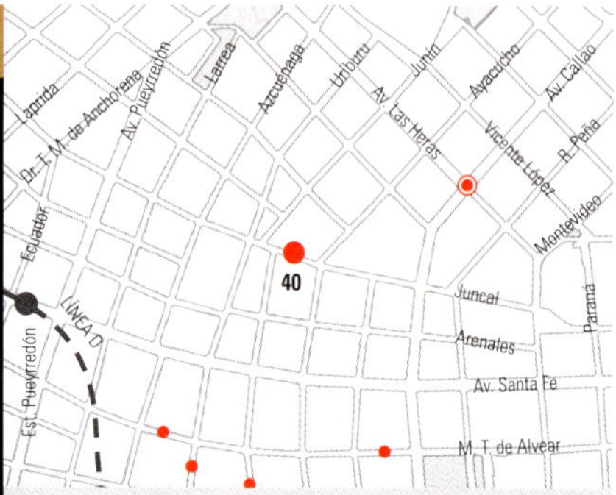


**LOCATION:** JUNCAL 2029
**TRANSPORTATION:** BUSES: 12, 37, 39, 60, 61, 62, 95, 101, 111, 124, 150, 152. SUBWAY STATION: FACULTAD DE MEDICINA (D LINE).

HOMAGE TO DISAPPEARED FILM PROFESSIONALS.

Argentine cinema experienced a boom during the last dictatorship. On the one hand, the military government gave political and economic backing to certain kinds of films. On the other, it imposed extreme censorship, promoted "black lists," and persecuted producers and actors with forced disappearances, imprisonment, or death. A tribute to disappeared film professionals can be found in the headquarters of the Union of the Argentine Cinematic Industry (SICA).

The military junta financed dozens of "racy" comedies inspired by the music hall genre as a bastion of its cultural policy. These accounted for a quarter of films premiered between 1976 and 1983. The years leading up to the coup, however, had seen the emergence of a counterhegemonic cinema that continues to influence producers and documentary filmmakers. Productions by Cine Liberación and Cine de la Base were the most emblematic of this genre.

In 1968, during the dictatorship led by Juan Carlos Onganía, Fernando "Pino" Solanas produced his first feature film, *La hora de los hornos* (The hour of the furnaces). Shot in secret, this documentary trilogy examined neocolonialism and violence in Argentina and Latin America as a whole. In 1969 Solanas founded the Cine Liberación group with Octavio Getino and Gerardo Vallejo. Together they promoted an alternative distribution network, circulating films through social and political organizations resisting the dictatorship. *La hora* won multiple international awards and was distributed in over 70 countries. Banned in Argentina, the film made a significant impact at international festivals and was well received by film critics. In 1971 Juan Domingo Perón invited the group to Madrid, where he remained in exile, to shoot two testimonial films, directed by Solanas and Getino, *La revolución justicialista* (The justicialist—or Peronist—revolution) and *Actualización Doctrinaria para la toma del* *poder* (Update on the doctrinal position for the seizure of power). In 1976, Solanas went into exile in Spain after being threatened by the Triple A* (Argentine Anticommunist Alliance). In 1980 he produced the documentary *La Mirada de los otros* (The gaze of others) in France.

Cine de la Base, linked to the PRT-ERP* revolutionary movement, was inaugurated in 1973 with *Los traidores* (The traitors) by Raymundo Gleyzer. Denouncing the corruption of union leaders who collaborated with the military and the bosses, it included performances by actors and workers who were committed activists. The group sought to take cinema to the places where its protagonists—construction workers, agricultural laborers, the dispossessed—lived. They set up ad hoc screening rooms in shantytowns, working-class neighborhoods, and apartments using wooden boards, benches, and chairs provided by the workers. These efforts facilitated screenings of such films as *Los traidores, Informes y testimonios* (Reports and testimonies, 1973), and *Operación Masacre* (Operation massacre, 1972), directed by Jorge Cedrón and based on the novel by Rodolfo Walsh (see "Corner of San Juan and Entre Rios," p. 96, and "Julio Troxler Street," p. 240). The group's goal was to create a national network for screening and distributing the films.

The group had already been raided and attacked even before the coup. After March 24, 1976, these experiments in documentary cinema were interrupted not only by censorship, but also by murders, disappearances, and the forced exile of several authors. The core of the Cine de la Base group remained in Argentina. Raymundo Gleyzer was in New York at the time of the coup, and he denounced it in several American media outlets. Upon his return, he was kidnapped at the entrance to the union building. A committee of filmmakers and actors protested his disappearance. Raymundo was detained at the El Vesubio* CDC along with the disappeared writer Haroldo Conti.

While "activist cinema" was hit hard by censorship and disappearances, supposedly "light" films became symbols of the era. Hugo Sofovich, the director most associated with this genre, screened more films during the dictatorship than any other director or screenwriter. These films promoted values and beliefs in keeping with the regime's repressive system. In most of them, the protagonist, inevitably male, accumulated power through mischief and brazenness, while women appeared only as "objects." Though usually depicted as more intelligent than the males, they depended on these men. Women's roles were limited to the character of the mother–wife or the prostitute. "In spite of its claims to defend Western and Christian values, the dictatorship evoked the culture of the brothel because it represented the best metaphor for the new social space that it was fostering" (*Radar*, "Operación Ja Ja," October, 2006).

Today, a commemorative plaque in the Union of the Argentine Cinematic Industry (SICA) pays tribute to Raymundo Gleyzer, disappeared in May 1976; Julio César Carboni, a lighting technician disappeared in May 1977; Alberto Imas, an assistant director disappeared in May 1977; and Enrique José Juárez, director of *Argentina, mayo de 1969: los caminos de la liberación* (Argentina, May 1969: The paths to liberation), from 1969, and *Ya es tiempo de violencia* (Now is the time for violence), also from 1969. Juárez, a delegate of the Luz y Fuerza union of electrical workers and a member of the national leadership of the Peronist Workers Youth Movement* (JTP, Juventud Trabajadora Peronista), disappeared on December 10, 1976, and was seen in the ESMA detention center (see p. 153).

"We don't make films to die, we make them to live, and to live better. And if we lose our life in the process, then others will come along to continue the work," declared Raymundo Gleyzer in the film *Raymundo* (2002), by the directors Ernesto Ardito and Virna Molina.

# 41. **Patricios First Infantry Regiment**



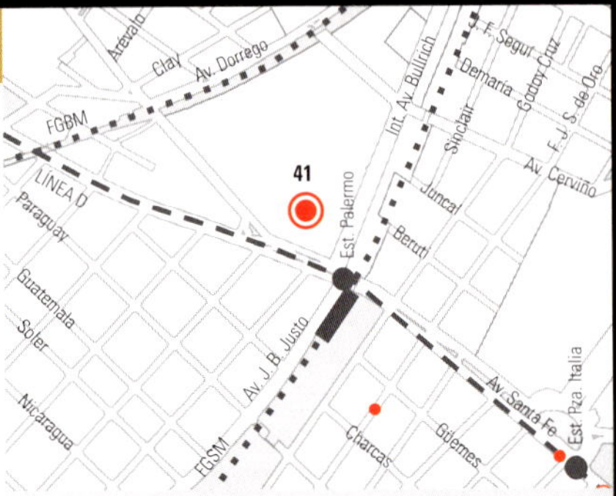


**LOCATION:** AV. BULLRICH AND AV. SANTA FE
**TRANSPORTATION:** BUSES: 12, 15, 29, 36, 39, 41, 55, 57, 59, 60, 64, 67, 68, 93, 95, 108, 111, 118, 128, 152, 160, 161, 166, 194. SUBWAY STATION: PALERMO (D LINE). TRAIN STATION: PALERMO (SAN MARTÍN LINE).

The Patricios First Infantry Regiment functioned as the First Army Corps headquarters during the dictatorship. A Clandestine Detention Center also operated there from 1976 to 1977. Although not all witnesses agree as to the precise location of the center within these premises, several testimonies do attest to its existence.

## The Clandestine Detention Center

According to the testimony of Rodolfo Peregrino Fernández, a former member of the Federal Police who testified before the Argentine Commission for Human Rights in Madrid (see "Coordinación Federal," p. 17), the Patricios Regiment contained cells where illegally detained prisoners were held: "The First Army Corps: in the headquarters of the Command Unit, located in the neighborhood of Palermo in the city of Buenos Aires, and whose main entrance is on Santa Fe, just a few meters from Av. Bullrich, the entrance hall of the main building led into a reception room. Behind a door that opened up onto a kind of gallery, there was a staircase that led down to the basement. Two small rooms below had been prepared as cells. They were used to hold people who had been kidnapped and were of special interest to Colonel Rowaldes [chief of the detention center's Special Task Group*]. Another officer had told him that Rowaldes was assistant to the commanding officer of the First Army Corps, charged with matters of 'subversion.' The day the declarant visited this prison, he managed to catch sight of at least two men" (Peregrino Fernández, 1983).

The book *El escuadrón perdido* (The lost squadron) by Captain José Luis D'Andrea Mohr (1998) contains information about conscripts disappeared from this site. Early in the morning of July 20, 1976, Darío Oscar Bedne left his home and made his way to the regiment, where he was performing

MAIN ENTRANCE TO THE PATRICIOS REGIMENT.

his military service. Later that morning, his family received a telephone call from the barracks asking why he had not shown up. When his father went to the barracks, another conscript informed him that Darío had indeed entered the building in the early morning hours. Nonetheless, Captain Conforti, Lieutenants Ferrero and Del Torchio, and the Regiment's leader, Colonel Lobaiza, all denied it.

Rubén Raúl Maggio was drafted into the regiment on March 19, 1976. On March 25, a day after the coup, family members met another conscript who asked them why Rubén had not returned to finish his term of duty. When Rubén's parents went to inquire at the barracks, they were told that he was considered "absent without leave." Some time later they found out through other conscripts that Rubén had been punished by a captain and had never gone off duty.

**Control of Clandestine Detention Centers in the city**

As part of its repressive strategy, the Armed Forces divided the nation's territory into five zones, which were in turn divided into subzones and areas of influence. In 1975 the government of Isabel Perón passed a series of decrees aimed at the "annihilation of subversion" and granted the Armed Forces control of all the nation's security forces. The Armed Forces created a Defense Council presided over by the Minister of Defense, subdivided the nation's territory, appointed officers in charge of each zone, and established the methods to be used against the guerrilla movements.

The five zone command units corresponded to the Army Corps jurisdictions that covered the entire national territory. These jurisdictions were as follows:

- Zone 1 (until 1979): the city of Buenos Aires, the northern and central regions of the Province of Buenos Aires (excluding certain towns) and the province of La Pampa;

- Zone 2: the provinces of Santa Fe, Entre Ríos, Corrientes, Misiones, Chaco, and Formosa;

- Zone 3: the provinces of Córdoba, Santiago del Estero, San Luis, Mendoza, San Juan, La Rioja, Catamarca, Tucumán, Salta, and Jujuy;

- Zone 4 (created later): the northern suburbs of Buenos Aires, including the districts of General San Martín, Escobar, General Sarmiento, Tigre, San Fernando, Pilar, Tres de Febrero, and Vicente López;

- Zone 5: the southern region of the province of Buenos Aires and the provinces of Neuquén, Río Negro, Chubut, Santa Cruz, and Tierra del Fuego.

The governing junta maintained these jurisdictions after the coup of 1976. The Command Unit of the First Army Corps, in charge of Zone 1, operated from the Patricios First Infantry Regiment. Generals Suárez Mason, Galtieri, and Montes commanded the unit in succession during the years of the dictatorship.

All state terror activities in Zone 1 were coordinated from this Command Unit, which issued instructions for kidnappings and for the police to deliberately "overlook" certain areas while Special Task Group operations were being carried out. Within Zone 1, the city of Buenos Aires was in turn subdivided into seven areas. A building belonging to the Patricios Regiment, at 480 Bullrich Street, contained the operational headquarters for Area 2. This office operated a Clandestine Detention Center on the premises and oversaw police precincts 9, 11, 15, 17, 19, 21, 23, 5, and 27 (see "Police stations as sites of illegal detention," p. 255). This area was under the command of the regiment's chief, a position occupied by Colonels Lobaiza, Saa, and Goitia.

### Compulsory military service

Illegal detentions had already been taking place within the regiment for some time. Hugo Giusti, who sympathized with the PRT-ERP* revolutionary organization, did his compulsory military service there in 1974. In his testimony he describes the torture methods used by the army to discipline conscripts: "As soon as you arrived, you started jumping . . . the asthmatic ones had to jump, and the lazy ones, too. If you had long hair, they took you aside, shaved your hair, and insulted you. That was the daily stuff. . . . My first punishment came in the Campo de Mayo* [military base] in a simulated attack. They told us there was going to be a guerrilla attack, and the guy who later became my torturer told us that while we were in our little tents, [Norma] Arrostito was going to come at us from one side, and [Roberto] Santucho from the other. They were going to riddle us with bullets during the night, killing the soldiers who were fighting for our country. Many of the men believed them, and those who didn't—like me—started to worry. The draft had become really oppressive. At that time, there were heavy clashes between the Army and the ERP [People's Revolutionary Army*]. The punishments were harsh: if a guard fell asleep, he would be "staked" [tied to stakes on the ground for long periods, with his arms and legs spread out], or buried up to his neck. Sometimes they forced the others to jump on him and beat him. The training took place in a climate of constant harassment and fear. It was no longer a question of "running, cleaning, and sweeping" [an Argentine expression for a conscript's usual mundane tasks] but of being prepared. You had to be awake, alert. Anyone could be a terrorist, including even your fellow conscript. There was one conscript from the PC [Communist Party], who had been sent to a cell. We became confidants, and I would take food to him. We would comfort one another" [AO 0539].

Giusti described his own detention as follows: "We entered the heart of the regiment. There they blindfolded me, they made me walk, they handcuffed me, and because they hadn't blindfolded me properly I saw that they were making me climb some wooden steps. I saw a gallery, rooms, and peeling walls. It was an abandoned house in the middle of the First Corps that I didn't know about because we had never gone that far. I've since learned that the place was also used as a clandestine [detention] center, and maybe it was already functioning as a clandestine center. But those words didn't exist at that time. Neither did the word "disappeared." They told my mother that I wasn't there, that I had left for the day and hadn't returned. Although the word "disappeared" didn't exist, I was being detained illegally within the First Corps. . . . Once I got upstairs, they put me in a room alone against the wall. They removed my blindfold and the captain said to me, 'From now on, you're in solitary confinement.' They left me standing there, blindfolded and handcuffed, with conscript soldiers watching over me, the same ones who had been with me in the barracks. . . . Later they removed the conscripts and instead used military police, officers from the military prison."

Giusti asked to speak to the head of the company, General López, but the general spat in his face, insulted him, and threatened him: "He said he wanted to see me and my family die. I could hear people screaming in the other rooms too; I didn't know who they were. I could hear a lot of movement."

While most testimonies about the Clandestine Detention Center in the Patricios Regiment date its existence to the years 1976 and 1977, Giusti's testimony has revealed that such illegal practices dated from before then.

More than 230 conscripts were disappeared during the last dictatorship. Compulsory military service was not abolished until 1995, following the murder in March 1994 of the conscript Omar Carrasco, who had been tortured in the Army Artillery Group 161 in the province of Neuquén.

# 42. **Dr. Cosme Argerich Central Military Hospital**

After being housed in a series of different buildings, the Central Military Hospital was inaugurated in the neighborhood of Palermo in September 1939. It began functioning as a clandestine maternity clinic soon after the coup of 1976 and became part of the dictatorship's repressive apparatus. While it maintained its regular activities, some restricted areas functioned as maternity wards where pregnant detainees awaited childbirth. These secret maternity wards served different purposes. Sometimes pregnant women detained in the Clandestine Detention Centers were transferred here to give birth to their babies. In other cases, women who were illegally kidnapped in the last months of pregnancy were taken directly to the wards. After giving birth, these women could be disappeared and their babies stolen and appropriated. In a small number of cases, women were released with their babies after being threatened.

Three cases of women who gave birth in the Central Military Hospital were reported before the National Commission on the Disappearance of Persons* (CONADEP, Comisión Nacional sobre la Desaparición de Personas). Two of these women remain disappeared, while the third was released along with her daughter. These births took place in 1977 and 1978.

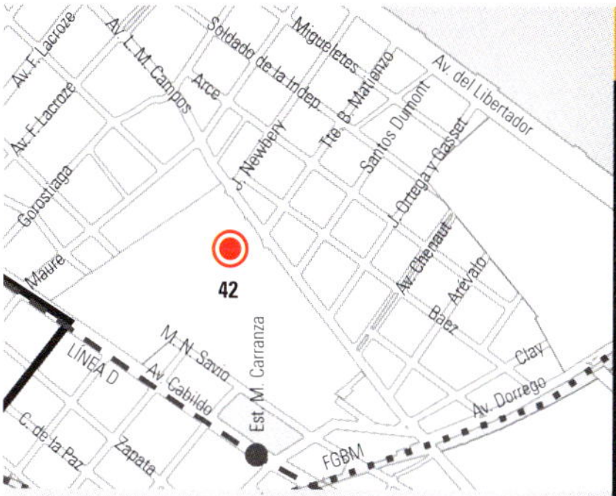


**LOCATION:** AV. LUIS MARÍA CAMPOS 726
**TRANSPORTATION:** BUSES: 15, 29, 55, 59, 60, 64, 118.

Laura Carlotto was one of these disappeared women. In 2004 the soldier Carlos Aníbal López declared in the Truth Trials* that Laura was taken from the Military Hospital without her son. "They told me to go and guard a woman and not to talk to her, because she was a subversive criminal. . . . I was three meters away from Laura. She was sitting quietly, without handcuffs. She had dark hair, big eyes, and a very sweet expression. I didn't know who she was. I found out years later when I saw her photo printed in a newspaper. The baby was there, in a crib at

the foot of the bed. . . . They gave Laura an injection that put her to sleep. They took her by wheelchair to an indoor parking lot and put her into a [Ford] Falcon. I went with them and brought the wheelchair back. When I got back, I passed a tall, thin man in the hallway; he wore glasses and was about twenty-five to thirty years old. He was carrying the baby in his arms. He was moving quickly toward the exit, carrying the baby in a furtive manner, not at all the way a family member would normally do."

**Systematic plan for the theft of babies**

Clandestine maternity wards played a crucial part in the systematic theft of babies. The frequent transfers of prisoners between these wards and the Clandestine Detention Centers attest to the depth of the repressive plan and the number of people implicated in the appropriation of children. In the human rights trials in 1996 relating to the appropriation of children, evidence presented included a list from the Naval Hospital of military families who were "on the waiting list for a child" as well as documents acknowledging donations of equipment to clandestine maternity wards made by private corporations who collaborated in the repression and the appropriation of babies (see "Mercedes Benz," p. 31).

Children kidnapped with their parents or born in the clandestine maternity wards were appropriated and registered as biological or adoptive children or else handed over to families linked to the repressive forces. In a handful of cases the children were left in orphanages, where families adopted them in good faith.

The Trials of the Military Juntas* in 1985 did not address the theft of babies. The prosecution did not include charges relating to the crimes of suppression of legal records, abduction, detention, and concealment of minors or forgery of public documents. These crimes were therefore not covered by the pardon* enacted by President Carlos Menem in 1989, which left open the possibility that military officials could still be charged for crimes relating to child abductions. New trials relating to the crimes of abduction and falsification of identity of minors took place in 1996 and proved that high-ranking officers had full knowledge of the systematic kidnapping of babies from political prisoners.

On July 5, 2012, a lengthy investigation into the appropriation of children finally concluded. The court found proof of the existence of a "systematic and widespread practice of removing, detaining, and hiding minors . . . within a broad plan of annihilation aimed at one sector of the civilian population. This policy was justified as part of the war against subversion." The former dictators Jorge Rafael Videla and Reynaldo Bignone were given sentences of fifty and fifteen years, respectively. The repressor Antonio Vañek was sentenced to forty years in prison, Jorge "El Tigre" Acosta received a thirty-year sentence, and Santiago Omar Riveros was condemned to twenty years. Jorge Magnacco, the obstetrician who attended to the women who gave birth in the ESMA, received a fifteen-year sentence.

**Abuelas de Plaza de Mayo**

Alcira Ríos was held prisoner along with Laura Carlotto, the daughter of Estela de Carlotto, the leader of the Abuelas de Plaza de Mayo (Grandmothers of the Plaza de Mayo). Ríos worked for more than twenty years as a lawyer for the Abuelas (see "Plaza de Mayo," p. 3). The Abuelas de Plaza de Mayo have been active since 1977 in trying to locate children kidnapped or born in captivity and return them to their families. They began by searching in hospitals, orphanages, and juvenile courts; later they turned to other people and institutions for help. "The Abuelas . . . went out to ask geneticists to help them by [developing a more accurate form of DNA test]. . . . This work resulted in the development of the 'grandparent index,' which is capable of determining a minor's family relationship even without the presence of the parents" [AO 0293].

The state had to construct the required investigative tools and pass laws to establish national mechanisms for locating and identifying these minors, who today are adults. Law 23.511, passed in 1987, created the National Genetic Data Bank (BNDG, Banco Nacional de Datos Genéticos). Housed in the Carlos Durand Hospital in Buenos Aires and reporting to the municipal government, this institution offers its services free of charge. It collects and stores genetic data that may be used to determine and resolve conflicts over family relationships; it also performs genetic tests when requested by the courts. Any blood relative of a disappeared child may request the BNDG's services. The bank's existence makes it possible to register the genetic map of each child's maternal and paternal family so that family relationships can be proven, no matter how much time lapses before a genetic test is requested. These tests establish the "grandparent index," which constitutes legal proof of a family relationship.

In 1989 the Abuelas helped to shape the International Convention on the Rights of the Child by advocating the adoption of the three so-called Argentine articles, which define a child's right to an identity and the state's obligation to protect this right. These articles were incorporated into Law 23.849 and included in the Argentine constitution as part of the reform of 1994.

Finally, in 1992 the National Commission on the Right to Identity (CONADI, Comisión Nacional por el Derecho a la Identidad) was created. Its mission is to search for and locate children appropriated during the last military dictatorship.

**Restitution**

The adoption process is governed by law. A child is the product of a mutual desire determined not only by blood ties. Adoption is based not only on the legality of the event itself but also on respect for the minor's family history. Appropriation of children is therefore a crime. It "constitutes the legal objectification of the child. For the child's own subjectivity, there is a difference between being the child of adults who wish to be parents and being the child of adults who wish to own a child. The bond between the appropriators and the child has been described as perverse because it is based on a lie about the child's origins." (H.I.J.O.S., 2009).

The Abuelas de Plaza de Mayo established new legal precedents once again with regard to illegal adoptions. Alcira Ríos explains the legal status of the appropriation of minors: "Adoptions of minors who were victims of forced disappearance are absolutely null and void because they were contracted through a fraudulent application of the law of adoption itself. These minors had not been abandoned; they had not been surrendered voluntarily to the state; they were not in a position to be adopted. They were minors who had been stolen, and crime confers no rights." She adds, "The 14 adoptions that were conducted in good faith still stand, because when adoptions took place in good faith we do not seek to overturn them, and the children end up with a kind of extended family."

Since 1977 the Abuelas have managed to locate 105 appropriated grandchildren. Their work transcends the individual cases; it also has a social impact because it helps resolve questions about the past and furthers the reach of justice. "When a former child exercises their inalienable right to recover their identity and history, this achievement carries more than individual meaning. Its implications are far broader because we are saying no to forgetting and no to impunity," observes Ríos. "And that is very healthy for Argentina." The adult who recovers his or her biological family and original history recovers the right to be free.

## 43. **Faculty of Social Sciences, UBA**

In the Rodolfo Walsh (see p. 196) auditorium on the second floor of the main building on Marcelo T. de Alvear Avenue, several plaques were dedicated to the disappeared who studied and worked within this Faculty. A plaque in remembrance of Roberto Carri was placed in 1989. In 1995, another plaque was dedicated to the disappeared from the Department of Communications, and in 1998, one was placed to recall those disappeared from the Department of Social Work. A fourth plaque pays tribute to Lucía Cullen.

**LOCATION:** AV. MARCELO T. DE ALVEAR, RECOLETA

## 44. **Faculty of Medicine, UBA**

Two placards in the cafeteria of the Faculty of Medicine remember the students who were disappeared from this institution. One, placed by the Union of Medical Sciences Students (CECiM), carries a list with the dates of the victims' disappearances. The other, signed by the Human Rights Secretariat of the Union of Medical Students (CEM), displays the following sentence along with the list of detained and disappeared students: "They may cut all the flowers, but they cannot keep spring from coming."

**LOCATION:** PARAGUAY 2155, RECOLETA

## 45. **Faculty of Economics, UBA**

On March 27, 1998, the Commission for the Reconstruction of Memory of the Faculty of Economics placed a list in the building's central courtyard bearing the following title: "To our companions who died and disappeared, you shall always be present." This same commission dedicated a lecture hall to Horacio Angel Simona.

**LOCATION:** AV. CORDOBA 2122, RECOLETA

## 46. **Plaque in the FUBA**

On the twentieth anniversary of the last military coup, the Buenos Aires University Federation (FUBA, Federación Universitaria de Buenos Aires) placed a bronze plaque just a few meters away from the Plaza Houssay (see p. 66) bearing the names of all those detained and disappeared from the University of Buenos Aires.

**LOCATION:** URIBURU 920, RECOLETA

## 47. Cristián Caretti

Cristián was one of the founders of the Union of Secondary School Students* (UES, Unión de Estudiantes Secundarios) in the 1970s. The paving stone dedicated in his memory bears the following inscription: "This is where Cristián Caretti, the 'Gringo,' was born and lived. Political activist disappeared by state terrorism on September 14, 1976. Family and friends. Neighborhoods for Remembrance and Justice."

**LOCATION:** URIARTE 2269, PALERMO

## 48. Eduardo Goldar Parodi

On March 10, 2007, a plaque was placed as a tribute to Eduardo Goldar Parodi in the house where he lived with his wife, Nora Codina, and his young son. Eduardo was kidnapped in Palomar. His wife was home with her son when she was kidnapped. The boy was rescued by neighbors. Nora was later released.

**LOCATION:** J. L. BORGES 2252, PALERMO

## 49. María Claudia Falcone School No. 7

With 250 votes in favor, students and teachers chose to name Secondary School No. 7 after María Claudia Falcone, a victim of the notorious Night of the Pencils, an operation involving the abduction, torture, and disappearance of high school activists in September 1976. A memorial paving stone was placed on November 26, 2007; a second was placed in the school's Yatay Street building. The Commission of Neighborhoods for Remembrance and Justice and the education community held activities and workshops.

**LOCATION:** MALABIA 2148, PALERMO

## 50. Daniel Antokoletz – Jorge Tranco

Daniel and Jorge were neighbors in the building where, on April 19, 2008, paving stones were placed to pay tribute to them. The first stones laid in 2006 were replaced by the Popular Assembly of Palermo. Daniel was a thirty-nine-year-old lawyer and teacher kidnapped on November 10, 1976. Jorge worked in the Güemes Clinic, the site of his kidnapping on September 17, 1976.

**LOCATION:** FRAY JUSTO SANTA MARIA DE ORO 2366, PALERMO

## 51. St. Gregory the Illuminator Church

On November 11, 2007, a plaque was placed to remember Armenians who had been detained and disappeared: "For the recovery of historical memory, truth, and justice." The Archdiocese of the Armenian Apostolic Church and family members of victims of detention and disappearance took part in a tribute ceremony dedicated to the "sons and daughters of the Armenian People who fell victim to state terrorism."

**LOCATION:** ARMENIA 1353, PALERMO

## 52. Gerardo Brugo Marcó

The Commission of Neighborhoods for Remembrance and Justice placed a paving stone as a tribute to Gerardo Brugo Marcó on the corner of the street where he was kidnapped on March 23, 1981.

**LOCATION:** CORNER OF SANTA FE AND J. L. BORGES, PALERMO

## 53. María Teresa Barvich

"Tere" was twenty-four years old when she was murdered in her home. During this action, her attackers kidnapped an injured companion and arrested three more. A paving stone was placed in her memory on November 4, 2007, thirty-two years after her murder, in the presence of her mother, Ema, her siblings Alicia and Rodolfo, and her nieces and nephews.

**LOCATION:** HONDURAS 4183, PALERMO

## 54. Eduardo Tejedor

Eduardo was kidnapped on May 3, 1978, as he was leaving the República de Irán School, where he taught. Twenty-eight years old at the time, he was a teacher and social worker. The Commission of Neighborhoods for Remembrance and Justice placed a paving stone as a tribute to him.

**LOCATION:** CABRERA 3484, RECOLETA

## 55. Revolución de Mayo School No. 15

On September 12, 2007, a plaque was placed to honor Alejandro Almeida, Martín Zukernik, "Fafa," "Gabi," and all of the students from this school who were detained and disappeared. Family members, fellow students, and friends undertook this initiative. Those in attendance included Alejandro's mother, Taty Almeida, a member of the Madres de Plaza de Mayo, and Daniel Filmus, then Minister of Education.

**LOCATION:** ECUADOR 1158, RECOLETA

## 56. Faculty of Law, UBA

An acrylic plaque dedicated by the Student Union in 1997 pays tribute to the students of the Faculty of Law and Social Sciences who were killed and disappeared during the last military dictatorship. The plaque reads, "They fought for a better world."

Another plaque placed in 2002 by students from the Faculty of Law honors disappeared students from the Faculty and bears their names, ages, and the dates of their kidnappings. The plaque reads, "They lived to transform reality. They lived for a University open to everyone. They lived to build a different country. They lived so as not to die."

**LOCATION:** AV. PTE. FIGUEROA ALCORTA 2263, RECOLETA

## 57. Carlos Prat – Sofía Cuthbert

A paving stone was unveiled at the site of the murders of Chilean general Carlos Prat and his wife, Sofía Cuthbert. Prat, former Commander in Chief and Vice President of Chile during the government of Salvador Allende, had been in exile from the dictatorship of General Augusto Pinochet at the time of his death. The dedication was organized by the Commission of Neighborhoods for Remembrance and Justice to commemorate the thirty-fourth anniversary of the murders. Participants in the ceremony included the couple's daughters, Cecila and María Angélica, and Ambassador Luis María Aguirre of Chile.

**LOCATION:** REPUBLICA ARABE SIRIA 3351, PALERMO

## 58. Tribute to Chilean Citizens

The Buenos Aires City Council paid tribute "to the Chilean citizens who disappeared and were murdered by State terrorism in Argentina" with a plaque placed in the Plaza República de Chile on September 13, 2001.

**LOCATION:** CORNER OF AV. DEL LIBERTADOR AND TAGLE, PALERMO

## 59. Dr. Ricardo Gutiérrez General Children's Hospital

In front of the office of the Medical Association several plaques pay tribute to hospital workers who were detained and disappeared. The hospital community dedicated one to the victims of state terrorism. Another pays tribute to the nurse Elena Arce Sahores, and a third honors Graciela Vallejo and Hugo Strejilevich, both doctors at the hospital.

**LOCATION:** CORNER OF GALLO AND PARAGUAY, RECOLETA

## 60. National Library

On December 9, 2007, a plaque was unveiled in the main hall of the National Library to pay tribute to disappeared library employees. This event was organized by the Library, the Permanent Commission of Tributes to Librarians and Library Employees who Disappeared and Were Murdered by State Terrorism, and the National Commission for the Protection of Community Libraries.

**LOCATION:** AGUERO 2502, RECOLETA

## 61. Julio César Juan

When he was disappeared from his home on March 12, 1977, Julio César was a twenty-four-year-old history student at the University of Buenos Aires and an employee of Yacimientos Carboníferos Fiscales, then the national coal company. The Commission of Neighborhoods for Remembrance and Justice placed a paving stone in his honor at the site of his disappearance.

**LOCATION:** AV. CORDOBA 2745, RECOLETA

## 62. José Figueroa Alcorta Secondary School No. 1

On the school's hundredth anniversary, June 28, 2007, a plaque was placed in tribute to former students who were detained and disappeared: Diana Feldman and Claudia Yankilevich, from the class of 1969, Andrea Yankilevich, from the class of 1979, and María Lourdes Noia, from the class of 1962.

**LOCATION:** AV. SANTA FE 2778, RECOLETA

## 63. President Roque Sáenz Peña Modern Languages Teacher Training School No. 1

On October 3, 2008, paving stones were dedicated to Lidia Amigo, Paloma Alonso, Marcela Goeytes, Cristina Navajas, and Betina Tarnopolsky. This event, organized by the education community, family members, and friends of the victims, the Commission of Neighborhoods for Remembrance and Justice, and the Student Union, included a dedication ceremony, music, poetry, and a display of photographs of those being remembered.

**LOCATION:** AV. CORDOBA 1951, RECOLETA

# SECTOR **3**

ALMAGRO, BALVANERA, BOEDO, AND SAN CRISTÓBAL

# 64. **Santa Cruz Church**

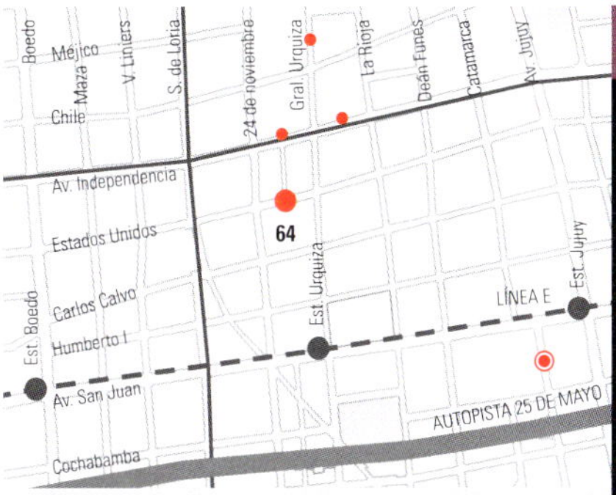


**LOCATION:** ESTADOS UNIDOS 3150
**TRANSPORTATION:** BUSES: 23, 32, 41, 75, 88, 96, 101, 118, 126, 127, 129, 155. SUBWAY STATION: URQUIZA (E LINE).

The Gothic-style Santa Cruz Church is located at 3150 Estados Unidos Street on a property granted to the Passionist Community in 1881. The church, inaugurated in 1894, was a meeting place for members of the Irish community and other residents from the neighborhood of San Cristóbal throughout the twentieth century. On March 12, 1977, it brought together another kind of community in the early years of state terrorism, when family members of the disappeared gathered here and initiated the most effective form of resistance to the dictatorship. The founding group of the Madres de Plaza de Mayo met here and in other churches on more than one occasion.

The Madres recall that they were invited to meet in the church by a group of young people who supported the families of the disappeared and who, for the most part, had ties to the Communist Vanguard*. Participants in the meetings included Remo Berardo, Gabriel Eduardo Horane, Angela Auad de Genovés, Raquel Bulit, Oronzo Vinci Mastroiácomo, Horacio Elbert, José Julio Fondevilla, Patricia Oviedo, Cecilia Vázquez, and Sister Alice Domon. The Navy set out to infiltrate this group in October and November 1977. Frigate Lieutenant Alfredo Astiz, using the name Gustavo Niño, began to attend Mass, ceremonies, and family meetings, claiming to be the brother of a man who had been disappeared.

On October 5 the Madres de Plaza de Mayo published their first paid announcement demanding information about their sons and daughters; from that point on, they became the main target of Special Task Group* 3.3.2 from the Navy School of Mechanics

SANTA CRUZ CHURCH.

GROUNDS OF THE SANTA CRUZ CHURCH.

TRIBUTE TO MADRES DE PLAZA DE MAYO ON THE 31ST ANNIVERSARY OF THEIR FOUNDING.

PAVING STONE COMMEMORATING THE TWELVE PEOPLE KIDNAPPED FROM THE CHURCH.

(see p. 153). On December 8, the Feast of the Immaculate Conception, a group of Madres arranged to meet with other family members in the church to finish preparing their second announcement. Astiz took part in the meeting; on his way out, he identified those who should be kidnapped by the task force by giving them a kiss goodbye. In an operation organized by Lieutenant Raúl Scheller, the task force kidnapped María Eugenia Ponce de Bianco, Esther Ballestrino de Careaga, Alice Domon, Raquel Bulit, Patricia Oviedo, Ángela Auad de Genovés, and Gabriel Eduardo Horane as they left the meeting.

The following day, December 9, as part of the same operation, they kidnapped Remo Berardo from his home and Horacio Elbert and José Julio Fondevilla at the intersection of Belgrano and Paseo Colón Avenues. Ten people were kidnapped in total.

On that same day another group of Madres who were working on their next announcement in the home of Eva Castillo found out about what had happened in the Santa Cruz Church. When one of the women expressed doubt about whether to go ahead with the second announcement, Azucena Villaflor insisted that they had to carry on; what they were doing made sense and they had to continue. They were standing at the entrance to the daily *La Nación* before the three o'clock deadline for submitting announcements.

On Saturday, December 10, Task Force 3.3.2 kidnapped Léonie Duquet, who was a French nun like Alice Domon. The Madres' second announcement

MASS CELEBRATED ON THE 31ST ANNIVERSARY OF THE FOUNDING OF THE MADRES DE PLAZA DE MAYO.

appeared on page 19 of *La Nación,* titled "For a peaceful Christmas, all we ask for is the truth."

That same morning, far away in Sarandí, in the province of Buenos Aires, Azucena Villaflor left her house to buy a copy of the morning paper. A Ford Falcon and a Renault 12 blocked her path just a few meters from her home, at the corner of Crámer Street and Avenida Mitre. As Enrique Arrosagaray explains in his biography of Villaflor, her screams alerted Pacífico Moyano, a neighbor who was on the street corner washing his school bus. When he looked toward the avenue, he saw Azucena lying on the ground, fighting with eight men who were forcibly dragging her toward a Falcon. He managed to call out to Oscar, the neighborhood mechanic who was working on the same block, but Oscar only saw the cars speeding away at top speed toward Buenos Aires.

The twelve people kidnapped in the same operation between December 7 and 8, 1977, were all taken to the ESMA (Navy School of Mechanics). They were not held there long, according to the testimony of several survivors (CONADEP, 1984).

On December 20, 1977, several corpses washed up on beaches in the southern part of the province of Buenos Aires, between the seaside resorts of Santa Teresita and Mar del Tuyú. Local authorities immediately ordered that they be buried in anonymous graves in the General Lavalle Cemetery (province of Buenos Aires).

MURAL IN FRONT OF THE CHURCH HONORING THE MADRES DE PLAZA DE MAYO.

Twenty-six years later, Judge Horacio Cattani authorized the Argentine Forensic Anthropology Team* (EEAD, Equipo Argentino de Antropología Forense) to carry out exhumations in the General Lavalle Cemetery. In 2005 the bodies of Azucena Villaflor de De Vincenti, Mary Ponce de Bianco, Esther Ballestrino de Careaga, Léonie Duquet, and Ángela Auad were identified; they had all been victims of "death flights"*.

Azucena Villaflor's ashes were scattered in the Plaza de Mayo (see p. 3). The remains of Ángela Auad, Léonie Duquet, Esther Ballestrino de Careaga, and Mary Ponce de Bianco were laid to the rest in the gardens of the Santa Cruz Church.

## 65. **Trees in Avenida San Juan**



Seventy-eight trees planted along more than twenty blocks of Avenida San Juan honor the disappeared of the neighborhood of San Cristóbal. Each jacaranda tree pays tribute to a person who lived, was politically active, or was kidnapped in the neighborhood. The initiative was launched by the association San Cristóbal Residents Against Impunity, which has also published a book containing the life stories of all the people disappeared from the neighborhood. According to the group, this work serves to perpetuate "their names, their stories, and their struggles for a fair, united, and free country" (2008).

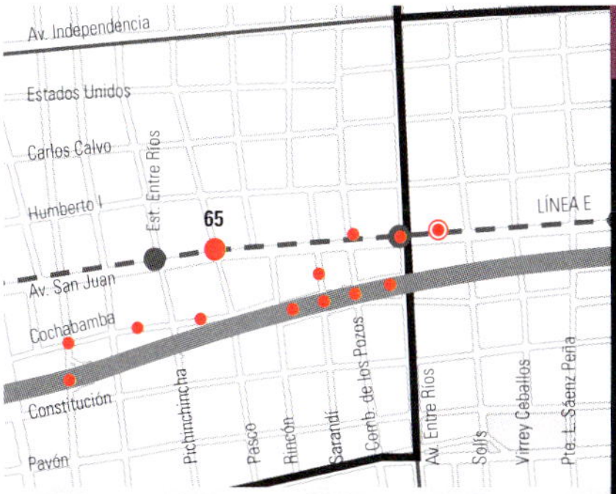


**LOCATION:** 1800 TO 2700 AV. SAN JUAN
**TRANSPORTATION:** BUSES: 4, 6, 12, 23, 37, 41, 50, 53, 61, 84, 95, 96, 97, 101, 102, 111, 126, 129, 143, 150, 151, 168, 188. SUBWAY STATIONS: ENTRE RÍOS, PICHINCHA, AND JUJUY (E LINE).

The association emerged in 1997, when it carried out an *escrache** (shaming protest) against neighborhood resident Héctor Vergés, a former intelligence agent who had participated in the repression. The group's members have worked since then to strengthen memory in the neighborhood. Their goal was to make "the sidewalks where [the neighborhood's disappeared] walked . . . speak about them." As they describe in the book, even though it was difficult to find all the names and addresses, it was far more challenging to collect testimonies: "Some days were hopeless, while others gave us strength." They knocked on doors, "asking the oldest residents, delving into the memory of the neighborhood" to put together each and every story. The association got help from human rights organizations and from the archive of the National Commission on the Disappearance of Persons* (CONADEP, Comisión Nacional sobre la Desaparición de Personas; see "Nunca Más Square and Cultural Center," p. 186). The Subsecretariat of Human Rights of the City of Buenos Aires and the Department of Green Spaces also provided assistance.

Ever since it began, the association San Cristóbal Residents Against

A WOMAN READS A PLAQUE HONORING ONE OF THE NEIGHBORHOOD'S DISAPPEARED.

Impunity has worked to make public the memory of those who were kidnapped in the neighborhood, including the writer Rodolfo Walsh, whose kidnapping site was marked by the association (see "Corner of San Juan and Entre Ríos," p. 96). The group's members have also worked on legal claims and demands for justice. They erected a ceramic portrait of Julio López in the Miramar bar at the corner of San Juan and Sarandí Streets. López, a survivor of disappearance during the dictatorship, disappeared again after testifying in court in 2006. This tile work was donated by workers from the Factory without Bosses (FaSinPat, or Fábrica sin Patrones, formerly known as Zanon), which has operated as a worker-run cooperative since 2001. These residents also succeeded in expropriating the building on Virrey Cevallos Street (see p. 36) that had operated as a Clandestine Detention Center during the dictatorship. It was recovered as a space of remembrance.

More than three hundred people gathered for a ceremony on March 24, 2004, to dedicate the trees that had been planted and to commemorate the neighborhood's disappeared. After the speeches were over, they visited each tree and read out the name of the person to whom it was dedicated, calling out, "Here with us, now and forever."

**Attacks**

Yet signs of intolerance soon surfaced, and those who opposed the commemoration chose an especially harsh way to express their disagreement. Just a few days after the ceremony, vandals cut down thirty-two of the trees and destroyed several of the stones bearing the names of the disappeared.

ONE VIEW OF THE STREET: SEVENTY-EIGHT TREES MAKE UP THE TRIBUTE.

MARKERS OF INTOLERANCE ON THE MEMORIAL STONES.

Faced with these attacks, the association of San Cristóbal Residents Against Impunity filed a legal complaint and organized a march. Then-President Nestor Kirchner condemned the vandalism through the General Secretariat of the Presidency and the Human Rights Secretariat. Although the attacks continued, the association decided to continue replacing trees and stones whenever necessary.

The meaning associated with public landmarks "is always open, subject to fresh interpretations and resignifications. [It may] be appropriated in new ways, forgotten or silenced, incorporated into daily routines or even ignored in the space of daily life" (Jelin and Langland, 2003). These landmarks are also vulnerable to attack, and such attacks represent one of the many forms of ideological struggle and political contestation at stake in the construction of historical meaning. The attackers seek to destroy symbolically not the monument itself, but what it represents: the memory of crimes and victims.

The people who promote remembrance and those who attack commemorative sites are all expressing collective understandings of the past. The trees and the plaques not only recall the disappeared but also keep alive the memory of the criminal act of disappearance. Those who galvanize memory by shaping urban space do so within "a field of confrontation and debate with conflicting interpretations and meanings" (Jelin and Langland, 2003). These conflicting memories leave physical marks that affect those who live among them. Yet the people who use violence leave a different kind of trace, a sign of intolerance that characterizes those who claim "to be the bearers of universal truth, by virtue of which they have the right to eliminate anything that contradicts that truth" (Schmucler, 2007b).

## 66. **Corner of San Juan and Entre Ríos**

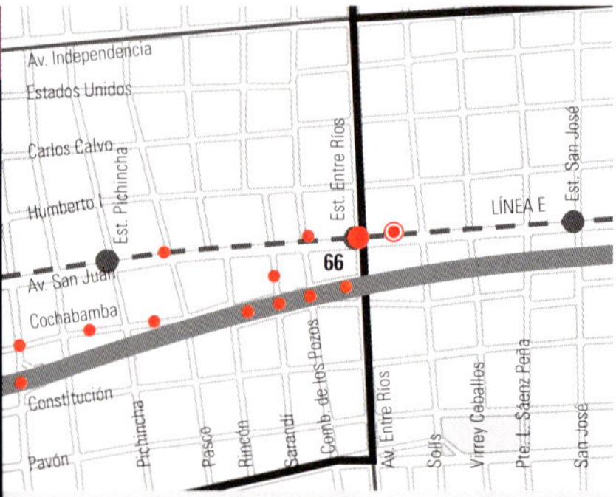


**LOCATION:** AV. SAN JUAN AND AV. ENTRE RÍOS
**TRANSPORTATION:** BUSES: 4, 6, 12, 23, 37, 50, 53, 84, 96, 126, 129, 150, 151.
SUBWAY STATION: ENTRE RÍOS (E LINE).

Rodolfo Walsh, a writer, journalist, and activist in the armed political movement known as the Montoneros*, was murdered on March 25, 1977, at the corner of Avenida San Juan and Avenida Entre Ríos by a Special Task Group* from the Navy School of Mechanics* (ESMA, Escuela de Mecánica de la Armada; see p. 153). His daughter, María Victoria Walsh, had been murdered by the repressive forces just a few months earlier, on September 29, 1976.

Lilia Ferreyra, Walsh's partner at the time, recalls that the first anniversary of the coup had become a decisive date for Rodolfo Walsh. On the one hand, March 24, 1977, marked the completion of a full-year cycle in the policies that Walsh had set out to analyze in detail in his "Open Letter to the Military Junta," one of the most precise and powerful denunciations of state terrorism ever written in Argentina. On the other hand, for his family the anniversary represented one year of survival in the midst of that devastating atmosphere. Walsh circulated his "Open Letter" clandestinely on the anniversary of the coup; it managed to reach many of its intended readers. Though he had planned to celebrate the day by sharing a barbecue with his other daughter and grandchildren, the festivities never took place.

The barbecue had been planned for Saturday, the twenty-sixth. Had it taken place, it would have been the first time in three years that Rodolfo and Lilia received people in their home. Their intense political activism and

THE CORNER WHERE RODOLFO WALSH WAS ASSASSINATED.

STENCIL "THAT MAN." THE WORDS ALLUDE TO THE SHORT STORY "THAT WOMAN," ABOUT EVA PERÓN.

the long months of living underground* had prevented them from doing so. Yet one day earlier, on Friday the twenty-fifth, a Special Task Group from the ESMA kidnapped Walsh from the corner of San Juan and Sarandí Streets, where two plaques now pay tribute to him. Walsh resisted his kidnapping by using his twenty-two caliber revolver to try to fend off eight men armed with automatic weapons. ESMA survivors have confirmed that Walsh was killed before reaching the Clandestine Detention Center; his body was riddled with bullets when it was brought in.

Walsh was born fifty years earlier, on January 9, 1927, into a family of Irish immigrants in Lamarque, in the province of Río Negro. He began working for the publishing house Editorial Hachette as a proofreader, anthologist, and translator before he turned thirty. His prestigious literary career began after he won the Municipal Literary Prize of the City of Buenos Aires in 1953 for his collection of detective stories titled *Variaciones en rojo* (Variations in red). However, as he describes in one of his most accomplished works, this relatively comfortable writing career was challenged on the night of June 10, 1956, by an episode of political violence.

Nine months earlier, in September 1955, a military coup led by General Pedro Eugenio Aramburu had overthrown the government of Juan Domingo Perón. On June 9, 1956, two officers loyal to Perón, Generals Valle and Tanco, launched a failed insurrection against Aramburu. The only battle took place in the city of La Plata and left three civilians dead.

Six months after the uprising Walsh learned through the testimony of a survivor that the military government had carried out a series of clandestine executions on the night of June 10. He immediately began to investigate the shooting deaths of civilians in the garbage dump in the municipality of José León Suárez. He published his initial results in various magazine articles and then, a year later, in the book entitled *Operación Masacre* (Operation massacre).

Subsequent editions of this work reveal the transformation of Rodolfo Walsh's political thinking, which paralleled the changes affecting most people in his generation. Walsh published new and significantly revised editions on three occasions: in 1964, after his experience of the Cuban Revolution; in 1969, after the mass student-worker uprising known as the Cordobazo*; and again in 1972, during an upsurge in popular political mobilization and activity by armed revolutionary organizations. The changes made to each edition reveal the broader changes of the era; and Walsh's political and literary choices attest to his intellectual and political commitment.

He published his second work of investigative journalism in the magazine *Mayoría* in 1958 and 1959. *El caso Satanowsky* (The Satanowsky case) focused on the murder of Marcos Satanowsky, the lawyer of Ricardo Peralta Ramos, co-owner of the daily newspaper *La Razón*. In the 1960s Walsh tried his hand as a playwright with works such as *La granada* (The grenade) and *La batalla* (The battle) and developed his fiction writing through several short story collections. He also continued to produce investigative journalism, now with a focus on organized labor. After a meeting with Juan Domingo Perón in Madrid, he and Raimundo Ongaro (the leader of the militant print workers' union) founded the newspaper of the independent workers' federation known as the CGT de los Argentinos*. Here, Walsh published a series of articles about the murder of metalworkers' union leader Rosendo García by interests linked to the corrupt union bureaucracy. These articles would later be published in the book *¿Quién mató a Rosendo?* (Who killed Rosendo?). Walsh visited and worked in shantytowns after joining the movement known as Grassroots Peronism* (Peronismo de Base). In the 1970s he joined the Peronist Armed Forces* (FAP, Fuerzas Armadas Peronistas), which led him to become a member of the armed Peronist movement known as the Montoneros.

The Montonero movement went underground after September 1974, and Walsh and his partner, Lilia Ferreyra, followed suit. Walsh founded the Clandestine News Agency (ANCLA, Agencia de Noticias Clandestinas) to receive and distribute information outside the mainstream media channels. He distanced himself from the Montonero leadership three years later. In a series of internal documents he criticized the creation of the Montonero Party and questioned the organization's preference for violence over political action. By December 1976 he had already drafted the outline for his "Open Letter to the Military Junta." In subsequent months he decided to return to writing and publish the letter under his own signature.

The writings of Rodolfo Walsh offer exceptional insight into the period after Peronism's overthrow in 1955. The trilogy including *Operation Massacre, The Satanowsky Case,* and *Who Killed Rosendo?* sheds light on the violent social and political relations between and within classes. The second and third books revealed confrontations within the ruling classes and between rival elements of the working class. *Operation Massacre,* on the other hand, crudely exposed the brutality with which the ruling sectors in Argentine society sought to discipline the working class.

# 67. **Small Squares (Plazoletas) – 25 de Mayo Freeway**

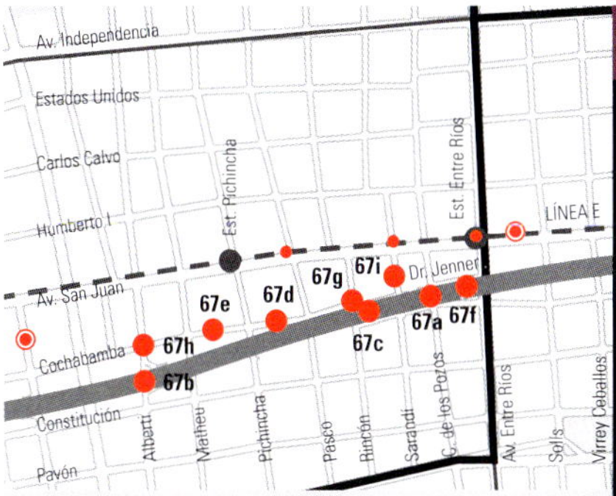


**LOCATION:** "25 DE MAYO" FREEWAY BETWEEN AV. ENTRE RÍOS AND AV. JUJUY
**TRANSPORTATION:** BUSES: 4, 6, 12, 23, 37, 50, 53, 84, 95, 96, 126, 150, 151, 188. SUBWAY STATIONS: ENTRE RÍOS AND PICHINCHA (E LINE).

Nine disappeared members of the Madres de Plaza de Mayo were honored in October 2003, when the Buenos Aires City Council decided to name a series of residual green spaces from the 25 de Mayo Freeway after them. Today these sites, which have been neglected by the government, contrast sharply with the monumental freeway conceived by the dictatorship's municipal government under the control of Brigadier Osvaldo Cacciatore.

### 67a. Plazoleta María Eugenia Ponce de Bianco

**LOCATION:** DR. JENNER 1900, BETWEEN COMBATE DE LOS POZOS AND SARANDI

María Eugenia was kidnapped with seven other people on December 7, 1977, as they were leaving a meeting organized by the Madres in the Santa Cruz Church (see p. 89). Her kidnappers belonged to a Special Task Group* from the Navy School of Mechanics (ESMA, Escuela Superior de Mecánica de la Armada; see p. 153); Frigate Lieutenant Alfredo Astiz reported to this force. The operation continued over the next days and resulted in the disappearance of five members from that founding group.

The Madres had been raising funds to publish an announcement in the newspapers; they had met in the church to count the money and collect signatures. This was when Lieutenant Astiz, who had infiltrated the group using the name Gustavo Niño, left the meeting early and kissed some of the Madres goodbye to identify them to their kidnappers. "I remember that I was leaving arm in arm with María Ponce," recalls María del Rosario de Cerruti, "and suddenly a group of men pounced on us. They pushed me and pulled Mary's arm

JENNER STREET BETWEEN COMBATE DE LOS POZOS AND SARANDÍ. LOCKED AT 3:00 P.M., THIS SMALL SQUARE ALSO SERVES AS A MUNICIPAL WORKSHOP.

PLAZOLETA ESTHER BALLESTRINO DE CAREAGA.

from mine. I was screaming; I didn't know what was going on. I kept asking, 'Why? Why?' and they said, 'This is a drug bust' " (Gorini, 2006).

At fifty-three years of age, María Eugenia was one of the most politicized members of the Madres, thanks to her experience in the Communist Party.

On December 20 several bodies were discovered on the coast in Santa Teresita, a beach resort in the province of Buenos Aires. María Eugenia and the other Madres had been thrown into the ocean in one of the "death flights"*. Many years later, on April 16, 2005, her body was identified through the meticulous work of the Argentine Forensic Anthropology Team* (EAAF, Equipo Argentino de Antropología Forense).

### 67b. Plazoleta Esther Ballestrino de Careaga

**LOCATION:** ALBERTI 1300, BETWEEN COCHABAMBA AND CONSTITUCION

Esther was one of the founding members of the Madres de Plaza de Mayo. Born in Uruguay, she grew up in Paraguay, where she was an activist in the Febrerista Revolutionary Party. She played a leading role in the struggle against dictator Higinio Morínigo during the 1940s. As a teacher and a doctoral fellow in biochemistry and pharmacology, she organized the Paraguayan Women's Movement and was its first secretary general. Persecuted for her political activism, she went into exile and settled in Argentina in 1947.

On June 13, 1977, Esther's youngest daughter, Ana María, was kidnapped and taken to the Clandestine Detention Center known as the Club Atlético; she was three months pregnant. Esther immediately approached the groups of family members who were beginning to organize to formulate their demands. Though Ana María was released soon afterward, Esther decided to continue fighting for the release of all those who had been detained and disappeared. This gesture was to help shape the future of the Madres de Plaza de Mayo. On December 8, 1977, Esther was kidnapped in the Santa Cruz Church by a Special Task Group and taken to the ESMA. After being held for ten days in a detention area within the attic known as *capucha* ("hood"), Esther was "transferred" (see ESMA, p. 153) along with others who had been kidnapped between December 8 and 10. They were thrown into the Río de la Plata in a "death flight." Esther's body was found soon afterward and buried in an unmarked grave in the General Lavalle Cemetery in the province of Buenos Aires. In 2005 the Argentine Forensic

PLAZOLETA MATILDE VARA DE ANGUITA.

PLAZOLETA DELIA AVILÉS DE ELIZALDE LEAL.

Anthropology Team (EAAF) identified her remains through genetic testing; they were then buried in the Santa Cruz Church.

### 67c. Plazoleta Matilde Vara de Anguita

**LOCATION:** SOUTH SIDE OF THE 25 DE MAYO FREEWAY, BETWEEN RINCON AND SARANDI

"As long as you are in prison, as long as you and Wanda are in prison, I will not leave Argentina" [AO.0131]. Matilde spoke these words to her son Eduardo when they discussed the possibility of her leaving the country. In 1978 he was being held in the La Plata Prison along with other political prisoners.

The repressive forces had held militants from the Montonero and PRT-ERP* armed movements, whom they considered their most important prisoners, in Blocks 1 and 2 of the La Plata Prison since the beginning of January 1977. These were known as the Death Blocks. Several prisoners were taken out alive in false "transfers" and then murdered in simulated escapes. This same method was used to kill legally detained political prisoners in other prisons around the country, such as Sierra Chica in the province of Buenos Aires and Resistencia, in the province of Chaco.

Matilde was active in the prisoner solidarity committee that carried out a number of activities: collecting money for the prisoners to use in the prison shop, overseeing security, and acting as a communication link to the outside world. The repressive forces regularly murdered detainees and kidnapped and disappeared family members. Matilde was kidnapped on July 24, 1978, at the age of sixty. That same day the guards seized letters she had sent to her son. Although Matilde's family never uncovered the precise circumstances of her kidnapping, they do know that prison agents were among the members of the Special Task Group responsible for her disappearance.

### 67d. Plazoleta Delia Avilés de Elizalde Leal

**LOCATION:** COCHABAMBA 2200, BETWEEN PASCO AND PICHINCHA

While Alberto Elizalde was being held in the La Plata prison, his mother, Delia Avilés de Elizalde, and his siblings Sofía and Felipe were kidnapped on January 20, 1977.

PLAZOLETA RAMONA GASTIAZORO DE BRONTES.

PLAZOLETA ANGELA MARÍA AIETA DE GULLO.

Alberto had been held captive in a number of different prisons since 1973: Villa Devoto, Caseros, Chaco, Río Gallegos, Rawson, Sierra Chica, and Unit 9 in La Plata. The family members of political prisoners had faced persecution and threats since 1974. That year, when Delia visited Alberto in the Río Gallegos Prison, security agents planted a gun under the pillow in her hotel room. She was imprisoned for several days as a result.

Delia and Sofía were active from 1975 in a committee that denounced the inhumane living conditions inside the prisons. On January 19, 1977, Delia went to La Plata to visit her son; she had been planning to present an appeal that same day to demand improved prison conditions. She told her son that she would be back the following week, but she did not appear on the twenty-sixth. The mother of another detainee informed Alberto that she had been kidnapped along with his brother and sister.

### 67e. Plazoleta Ramona Gastiazoro de Brontes

**LOCATION:** COCHABAMBA 2300, BETWEEN PICHINCHA AND MATHEU

A task force kidnapped fifty-year-old Ramona Gastiazoro de Brontes from her home in Ciudadela on March 9, 1977. She was taken to the Clandestine Detention Center that operated inside the Campo de Mayo* military base. Her son, José Brontes, was an activist in the Peronist Workers Youth Movement* (JTP, Juventud Trabajadora Peronista) and in the armed Montonero movement. He was kidnapped on May 13, 1975, and was disappeared for just over one day in Coordinación Federal (see p. 17) before being legally recognized as a political prisoner. He passed through several prisons, including Sierra Chica, Rawson, Villa Devoto (see p. 199), and Unit 9 in La Plata, before being released on October 30, 1983.

### 67f. Plazoleta Angela María Aieta de Gullo

**LOCATION:** DR. EDUARDO JENNER 1800, BETWEEN ENTRE RIOS AND COMBATE DE LOS POZOS

In a joint operation involving several Special Task Groups, the repressive forces kidnapped the mother and wife of Dante Gullo, leader of the Peronist Youth Movement (JP, Juventud Peronista), on August 5, 1976. In Buenos Aires, a group of heavily armed men burst into the Gullo family home at 1900 Cachimayo Street, coming in through the front door, the back, and over the roof. They took

PLAZOLETA IRENE ORLANDO.

PLAZOLETA HAYDEE ROSA CIRULLO DE CARNAGHI.

away Dante's mother, Angela María. At exactly the same time, another Special Task Group kidnapped Dante's wife, Graciela Ojeda, in Colón, in the province of Entre Ríos. Dante himself had been held captive since April 1975. Graciela Ojeda was released, but Angela María, who had been fighting for the release of her son and all political prisoners, was taken to the ESMA and later thrown into the Río de la Plata. Angela María's youngest son, Salvador Gullo, was kidnapped in April 1979 and remains disappeared to this day (see p. 232).

### 67g. Plazoleta Irene Orlando

**LOCATION:** CORNER OF RINCON AND COCHABAMBA

Irene Orlando was kidnapped at the age of sixty-four by a Special Task Group in the town of San Martín in the province of Buenos Aires. It was December 1977. Irene, a psychologist, was searching for her son Mario Tempone and her daughter-in-law, both of whom had been disappeared. Several survivors, including Victor Basterra, who managed to smuggle photographs of prisoners out of the ESMA, have testified to having seen her at this Clandestine Detention Center, where she was forced to work in the storeroom sorting clothes. Irene remains disappeared to this day.

### 67h. Plazoleta Haydée Rosa Cirullo de Carnaghi

**LOCATION:** ON THE EVEN-NUMBERED SIDE OF ALBERTI STREET, BETWEEN COCHABAMBA AND THE 25 DE MAYO FREEWAY EXIT

Haydée had a long history of political activism. She was a member of the women's branch of the Peronist Leadership Council (Consejo Superior Peronista) and was active in the Peronist Resistance*, where she was known as Tía Tota (Aunt Tota). In an interview in July 1974, the day of Juan Domingo Perón's funeral, Haydée stated, "I loved Perón very much. If only I hadn't loved him so much. . . . I dedicated my youth to him, just like my husband and our entire generation. We gave our children to him. And you don't give over your children to a cause just like that. . . . Before, when I was young, I wasn't afraid of anything. But once I had kids, things were different. I was afraid for them. The other day, while I waited endlessly to pay my last respects to Perón, I was not afraid for my children. In spite of that whole apparatus deployed by the army and the police, I knew that the kids would be all right because my fellow activists were going to watch over them. That's a beautiful thing, isn't it?" (*La Causa Peronista,* 4, 5).

THESE SMALL SQUARES ARE POORLY MAINTAINED.

Haydée was kidnapped on August 4, 1976, with her daughter Carmen, who was in ninth grade. They were held for a time in the Clandestine Detention Center known as Coordinación Federal. In 2000 the Argentine Forensic Anthropology Team identified them as two of the victims of the Fátima Massacre*.

### 67i. Plazoleta Elsa Rabinovich de Levenson

**LOCATION:** NORTH SIDE OF THE 25 DE MAYO FREEWAY, BETWEEN SARANDI AND RINCON

Elsa Rabinovich de Levenson was kidnapped and taken to the ESMA in 1977. Her grandson was abducted in the same operation, though Elsa's husband, Gregorio Levenson, managed to recover him after several years of searching. Gregorio's and Elsa's sons Miguel Alejo and Bernardo had founded the Revolutionary Armed Forces* (FAR, Fuerzas Armadas Revolucionarias) in its initial period, when it served as a support group for Ernesto "Che" Guevara's Bolivia campaign. Miguel Alejo died of a heart attack on December 19, 1970, following a failed combat operation. Bernardo died in combat during the last dictatorship while defending a communications center belonging to the armed Montonero movement located at 700 Yatay Street in the neighborhood of Almagro. Elsa was the victim of a "death flight"*.

# 68. **Tribute to Jorge Julio López in the Miramar Bar**



On March 19, 2007, the association San Cristobal Residents Against Impunity (Vecinos de San Cristóbal contra la Impunidad) placed a ceramic plaque to honor Jorge Julio López and demand that he be found alive. The tile work was erected on the facade of the Miramar Bar at the corner of Avenida San Juan and Sarandí Sreet. It was made by workers from the Factory without Bosses (FaSinPat, or Fábrica sin Patrones), a worker-controlled factory located in Neuquén that each year produces a ceramic tile with a sociopolitical theme.

**LOCATION:** AV. SAN JUAN AND SARANDÍ
**TRANSPORTATION:** BUSES: 4, 6, 12, 23, 37, 50, 53, 84, 96, 126, 129, 150, 151. SUBWAY STATION: ENTRE RÍOS (E LINE).

López was kidnapped twice, the first time by members of the State Security Forces on October 27, 1976, during the last military dictatorship. The circumstances of the second kidnapping remain unclear, but the assailants were allegedly linked to the Buenos Aires provincial police. It occurred on September 18, 2006, a few months before the twenty-third anniversary of the return to democracy in Argentina. López, disappeared under a democratic government, was kidnapped after testifying in a trial against people accused of participating in the repression of the military dictatorship.

**Detained and disappeared during the dictatorship**

At the time of his first captivity, López was disappeared and detained in the Clandestine Detention Center known as the Pozo de Arana* (Arana Pit), located within the Military Detachment of the Anti-Rustling Department of the provincial police, on the outskirts of the city of La Plata, Buenos Aires Province. From there he was moved to Police Stations 5 and 8 in La Plata*, and later to Prison Unit No. 9 in the same city. He was released on July 25, 1979.

When he testified in the trial against the man responsible for his first disappearance, López made the following remarks about his illegal

MIRAMAR BAR. CERAMIC PLAQUE DEMANDING THAT LÓPEZ BE RETURNED ALIVE.

MURAL ON THE AV. DE MAYO NEAR THE PLAZA DE MAYO.

STENCIL PORTRAIT OF JORGE JULIO LÓPEZ.

"DISAPPEARED UNDER DEMOCRACY." STENCIL ON THE AV. DE MAYO.

detention: "I think they kidnapped me because I helped the boys [referring to members of the Montonero guerrilla movement]. I collaborated with those who went out into the streets (after the coup of March 24), not with the leaders like [Mario] Firmenich who walked away with the organization's money" (*Clarín,* September 23, 2006).

López had arrived in La Plata from the town of General Villegas, in the north of the province of Buenos Aires. He lived in the neighborhood of Los Hornos in the mid-1970s and worked in construction. As a Peronist militant, he participated from 1974 to 1976 on the fringes of the Montonero* movement, more precisely in a grassroots movement known as the Unidad Básica Pablo Maestre. There he met Patricia Dell'Orto and Ambrosio De Marco, a married couple who were kidnapped one week before him and with whom he shared time in captivity.

The man in charge of the sites where López was detained during this first period of captivity was Miguel Osvaldo Etchecolatz, Director of Investigations of the Buenos Aires Police from 1976 to 1977. Etchecolatz directed twenty-one Clandestine Detention Centers and worked as the right-hand man of General Ramón Camps, Chief of Police during the same period.

**Disappeared under democracy**

On June 20, 2006, the Federal Oral Tribunal No. 1 of La Plata initiated legal proceedings against Etchecolatz. It was one of the first human rights trials to take place in the country after the National Congress overturned the so-called impunity laws (the Full Stop Law* and the Law of Due Obedience*) in 2003. During the trial Jorge Julio López described in detail how he had been tortured by Etchecolatz and others. He also testified that the Special Task Group* under Etchecolatz's control murdered Patricia Dell'Orto and Ambrosio de Marco.

BALLOONS WITH JORGE JULIO LÓPEZ'S IMAGE DURING THE RESISTANCE MARCH OF DECEMBER 2006.

López was kidnapped again three months later, shortly before the thirtieth anniversary of his first illegal detention. He had planned to go to court that day to listen to the proceedings. Jorge Julio López was seventy-six years old at the time of his second kidnapping; he remains disappeared, and there is no information about his whereabouts.

On September 19, 2006, the Federal Oral Tribunal No. 1 of La Plata sentenced Etchecolatz to life imprisonment for crimes against humanity. For the first time, the legal definition of genocide was used to describe the acts of state terror in Argentina.

The next day, September 20, 2006, the daily newspaper *Página/12* ran the headline, "López Is Still Missing." Two days later, after the intervention of the federal government, the provincial Minister of Security, León Arslanián, announced a two-hundred-thousand-peso reward to anyone who could provide information about López's whereabouts. One week later he removed from duty thirty-six officers and non-commissioned officers from the province of Buenos Aires with connections to the Clandestine Detention Centers directed by Etchecolatz during the last dictatorship. On September 23, while members of the security forces searched the country for López, a massive demonstration took place in front of the building housing the Government of the Province of Buenos Aires demanding that he be found alive. The demand was reiterated on the twenty-eighth, when a huge crowd marched from the National Congress to the Plaza de Mayo. Within a few months the reward was raised to one million pesos.

López's second disappearance reveals the continuities of the repressive state terror apparatus under democratic rule. Even the provincial governor at the time, Felipe Solá, did not rule out the possibility that police officers may have been involved. The circumstances surrounding the disappearance point to the possibility that security forces were involved and that we are dealing with a political kidnapping related to the trial of Etchecolatz and his relationship with the Buenos Aires provincial police. It is difficult to imagine another group in Argentina with the operational capacity to kidnap someone without leaving a trace and then keep him "disappeared" during an intense search carried out by all of the country's intelligence and security forces. It is particularly remarkable that no evidence has been leaked in spite of the size of the reward.

### The survivors' voices

López's second forced disappearance shows that the repressive apparatus created by those responsible for state terrorism was not entirely dismantled after the return of democracy. It also demonstrates that political authorities have been negligent in their protection of witnesses and have been powerless to investigate the security forces that are supposed to be under their control.

At the same time, however, this unprecedented disappearance highlights the importance these testimonies by survivors of the Clandestine Detention Centers hold for the functioning of the democratic process.

The activism undertaken first by family members of the disappeared and then by human rights organizations marked the first step in the recovery of the rule of law. That important first step took shape in the demands made by the Madres de Plaza de Mayo and the Abuelas de Plaza de Mayo. After 1977 their marches created the first tiny opening in the dictatorship's state of exception. That first crack made visible the criminal acts of the dictatorship: the systematic and forced disappearance of persons. The military's attempt to erase the existence of its victims denied the very possibility of living together as a community. Later, the voices of those rare survivors of the concentration camps' horror were also heard. Argentine society was able to take the unprecedented step of prosecuting the military juntas because a handful of survivors were willing to appear before the courts. The act of testifying about what happened during the period of state terrorism constitutes the foundation of whatever democracy may exist in Argentina. Jorge Julio López disappeared because he stepped forward as a witness.

One plaque pays tribute to him in the Miramar Bar, another in the Plaza de Mayo. The memorials bearing his name, like those that recognize other victims of detention and disappearance, expose the tensions between past and present. In the months after his kidnapping, broad sectors of society took part in demonstrations that demanded he be "found alive," reviving the old slogan: "aparición con vida." Stenciled images of his face appeared on hundreds of building facades in Buenos Aires and many other cities throughout the country. At the same time, several groups of street artists came up with new kinds of actions within the urban environment to voice the demand for his reappearance. One of these involved adding question marks to the title of the report by the National Commission on the Disappearance of Persons*, transforming it from *Never Again* to *Never Again?* (*¿Nunca más?;* see "Nunca Más Square and Cultural Center," p. 186). Over time, the demands surrounding López's disappearance became more muted. His name is now rarely mentioned in the media, and the country's leaders have never taken responsibility for the case.

## 69. *Abrazo* (*The Hug*). Sculpture the ATE

This sculpture was inaugurated in the headquarters of the Association of State Employees (ATE, Asociación de Trabajadores del Estado) twenty years after the last military coup to remember the 144 disappeared members of this union. Cristina Terzaghi made the work out of 144 stainless steel rods intertwined with a structure of stainless steel sheets. The three-meter-high sculpture is located in the garden of the ATE headquarters; a plaque next to it bears the names of the disappeared employees. When the wind blows through the sculpture, the steel rods produce a sound evoking the presence of the disappeared that can be heard throughout the building.

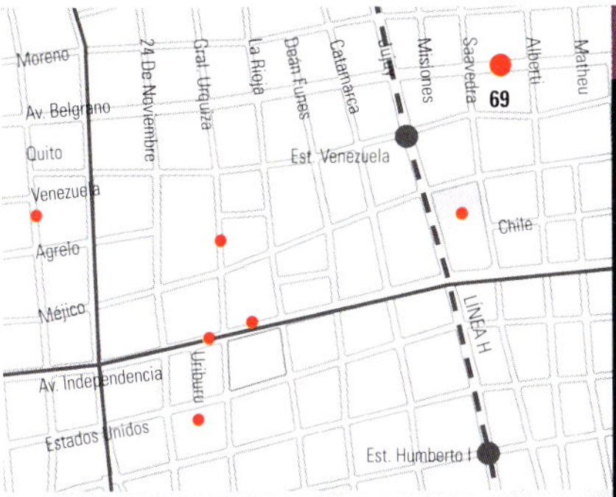


**LOCATION:** AV. BELGRANO 2523
**TRANSPORTATION:** BUSES: 2, 56, 61, 62, 84, 88, 95, 98, 118, 129, 168, 188. SUBWAY STATIONS: ALBERTI (A LINE) AND VENEZUELA (H LINE).

During the period of state terrorism the leaders of the ATE supported the military government's policies. The union was recovered by its membership after the return to democracy. In the 1990s members founded the Confederation of Argentine Workers (CTA, Confederación de Trabajadores Argentinos), a federation of militant unions that provided an alternative to the pro-government General Confederation of Labor (CGT, Confederación General del Trabajo). The CTA fought against the neoliberal policies enacted under the President Carlos Saúl Menem. Among the many ATE leaders who have influenced Argentine politics, of particular note is Germán Abdala. Secretary of the CTA office in Buenos Aires in the 1980s, Abdala went on to win a seat in Congress representing the city. He was a member of the Group of Eight, a dissident faction in the Chamber of Deputies that broke with the pro-government bloc to protest the government's neoliberal policies. In December 1990 President Menem granted pardons* to military officers and civilians implicated in the violence of the 1970s, thereby freeing the generals who had been imprisoned a few years earlier. Abdala, faithful to his political roots, resigned his seat in Congress and his membership in the Justicialist Party.

SCULPTURE IN THE COURTYARD OF THE ATE HEADQUARTERS.

Many ATE employees suffered persecution and kidnapping during the dictatorship. The government did not intervene in the union because its General Secretary, Juan Horvath, reported directly to the junta. Alberto Giudice, founder of the ATE offices in Buenos Aires, recalls, "The day after the coup, Horvath convened a Council meeting and told us that the military was going to be in charge for about twenty years, and that he was thinking of supporting them. He even boasted that [General Antonio] Massera had met with him in his underwear. So he traveled to Geneva to declare his support for the military government at the International Labor Organization. That was the breaking point; that was when we founded ANUSATE [National Association for Unity and Solidarity with the ATE]."

At an ATE Congress near the end of 1976 many delegates from the interior provinces declared their opposition to Horvath. Delegates from the Buenos Aires offices who had joined in this opposition were sanctioned and expelled from the union. They founded ANUSATE the next year. They were able to use the Casa de Nazareth, next to the Santa Cruz Church, for their meetings, the first of which took place on Friday, December 9, 1977. A Special Task Group* from the ESMA had kidnapped seven human rights activists from the steps of the church the previous day (see "Santa Cruz Church," p. 89).

When the last military dictatorship dissolved the CGT (General Confederation of Labor), the labor movement split into two groups: the National Labor Commission (CNT, Comisión Nacional de Trabajo), which included unions that had opted for conciliation and dialogue with the military, and the National Commission of the Twenty-five, who maintained a distance from the government. ANUSATE joined this second group.

The economic model promoted by the military government's Ministry of the Economy, José Alfredo Martínez de Hoz, favored the financial sector and those groups with the greatest concentration of capital, and hurt small and medium-sized businesses.

The military government replaced the CGT leadership in one of its first decrees. The law intervening in the CGT banned union elections, assemblies, and conferences. Union leaders who were compliant with the military could see their terms extended. In September 1976 the government passed a law prohibiting direct action by unions and imposed a prison sentence of up to ten years for incitement to strike. This attack on labor gains that had been won through many decades of organizing deepened in 1979, when the government extended the length of the standard working day.

The National Commission of the Twenty-five launched its first general strike that year; its organizers were imprisoned for months. A second general strike was declared on July 22, 1981, under the junta leadership of General Roberto Eduardo Viola. The third and largest took place on March 30, 1982, during the military leadership of Leopoldo Fortunato Galtieri. On this occasion, demonstrating activists and workers met with brutal repression as they made their way toward the Plaza de Mayo. Three days later the military occupation of the Malvinas (Falkland) Islands eclipsed the political impact of that strike and of the street clashes between workers and military forces (see "Plaza de Mayo," p. 3).

A succession of strikes took place after the war. A general strike declared on December 6, 1982, was the first to attract the support of all union organizations. Equally large strikes took place on March 28 and October 4, 1983.

Elections were called in ATE after the return to democracy in 1983. Víctor de Gennaro, the ANUSATE candidate, finally defeated Juan Horvath, who had held power for twenty years.

# 70. **Plaza Julio César Fumarola**

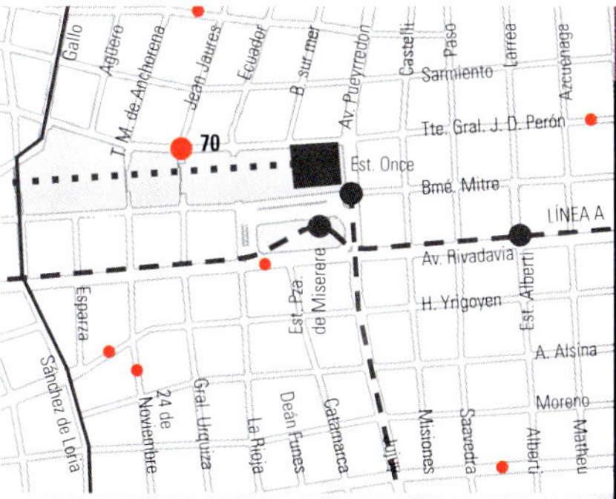


A group of residents managed to convert a vacant lot in the neighborhood into a public square for the community. This space, which had lain abandoned for years, was temporarily named "La plaza del mientras tanto" (The meanwhile square) until they decided to name it after Julio César Fumarola, a local resident and professional photographer who had been murdered in 1974 by the Triple A* (Argentine Anticommunist Alliance; see "Coordinación Federal," p. 17).

**LOCATION:** TTE. GRAL. J. D. PERÓN AND JEAN JAURÉS
**TRANSPORTATION:** BUSES: 5, 19, 24, 26, 32, 61, 62, 64, 68, 71, 75, 86, 88, 98, 101, 104, 105, 115, 118, 124, 129, 132, 151, 165, 168, 194. SUBWAY STATIONS: ONCE (H LINE) AND MISERERE (A LINE). TRAIN STATION: ONCE (SARMIENTO LINE).

Fumarola was born in the neighborhood of Balvanera and lived most of his life in a typical neighborhood house on 24 de Noviembre Street. The poet Alfredo Carlino, who was Fumarola's friend, bought the house and lives there today. In November 2007 the Association of Residents for Remembrance and Justice (Vecinos por la Memoria y la Justicia) dedicated a paving stone as a tribute to the photographer (see p. 123).

"I met Julio César here in the neighborhood," recounts Carlino, who worked alongside Fumarola in his early years as an activist. He describes how they used to meet in the Perla Nueva bar and coffee shop across from the Plaza Miserere, where a supermarket stands today. "We would go there to read, write, and hold meetings. We were like brothers."

A few hours after he was kidnapped early in the morning of February 6, 1974, Fumarola's body was discovered in the area of Ezeiza, near the famous public swimming facilities. These large swimming pools had been inaugurated that summer by the Ministry of Social Welfare led by José López Rega, founder of the Triple A paramilitary organization. The organization's arsenal was stored in the basement

PLAZA JULIO CÉSAR FUMAROLA.

THE PLAZA'S INAUGURATION.

ALFREDO CARLINO RECITES A POEM IN MEMORY OF HIS FRIEND FUMAROLA.

of the Ministry building, where one would expect to find blankets or other items required by a social assistance agency. The building also contained a prison. An orderly showed the red- and orange-painted bars to Jorge Watts, a survivor of the Clandestine Detention Center known as El Vesubio* who worked in computing and often visited the Ministry. He told Watts, "This is the Minister's prison. . . . His enemies are here."

Julio César's brother could not recognize his body; he had been shot more than sixty times, mainly in the face. Fumarola had worked as a photographer for the advertising industry. He was thirty-three years old and had two children.

### "The meanwhile square"

At the dedication ceremony in the square, Miguel Germino, the editor of the neighborhood newspaper *Primera Página,* recalled the residents' early efforts to transform the empty lot into a green space: "We removed cobblestones, we planted trees, we built flowerbeds, we brought in topsoil, and we cared for this small square for over two years." They tried to get the space officially recognized and named; together they made the decision to pay tribute to their neighbor by naming it after Julio César Fumarola.

In the case of the Plaza Julio César Fumarola, as in other parts of the city, the initiative to reshape the urban landscape by constructing a site of remembrance came from the neighborhood itself. This commemorative gesture reconnecting everyday space to a past that people had tried to forget also requires the state to safeguard the work begun by the residents. Germino therefore approached the civil servants in attendance at the inauguration ceremony to highlight a problem afflicting most of these green spaces: "This square was abandoned until two days ago. It hadn't been watered. It had no electricity and no caretaker. It was overrun by dogs and attacked by vandals who destroyed its playground equipment, benches, and fencing." He explained that the square had been cleaned up and painted in time for the officials' visit. Yet, he added, "This square shouldn't have to wait for public ceremonies to get some regular maintenance."

A PAVING STONE IS PLACED IN FUMAROLA'S MEMORY.

### The Triple A

Juan Domingo Perón convened the second press conference of his presidential term one day after Fumarola's murder. Ana Guzetti, a journalist from the newspaper *El Mundo,* questioned the president about the murder and the government's inaction in the face of such attacks:

"Mr. President: At your first press conference with us, I asked you what measures you were going to take to curb the escalation of fascist attacks on social and political activists. . . . Within two weeks, bombings were launched against exactly twenty-five Peronist neighborhood centers (Unidades Básicas), which hardly represent the far left. Twelve activists died, and yesterday we learned that a photographer had been murdered. Clearly, all this is the work of far-right paramilitary groups."

"Are you prepared to take responsibility for what you are saying?" responded President Perón. "You are going to have to prove your claims about paramilitary groups," he threatened. He then asked for the journalist's identification, "so that the Ministry of Justice [could] launch legal proceedings" against her.

The Association of Buenos Aires Journalists called for a strike to protest Fumarola's murder; the Federal Police then arrested the organization's leaders. *El Mundo* was shut down just over a month later, on March 15, 1974.

The Triple A had first emerged publicly with an attack on the Radical Party senator Hipólito Solari Yrigoyen on November 21, 1973, just after Perón took office. The bomb exploded in the parking lot of the Congress building, and the senator miraculously survived his injuries (see "Coordinación Federal," p. 17).

The Triple A issued its first public announcement one week before Fumarola's kidnapping and murder; it contained a list of the individuals the organization had sentenced to death. The text sent to the main media outlets was succinct: "Those who are named shall be executed wherever we find them." There followed a list of twenty-one names of elected officials, lawyers, guerrilla leaders, union activists, a bishop, and the editors of the newspapers *Noticias* and *El Mundo.*

# 71. **Mural in the National Congress**

**LOCATION:** AV. RIVADAVIA 1851
**TRANSPORTATION:** BUSES: 6, 7, 12, 37, 50, 56, 60, 64, 86, 105, 186. SUBWAY STATION: CONGRESO (A LINE).

"Where are you, Daddy?" With this question Carolina López Forastier expressed how much she had missed her father as a little girl after his arrest early in the morning of March 26, 1976. The artist Mónica Corrales used her words as inspiration for the mural *Soledades y ausencias infantiles – 30 años* (Thirty years of children's loneliness and loss), installed in front of the Juan Carlos Pugliese Annex of the Chamber of Deputies.

Leopoldo López Forastier was a Supreme Court judge when he was arrested in 1976 and incarcerated under National Executive Power* (PEN, "a disposición del Poder Ejecutivo Nacional"). In 1980 he regained his freedom in and founded an office of the Permanent Assembly for Human Rights that same year in the province of Misiones.

"This is a tribute to all of those who suffered this terrible experience," said the mural's creator. The image of a crying girl that Corrales chose for the mural was inspired by a text written by López Forastier, part of which is reproduced in the work. "I was moved by this issue. She had not had a childhood because she had been searching for her father. . . . [She] had lost her toys," says Corrales.

Construction of the annex building where the mural is displayed began under the military government, which sought to create a pseudo-institutional structure in order to hold onto power. The building was completed after the return to democracy, when Carlos Pugliese was president of the Chamber of Deputies. The building "lacked a space for the remembrance of these events," says Corrales. For the artist, it is "an honor that [the mural] is in such a prominent location where thousands of people pass through every day." She envisions that it will enable "future generations of Congress members to hold onto the memories. They must not forget what happened."

During the inaugural ceremony on March 23, 2006, each person was given a palette knife so that he or she could contribute symbolically to the artwork and fulfill the meaning of its final sentence: "Now we are all here. Let every tear that has been shed serve to keep memories alive and maintain the power of the message: *Nunca más* [Never again]."

MURAL HONORING THE DISAPPEARED AT AV. RIVADAVIA 1851.

# 72. **José María Ramos Mejía Hospital**

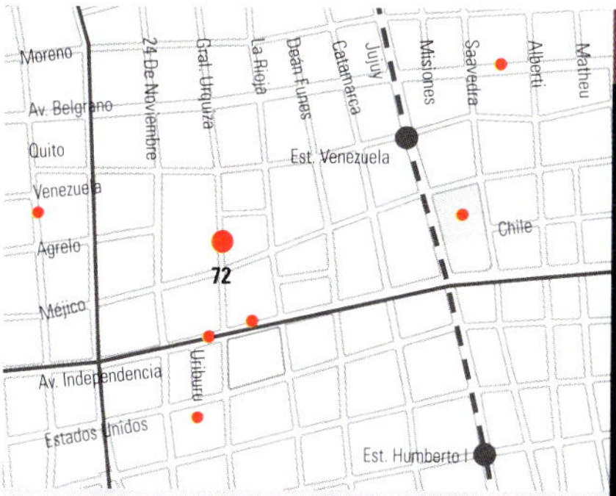




**LOCATION:** URQUIZA 609
**TRANSPORTATION:** BUSES: 23, 41, 61, 62, 75, 84, 88, 96, 101, 118, 129, 155, 188. SUBWAY STATIONS: URQUIZA (E LINE) AND VENEZUELA (H LINE).

Nine plaques pay tribute to workers from the Ramos Mejía Hospital who were detained and disappeared. One was dedicated by the Buenos Aires City Council, another by the hospital's union committee, and seven more by the Commission of Neighborhoods for Remembrance and Justice. These last plaques remember Norma Beatriz Leiva, a doctor kidnapped in August 1977; Eleonora Cristina, an employee and PRT-ERP* militant who was kidnapped at the age of twenty-five; Jorge Calvo, a doctor abducted in 1977 when he was twenty-seven years old; Mario Marzocca, a laboratory technician kidnapped in July 1978; Teresa Lajmanovich, a medical resident kidnapped when she was twenty-four; the neurologist Eduardo O'Neill and Pablo Linber, both kidnapped on September 20, 1977.

The hospital had originally been established in the sheds used to quarantine victims of three devastating epidemics that spread through Buenos Aires from 1867 to 1871. According to the census of 1869, the last of these, a yellow fever epidemic, caused 13,725 deaths out of a population of 177,787. In 1868, under the presidency of Domingo Faustino Sarmiento, Governor Adolfo Alsina opened a system of ditches and began to set up a sewage system as a response to the outbreak of cholera. In this period, the richest families began to move to the northern part of the city.

The hospital, at first named San Roque, was inaugurated in 1883. In 1914 it was given the name Ramos Mejía to honor one of the first doctors and intellectuals to call for the establishment of a public health system.

RAMOS MEJÍA HOSPITAL.

THE PLAQUES ARE LOCATED TO THE LEFT OF THE HOSPITAL'S MAIN ENTRANCE.

## State terrorism and health professionals

As explained in an Amnesty International report from May 1978, Argentina was considered one of Latin America's most developed countries in terms of health care before the military coup. It had the best medical schools in the region, and its health professionals were highly qualified. By mid-1976 various measures taken by the military government had turned most health professionals into active opponents of the policies of the Public Health Secretariat. These included dismissals, transfers, and the beginnings of a system of hospital fees that left thousands of people outside the health system.

The official response was swift. Over 250 health workers disappeared or were murdered. The dictatorship aimed its attacks at the numerous associations that represented health workers. Members of the Argentine Federation of Resident Doctors and Psychologists, including Norma Beatriz Leiva and Eduardo O'Neill, suffered persecution and disappearance. Members of the Federation of Psychiatrists and the Buenos Aires Association of Psychologists also disappeared and were persecuted.

## Posadas Hospital

On March 29, 1976, five days after the coup, a hundred soldiers burst into the Posadas Hospital and arrested over sixty people, many of whom were briefly detained and disappeared in the facilities of Coordinación Federal (see p. 17). Twelve people working in the Posadas Hospital were kidnapped in a series of operations in November of that year. These included Dr. Jorge Roitman, an infectious disease specialist from the polyclinic who was taken from his nearby home, hooded, and tortured in front of his wife and daughters.

Two years later, in May 1978, a boycott organized in France targeted the Twelfth Annual Cancer Congress that was due to take place in Buenos Aires in October of that year. By that time the practices of state terrorism in Argentina were known around the world. The Congress, like the even more notorious Football World Cup in 1978, was organized in order to improve Argentina's international image. It was condemned by thousands of professionals in the international scientific community. Professor León Schwarzenberg wrote a letter to forty thousand doctors denouncing torture and asking them to join the boycott. The letter, which also condemned the doctors who were participating in the torture sessions, was published in *Le Monde* on May 3, 1978.

## 73. **Beatriz Le Fur**

Beatriz was an activist in the Commission of Family Members of Student and Trade Union Political Prisoners. Working from a local coffee shop known as the Gildo bar, she received reports of detentions, prepared writs of habeas corpus*, and shared information with family members. On June 9, 2006, the Commission of Neighborhoods for Remembrance and Justice of Almagro—Balvanera dedicated a paving stone to her at this corner.

**LOCATION:** CORNER OF AV. CORRIENTES AND MEDRANO, ALMAGRO

## 74. **Hugo Penino – Cecilia Viñas**

Cecilia was seven months pregnant when she was kidnapped along with Hugo. Both were taken to the ESMA (see p. 153), where Cecilia gave birth to a son in September 1977. He was appropriated by Jorge Vildoza, who named him Javier and brought him up as his own child. Javier discovered his true origins in 1998 (see p. 77).

**LOCATION:** AV. CORRIENTES 3645, ALMAGRO

## 75. **Miguel Arcuschin – Noemí Jansenson**

Miguel and Noemí were kidnapped on September 13, 1976, by a group of men in civilian clothes who burst into their home. The couple had been students at the Carlos Pellegrini Advanced School of Commerce (see p. 61). They had married on December 22, 1975, and Noemí was three months pregnant. Neither they nor their child has ever been heard of again.

**LOCATION:** COLOMBRES 31, ALMAGRO

## 76. **Victor Hugo Acosta "El Cordobés"**

On September 16, 2006, the Commission of Neighborhoods for Remembrance and Justice dedicated a paving stone to Victor Hugo Acosta in front of the house where he lived and where he was kidnapped on September 16, 1977. Victor Hugo was twenty-seven years old, worked at the Stock Exchange, and studied psychology. He was seen in the Clandestine Detention Center known as the Club Atlético (see p. 129).

**LOCATION:** GUARDIA VIEJA 4572, ALMAGRO

## 77. Silvio Frondizi – Luis Angel Mendiburu

On September 27, 1975, a group of commandos kidnapped Silvio, brother of former Argentine president Arturo Frondizi. His wife's screams alerted her son-in-law Luis Angel, who tried to defend him. Luis was shot and died a few hours later in the Italian Hospital. The Triple A* claimed responsibility for the crime (see p. 17). Silvio's body was discovered in Ezeiza.

**LOCATION:** TTE. GRAL. J. D. PERON 4474, ALMAGRO

## 78. Graciela Mellibovsky

Graciela was kidnapped on September 25, 1976, as she was on her way to meet some fellow activists. She was twenty-nine years old. She had been a student at the Buenos Aires National School (see p. 43) and had a degree in political economy. On December 12, 2006, the Commission of Neighborhoods for Remembrance and Justice of Almagro—Balvanera dedicated a paving stone in her memory.

**LOCATION:** CORNER OF ACUNA DE FIGUEROA AND AV. CORRIENTES, ALMAGRO

## 79. Irene Belocchio – Rolando Pizoni

Rolando was twenty-eight years old when he was kidnapped. He became an activist in the Peronist University Youth Movement* (JUP, Juventud Universitaria Peronista) while studying engineering. In 1976 he met Irene, and they had a son named Carlos. Irene worked in the Banco Galicia, where she was a union delegate. The bank lent her money to study business administration at the Argentine University of Business (UADE, Universidad Argentina de la Empresa). She was twenty-five years old when she was kidnapped.

**LOCATION:** MARMOL 498, ALMAGRO

## 80. Gustavo Juárez

Gustavo was kidnapped on August 12, 1977. He was nineteen years old, had been a student at the Buenos Aires National School (see p. 43), and was a member of the Union of Secondary School Students* (UES, Unión de Estudiantes Secundarios). Although he lived at 4000 Av. Rivadavia, the paving stone that pays tribute to him was placed on a street corner where he often spent time: "Here walked Gustavo Juárez."

**LOCATION:** HIPÓLITO IRIGOYEN AND YAPEYÚ, ALMAGRO.

## 81. Alejandro Goldar Parodi

Alejandro was eighteen years old when he disappeared early in the morning of July 7, 1976. He was kidnapped as he was leaving the home of his girlfriend, Malena Gallardo, who is also disappeared. Goldar Parodi had been heading to the cinema to meet his friends Juan Marín, Hugo Tosso, and Pablo Dubcovsky, who had also left their respective homes. All four friends remain disappeared to this day.

**LOCATION:** HIPOLITO YRIGOYEN 3708, ALMAGRO

## 82. Alicia Cosaka

A plaque was placed at the entrance to Alicia Cosaka's home on April 23, 2007, following an initiative by the Commission of Neighborhoods for Remembrance and Justice. Alicia had attended high school at Normal School No. 8 in San Cristóbal. At the time of her kidnapping on June 29, 1976, she was studying architecture.

**LOCATION:** VIRREY LINIERS 548, ALMAGRO

## 83. Daniel Hopen – Evangelina Carreira

On August 17, 1976, Daniel and Evangelina were kidnapped in front of their home. Evangelina worked in advertising. Daniel had begun his career as an activist in the Student Union of the Urquiza School. He was a professor of sociology and a member of the Academic Council of the Faculty of Philosophy and Letters. They were last seen in the Clandestine Detention Center known as Coordinación Federal (see p. 17).

**LOCATION:** MEDRANO 441, ALMAGRO

## 84. Teresa Israel Cultural Center

Teresa was twenty-four years old when she was kidnapped on March 8, 1977. A plaque honoring her was placed in the Cultural Center that bears her name. It reads, "Communist Party militant in Almagro. Lawyer and member of the Argentine League for Human Rights. For Teresa and the other thirty thousand, we continue the fight for national liberation. Residents of Almagro and Balvanera."

**LOCATION:** CORNER OF HUMAHUACA AND ACUÑA DE FIGUEROA, ALMAGRO

## 85. **Plaza Almagro**

On November 12, 2007, paving stones were placed in the Plaza Almagro to pay tribute to five people from the neighborhood who had been detained and disappeared: José Felipe Caridi, Elizabeth Franco, María Cristina Lennie, Nelly Esther Ortiz, and Julio Luis Vanodio. The Commission of Neighborhoods for Remembrance and Justice of Almagro—Balvanera participated in the event along with family members, friends, and neighbors.

**LOCATION:** CORNER OF SARMIENTO AND SALGUERO, ALMAGRO.

## 86. **Daniel and Arturo Daroqui**

On November 17, 2007, family members, friends, and the Commission of Neighborhoods for Remembrance and Justice dedicated the paving stone honoring these brothers in front of the house where they lived. They were both kidnapped in the Federal Police Headquarters (see p. 40) on July 15, 1977, as they were going to pick up their passports. In September of that same year, a military operation kidnapped their older brother, Juan Carlos, who remains disappeared.

**LOCATION:** AV. DIAZ VELEZ 3986, ALMAGRO.

## 87. **Hugo and Abel Strejilevich**

Hugo was an actor, a medical resident, and a union delegate in the Ricardo Gutiérrez Children's Hospital. On the day of his kidnapping, he committed suicide by swallowing a cyanide pill. His body was found years later, buried in a mass grave in the Chacarita municipal cemetery. Abel had studied at the Carlos Pellegrini Advanced School of Commerce. He was injured in the leg as he tried to escape his kidnappers.

**LOCATION:** AV. CORRIENTES 3860, ALMAGRO.

## 88. **José María Torres Advanced Normal School No. 7**

On March 28, 2008, a paving stone was dedicated to former students Dorita Falco, Teresa Israel, and María Delia Leiva. The ceremony, organized by the educational community of Normal School No. 7, along with Commercial School No. 25 and the Commission of Neighborhoods for Remembrance and Justice, took place at the entrance to the school. Attendees included family members and friends of the three women as well as students and administrators of the school.

**LOCATION:** AV. CORRIENTES 4261, ALMAGRO.

## 89. **Union of Advertising Employees**

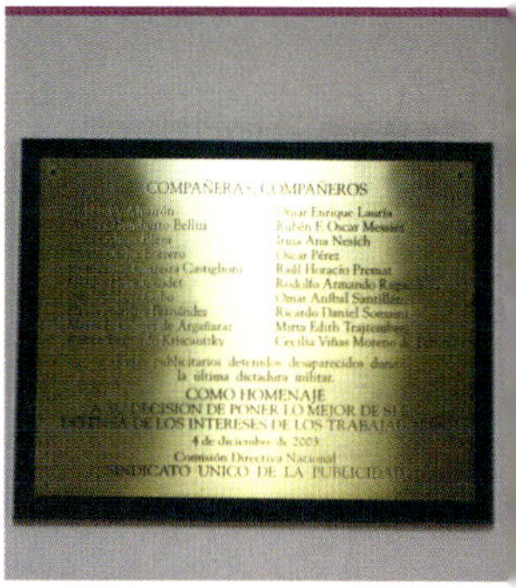


The Human Rights Commission and National Governing Committee of the Union of Advertising Employees (Sindicato Unico de Publicidad) paid tribute to detained and disappeared union members with a plaque dedicated jointly in 1987. The building's main hall was also named for Hilda Fernández, a union delegate detained and disappeared on January 21, 1977.

**LOCATION:** TTE. GRAL. J. D. PERON 2385, BALVANERA

## 90. **Argentine Judicial Federation**

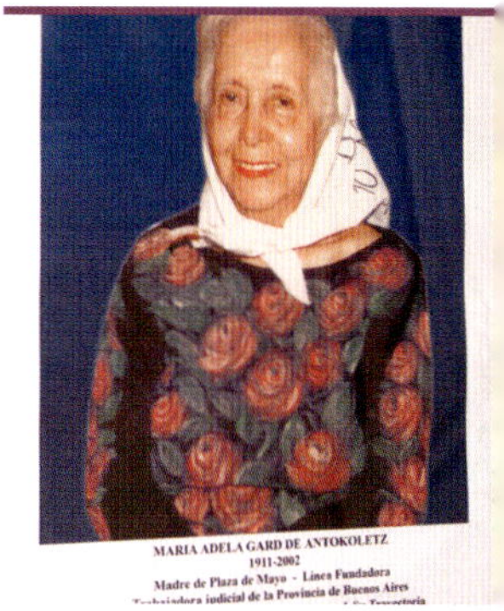


In March 2002 employees of the Federation placed a plaque "in remembrance of our fellow judicial employees who disappeared during the military repression." On October 22, 2004, tribute was paid to María Adela Gard de Antokoletz, a judicial employee and member of the Founding Line of the Madres de Plaza de Mayo. During the ceremony, a photograph donated by her daughter was placed at the site.

**LOCATION:** RINCON 74, BALVANERA

## 91. **Faculty of Psychology, UBA**

In November 1984 the Human Rights Commission of the Faculty's Student Union dedicated a plaque to detained and disappeared students. It reads, "Their struggle is our struggle!"

Another plaque was installed on the ground floor of the building in recognition of the work carried out by the Madres de Plaza de Mayo, following an initiative by the Student Union, the Argentine University Federation, and the Buenos Aires University Federation. The plaque reads, "In the midst of all the madness, the injustice, and the cruelty, they rose up twenty-one years ago . . . and they continue to march for the thirty thousand disappeared, demanding remembrance, truth, and justice."

On June 27, 2002, a third plaque was dedicated, bearing the following text: "On the night of July 29, 1966, known as the Night of the Truncheons [La noche de los bastones largos], many university students escaped the repression unleashed against public universities in Argentina. The Faculty of Psychology . . . pays tribute here to those whose sacrifices kept alive the flame of freedom of thought, the foundation of the university spirit."

**LOCATION:** INDEPENDENCIA LOCALE, AV. INDEPENDENCIA 3065, BALVANERA

## 92. Tribute in the AMIA

On December 7, 2004, the Jewish–Argentine Mutual Association (AMIA, Asociación Mutual Israelita Argentina) held a ceremony paying tribute to the nineteen hundred members of the Jewish community who had been detained and disappeared. At the event, then-President Nestor Kirchner unveiled a high-relief sculpture made by Sara Brodsky, the mother of Fernando Brodsky, who was detained and disappeared on August 14, 1979.

**LOCATION:** PASTEUR 633, BALVANERA

## 93. Tribute in the ATE – CONICET

In March 1996, twenty years after the coup, employees of the National Scientific and Technical Research Council (CONICET, Consejo Nacional de Investigaciones Científicas y Técnicas) paid tribute to Dante Guede with a plaque to remember him and to condemn crimes against humanity. Ten years later, another plaque was installed to "renew our commitment to our fallen colleagues."

**LOCATION:** AV. RIVADAVIA 1917, BALVANERA

## 94. Bartolomé Mitre School No. 5

In remembrance of former students and teachers from this institution who were disappeared, the educational community and school administrators installed a plaque on September 16, 2006, on what was named the Wall of Memory. It reads, "We embrace you and continue to search for you." This initiative was recognized for its social and educational significance by the Buenos Aires City Council.

**LOCATION:** VALENTIN GOMEZ 3163, BALVANERA

## 95. Carmen Mabel Muñoz

Mabel was a social worker and law student. She assisted the families of those who had been detained and wrote claims of habeas corpus*. At the time of her kidnapping her daughter Clarisa managed to escape with the help of her grandmother Carla. José María Galán, Clarisa's father, was detained some time later and released in 1983. Since October 14, 1986, a paving stone has stood at the entrance to her house in her memory.

**LOCATION:** SAN LUIS 3162, BALVANERA

## 96. Federation of University Professors

Thirty-one years after the coup a remembrance plaque was installed to pay tribute to disappeared university professors. Participants included the Federation of University Professors (FEDUN, Federación de Docentes de las Universidades), the Faculty Association of the University of Buenos Aires, and representatives of government and human rights organizations. The ceremony included an exhibit of paintings drawn from the *Propaganda Negra* (Black propaganda) exhibit.

**LOCATION**: AV. CORDOBA 2429, BALVANERA

## 97. Eva Núñez

Eva studied law and worked in a toy factory. In April 1975 she gave birth to Pablo Oscar, the son of Pablo Videla, who was detained in Rawson prison at the time. She was kidnapped three months later. Pablo learned of Eva's disappearance and of his son's birth three years later, through his brother-in-law Angel, who was detained in another prison.

**LOCATION:** CORNER OF AV. CORRIENTES AND PASTEUR, BALVANERA

## 98. Julio César Fumarola

Julio César lived on 24 de Noviembre Street. A paving stone placed on the sidewalk of his former home pays tribute to him. His friend, poet Alfredo Carlino, now lives in the house. Fumarola's children, family members, and friends were present at the ceremony. Fumarola worked as an advertising photographer and was kidnapped on February 6, 1974. His body was discovered near the public swimming pools in Ezeiza (see p. 17) with more than sixty bullet wounds.

**LOCATION**: 24 DE NOVIEMBRE 163, BALVANERA

## 99. María del Carmen Serrano

María worked as a rural teacher. She graduated from the School of Social Work in Mar del Plata, where she worked at the National Institute of Epidemiology. In May 1977 she moved to the city of Buenos Aires, where she practiced at the No. 5 Health Center in Caseros. She was kidnapped one month after her arrival in the city. On November 13, 2007, a plaque was placed in her remembrance.

**LOCATION:** AV. RIVADAVIA 2970, BALVANERA

## 100. Mirta Barragán – Leonardo Sampallo – Ana Bonato – Eduardo Arzumendi

On December 28, 2007, a paving stone was dedicated in their memory. At the ceremony, speeches were given by the children of the four people being honored: María Eugenia, the daughter of Mirta and Leonardo (born in captivity and appropriated for twenty-four years); Gustavo, the son of Mirta; and Eugenia and Manuel, the children of Ana María and Emilio.

**LOCATION:** VIAMONTE 2565, BALVANERA

## 101. Gerardo Strejilevich

A plaque was installed on March 2, 2008, at the entrance to the house where Gerardo lived. At the time of his disappearance on July 15, 1977, he was studying physics and teaching at the National Technological University. He was about to defend his thesis, written in the National Atomic Energy Commission. He was kidnapped along with his girlfriend, Graciela Barroca, and a fellow student named Daniel Lázaro Rus.

**LOCATION:** AV. CORRIENTES 2583, BALVANERA

## 102. Café Los Angelitos

A paving stone was installed on April 26, 2008, as a tribute to Jorge "Nono" Lizazo, Oscar Lagrotta, Jorge Alberto Niemal, and María del Carmen "China" Núñez. Nono and China were shot as they entered the café on April 26, 1976. María del Carmen was killed in the same operation, and Jorge was injured and kidnapped, together with husband and wife Graciela de Lagrotta and Jorge Niemal. Graciela was later freed.

**LOCATION:** CORNER OF AV. RIVADAVIA AND RINCON, BALVANERA

## 103. Plaza de México y Saavedra

In 1975 a group of young people turned the vacant lot at the corner of México and Saavedra Streets into a small park. Eight of them (Marcelo Pardo, Diego Beigbeder, Nora Friszman, Isidoro Feldman, Jorge Fukman, Rodolfo Sarmiento, Daniel Echeverría, and Sergio Cetrángolo) were detained and disappeared. Plaques bearing their names and the dates of their kidnappings were installed in their honor on the park's bandstand.

**LOCATION:** CORNER OF MEXICO AND SAAVEDRA, BALVANERA

## 104. **Faculty of Psychology, UBA**

The Secretariat of Popular Solidarity and the grassroots organization H.I.J.O.S.* (Children for Identity and Justice Opposed to Forgetting and Silence) created a mural on the grounds of the Faculty of Psychology's building on Hipólito Yrigoyen Street as a tribute to disappeared students. The mural contains a list of the students' names and the dates of their kidnappings, along with the following inscription: "With our fellow students in our hearts, the struggle in our hands, and our hope in the People."

**LOCATION:** HIPOLITO YRIGOYEN 3238/46, BALVANERA

## 105. **Café Buenos Aires**

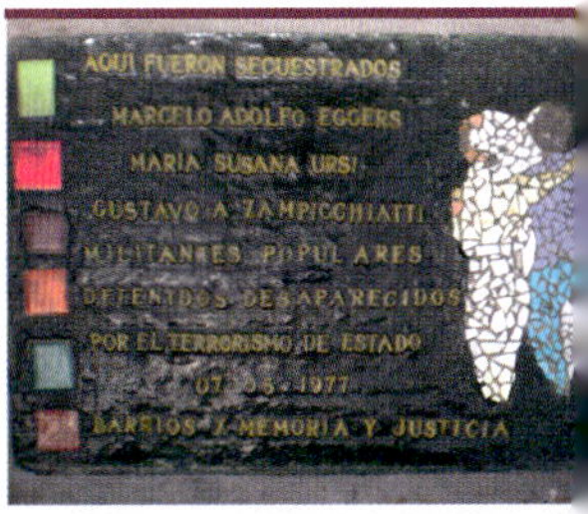


On May 7, 1977, psychology students Marcelo Eggers, María Susana Ursi, and Gustavo Alfredo Zampicchiatti were kidnapped in a coffee shop near the Faculty. Marcel was twenty-two years old. His wife Susana was twenty-six and Gustavo was twenty. A dedication ceremony unveiling a plaque in their honor took place on May 3, 2008, with family members and friends in attendance.

**LOCATION:** CORNER OF AV. INDEPENDENCIA AND URQUIZA, BALVANERA

## 106. **Domingo Faustino Sarmiento Advanced Normal School No. 9**

Paving stones were installed in the sidewalk in front of the school on July 15, 2008, to remember teachers Nélida Ardito, kidnapped on October 12, 1976, and Inés Cobos, kidnapped on September 1, 1976. A poster with their photos figured prominently in the ceremony, held in the school's foyer, where students were joined by Inés's mother, Carmen, and her sister, Noemí.

**LOCATION:** AV. CALLAO 450, BALVANERA

## 107. **Carlos "Turco" Abadi**

Carlos was a twenty-five-year-old psychology student when he was kidnapped on May 6, 1977, at the corner of Moreno and Alberti Streets. He was seen in the Clandestine Detention Center known as the Club Atlético (see p. 129). On May 18, 2008, a plaque was installed in his memory on the sidewalk in front of the building where he lived. His sister Reina and local residents of Almagro and Balvanera remembered him by sharing stories about his political activism.

**LOCATION:** AV. CORRIENTES 2370, BALVANERA

## 108. Tribute in the APSA

Thirty years after the coup, a plaque was unveiled in the head offices of the Association of Argentine Psychiatrists (APSA, Asociación de Psiquiatras Argentinos) as a tribute "to detained and disappeared mental health workers." A list with over one hundred names honors the psychologists and psychiatrists who were victims of state terrorism.

**LOCATION:** RINCON 355, BALVANERA

## 109. Aníbal Eduardo Gadea

"Anibal lived and was kidnapped here." A ceremony was held on September 30, 2007, to unveil a paving stone installed in tribute to Aníbal. Speeches were given by his friends, fellow students from the Calasanz School, and his brother Fernando Gadea. At the time of his disappearance, Aníbal was studying history at the Faculty of Philosophy and Letters and was a Catholic seminarian.

**LOCATION:** CASTRO 1408, BOEDO

## 110. Norberto Hugo Palermo

On October 14, 2007, a paving stone was installed in República de Entre Ríos School No. 23, where Norberto had been a student. His sister Silvia and teacher Daniel Ferro gave speeches during the ceremony. Other participants included Norberto's father, the educational community, and the Commission of Neighborhoods for Remembrance and Justice. Norberto disappeared while he was carrying out his compulsory military service in the Cavalry School of the Campo de Mayo* military base.

**LOCATION:** BOEDO 1935, BOEDO

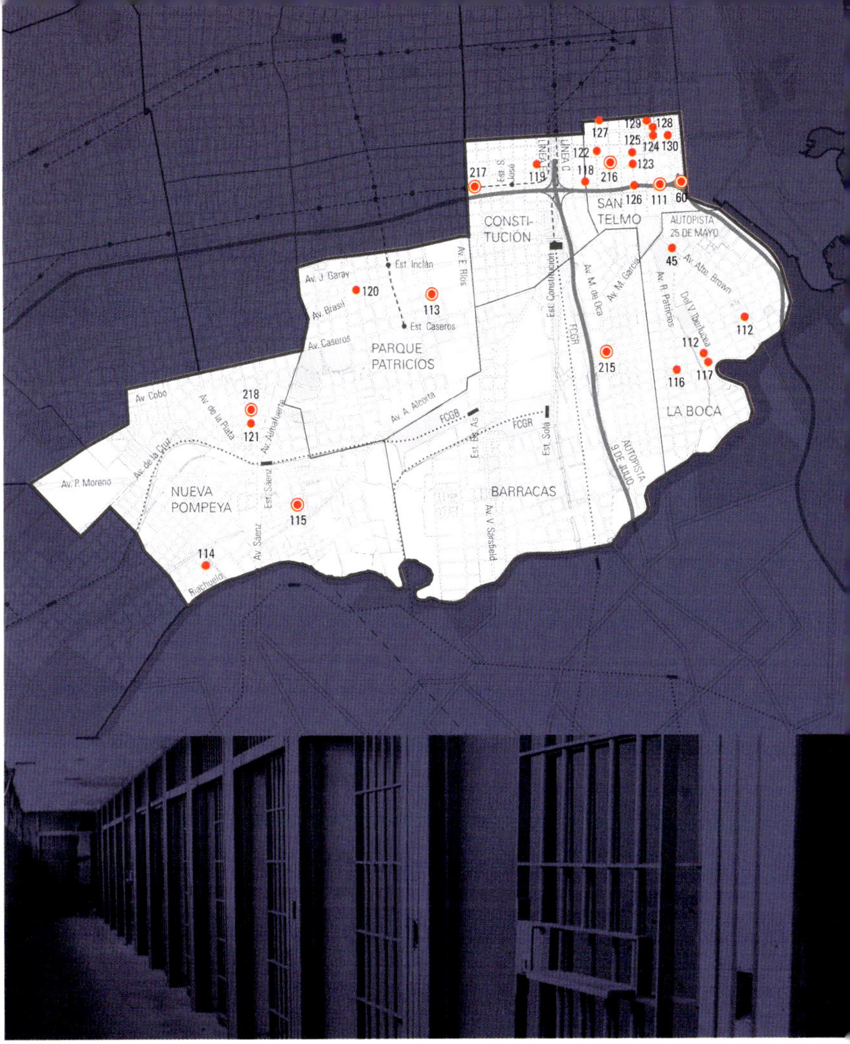

# SECTOR **4**

CONSTITUCIÓN, BARRACAS, LA BOCA, PARQUE PATRICIOS, NUEVA POMPEYA, AND SAN TELMO

## Introduction

The Clandestine Detention Center known as the Club Atlético operated between February and December 1977 in the specially prepared basement of a three-story building on Avenida Paseo Colón, between San Juan and Cochabamba Streets. The building was evacuated within a few months and demolished to make way for the 25 de Mayo Freeway, one of two highway projects built by the last dictatorship. Visitors can view an ongoing archaeological excavation at the site that has partially uncovered the clandestine center from beneath a mountain of earth and rubble.

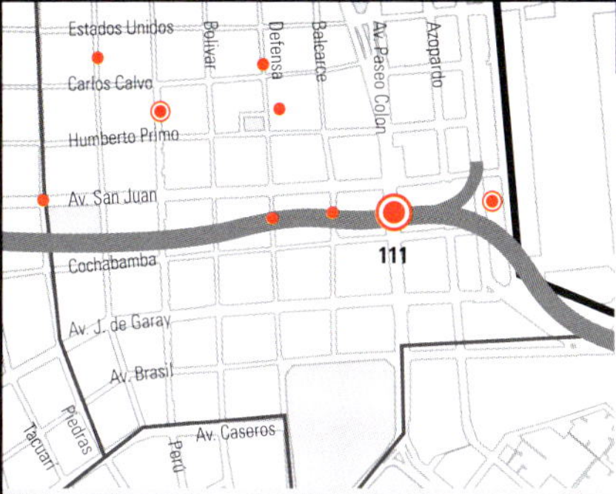


**LOCATION:** AV. PASEO COLÓN AND COCHABAMBA
**TRANSPORTATION:** BUSES: 4, 20, 33, 61, 62, 64, 74, 86, 93, 129, 130, 143, 152, 159.

## The clandestine center

"From now on, you have no names." Carmen Aguiar de Lapacó heard these words when she entered the Club Atlético with her daughter, her daughter's boyfriend, and her nephew. They had all been kidnapped from Carmen's house in the early hours of March 16, 1977, as they were chatting around the dinner table.

Their kidnappers blindfolded them and took them into the center, assigned them each a letter and number, and led them down some stairs to the basement. They then shackled their feet and gave them their padlock numbers to remember. Carmen and her nephew were released three days later; her daughter and daughter's boyfriend remain disappeared. "I've done everything possible first to find them alive, then to demand justice, and now to make sure they are remembered. This remembrance is essential," says Carmen, one of the founders of the Madres de Plaza de Mayo (Mothers of the Plaza de Mayo, see p. 3) and of the Center for Legal and Social Studies (CELS, Centro de Estudios Legales y Sociales) [AO0045].

THE FORMER CLANDESTINE DETENTION CENTER KNOWN AS THE CLUB ATLÉTICO.

New arrivals were nearly always taken directly to the "operating room" (*quirófano*) or torture room. Prisoners were punished for laughing, crying, expressing any feelings, or trying to uncover their eyes. "The torturers would play ping-pong between torture sessions," recalls journalist and survivor Marta Vassallo [AO.0270].

The basement had neither ventilation nor natural light; water trickled constantly down the walls and across the floor. "As soon as you entered, you thought you wouldn't be able to stand it," recalls Marta Vasallo. The Clandestine Detention Center had forty-one cells, three torture rooms, a guard's room, an infirmary, a kitchen, a laundry room, showers, and a place where the prisoners could be gathered together. It had room for two hundred people; more than fifteen hundred prisoners are estimated to have been held there over the years. An average of six or seven people were taken there every day, although at times the figure was as high as twenty.

Two cells were for solitary confinement. Adriana Friszman was held in one for a week: "When I arrived, I was shocked to see that it was underground," she recalls. She knows the place only through its sounds because of her isolation: "You could hear interrogations, typewriters, people screaming. It was a nightmare" [AO.0337].

Marta Vasallo, who was released on Christmas Eve, saw the Christmas tree set up by the torturers during the center's final month of operation. As they prepared to evacuate the Club Atlético to make way for the freeway construction, the military forces began to build another center, El Olimpo (see p. 215). All the furnishings, prisoners, and security forces were moved temporarily to the Clandestine Detention Center known as El Banco*, in the province of Buenos Aires. The rest of the building was used for the Supply Department and Distribution Division of the Federal Police. Police supplies, including bits of uniform, shoes, hats, and truncheons, have been found during the excavations.

**Anti-Semitism**

Jewish prisoners were treated with particular cruelty in this detention center. Sometimes the security forces asked prisoners for their family names and picked out only the Jews for torture. The methods used involved not only physical torture; Jewish prisoners were also objectified and treated as animals in a manner that recalled the language used by the Nazis.

Carmen Lapacó recalls that during one interrogation session she was asked why her house contained so many books by Jewish authors. She replied that she was more interested in authors' subject matter than in their religion. When they asked why she had so many Jewish names in her address book, she made a mistake that she says she will always regret. She replied that they must have been the names of her husband's relatives. "I didn't realize at the time that they were such Nazis, so anti-Semitic," she reflects. One of the torturers told her daughter Alejandra, "Oh, so you're Jewish? We're going to make soap out of you."

**Recovering the site**

Part of the 25 de Mayo Freeway was built on top of the part of the building containing the individual cells, or "tubes" (*tubos*), and the torture rooms. It is impossible to complete the excavations begun in 2002 because the remains of the Clandestine Detention Center were used in the freeway's foundations.

Survivors first presented a formal request to excavate the site in 1985 and by 2003, constant pressure from former prisoners, family members, activists, and

PILLAR WITH A MURAL BY THE TÓTEM GROUP ON THE SITE OF THE FORMER CLANDESTINE DETENTION CENTER.

SILHOUETTE REPRESENTING THE DISAPPEARED ON THE GROUNDS OF THE FORMER CLANDESTINE DETENTION CENTER.

local residents finally prompted Buenos Aires city government to lay the legal foundation for the site's recovery as a place of remembrance. The archaeological excavations had begun the year before. In 2005 Buenos Aires City Council declared the archeological remains a historic site and gave permission for further archeological work as well as the recovery of documents and testimonials.

Thousands of homes were expropriated and hundreds of families evicted to build fifteen kilometers of high-speed freeway lanes, as laid out in the "Urban Freeway Plan," which projected the dictatorship's repressive logic onto everyday life. This drastic urban renewal campaign, which included mass eradications of shantytowns, was led by Brigadier General Osvaldo Andrés Cacciatore, mayor of Buenos Aires for most of the dictatorship. Thousands of families were expelled from the precarious settlements where they lived, many of them simply dumped in vacant lots outside the limits of the capital (see "Plaza Houssay," p. 66).

The excavations uncovered the original building's structure, which made it possible to reconstruct half the partition wall that had bordered the solitary confinement cells and reveal many messages written there. This project marks the first use of archaeological methods in research on the history of the last military dictatorship.

An enormous silhouette representing the disappeared can currently be seen on the grounds beneath the freeway, near the archaeological dig. Local residents, survivors, and social activists gather at this site every year to light candles and pay tribute to the disappeared.

The Tótem group has painted a mural on one of the freeway's support columns near the remains of the Club Atlético's basement. It shows human figures with their arms raised in an attempt to escape confinement and isolation.

On November 3, 2007, a park named Space for Remembrance (Espacio por la Memoria) was inaugurated on the other side of the Paseo Colón, across from the former Clandestine Detention Center. It remained unfinished and closed to the public until 2010, when it was reopened with the name "30,000 compañeros."

# 112. **Murals in La Boca**

**LOCATION:** *MILITANTES POPULARES DETENIDOS-DESAPARECIDOS DE LA BOCA* (DISAPPEARED GRASSROOTS ACTIVISTS FROM LA BOCA) AT OLAVARRÍA AND GARIBALDI; *JUICIO Y CASTIGO* (JUDGMENT AND PUNISHMENT) AT SUÁREZ 300.
**TRANSPORTATION:** BUSES: 20, 29, 33, 46, 53, 64, 86, 152, 159.

In 2007 a mural titled *Juicio y Castigo* (Judgment and punishment) was unveiled at 300 Suárez Street to pay tribute to the thirty-year struggle of the Founding Line of the Madres de Plaza de Mayo (see "Plaza de Mayo," p. 3). The Germán Abdala Association of the Argentine Workers' Central (Central de Trabajadores Argentinos) initiated the work through the Trizkelión muralist group. The young artists who participated in the inauguration reclaimed mural painting as a form of popular expression and a tool for education, critique, and social transformation.

"We wanted to illustrate society's judgment," explains the muralist Pablo Murías. "That's why we showed the Madres on top of a platform with the scales of justice, the People's justice, and those responsible for the coup—military officers, priests, and businessmen—underneath. There is also a figure of a man with a shotgun being restrained by another man, which reflects hatred, but not vengeance. That is why the work is called *Juicio y Castigo*" (CTA Press Agency, October 11, 2007). This commentary points to a common feature of Argentina's human rights struggle: the victims of state terrorism have never taken justice into their own hands. On the contrary, they have always pressured the state to take responsibility for judging those accused of human rights violations.

The mural also depicts different figures representing political and social groups who were implicated in state terror: generals from the Armed Forces, businessmen (see "Mercedes Benz," p. 31), agents from the Special Task Groups*, and a representative of the Church.

*JUICIO Y CASTIGO* (JUDGMENT AND PUNISHMENT), MURAL ON THE CALLE SUÁREZ.

MURAL IN THE PLAZOLETA BOMBEROS VOLUNTARIOS, LA BOCA.

The work also includes part of the "Open Letter to the Military Junta," written by disappeared writer Rodolfo Walsh on the first anniversary of the coup (see "Corner of San Juan and Entre Rios," p. 96). In this excerpt Walsh asks the Commanders in Chief of the three branches of the Armed Forces to reflect upon "the abyss into which they are leading the country with their illusion of winning a war that would only begin again in a new form even if they managed to kill the last guerrilla fighter. Because the causes driving the resistance of the Argentine people for over twenty years would not disappear, but would be aggravated by the memory of their abuses and the revelation of the atrocities committed."

Another mural in the small square at Olavarría and Garibaldi Streets pays tribute to the neighborhood's disappeared. A group of residents and social organizations from La Boca organized a group of volunteers to spend a day restoring the mural, which has been painted over with other forms of urban expression on more than one occasion. This work evokes the name of the report by the National Commission on the Disappearance of Persons* (CONADEP, Comisión Nacional sobre la Desaparición de Personas; see "Nunca Más Square and Cultural Center, p. 186) and includes a list of nineteen neighborhood residents who had been identified as disappeared. One group participating in these activities is Memoria de la Boca, which is part of the coordinating committee of the Commission of Neighborhoods for Remembrance and Justice. This group has been working for years in La Boca, reconstructing the life histories of neighborhood activists detained and disappeared or murdered by agents of state terrorism. Its goal is to dedicate paving stones to each and every one of the disappeared, to leave traces of these people in the places where they lived, worked, and were politically active.

## 113. **Former Prison Unit 1 in Caseros**

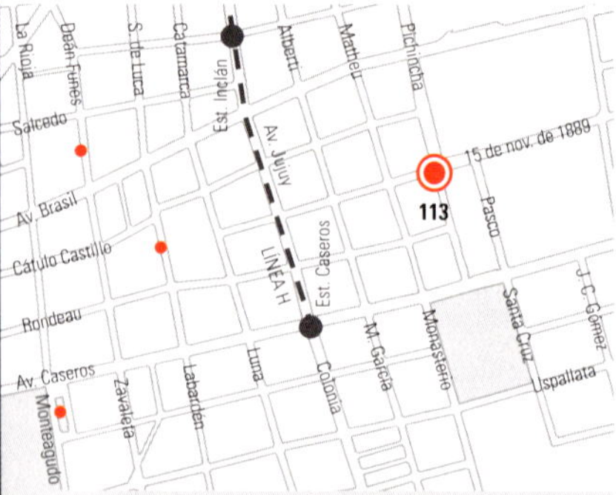


**LOCATION:** PICHINCHA AND 15 DE NOVIEMBRE
**TRANSPORTATION:** BUSES: 4, 6, 61, 95, 97, 118, 134, 143, 188. SUBWAY STATION: CASEROS (H LINE).

Dictator Jorge Rafael Videla inaugurated the Caseros Prison on April 23, 1979, in the neighborhood of Parque Patricios. Like many other prisons in the country, it housed large numbers of political prisoners during the last military dictatorship. With two twenty-two-story towers, two basements, and a total floor space measuring 85,000 square meters, it was the largest prison in South America at the time of its inauguration. It contained 2,096 individual cells, 14 elevators, 16 recreation yards, and 20 workshops. Criticized for its repressive design, it was closed in 2000, and two years later Buenos Aires city government ordered its demolition.

Prisons had been used to detain political prisoners long before the coup of 1976. During the previous military dictatorship of Rafael Onganía, which lasted from June 28, 1966, to May 25, 1973, prisons had held members of militant labor unions, guerrilla organizations, and a variety of political and student associations. President Héctor Cámpora issued an amnesty releasing the political prisoners during the restoration of democratic government in 1973. Yet in subsequent years prisons were again used to detain political prisoners. According to reports by Amnesty International, political prisoners numbered between five and six thousand by the end of 1976.

Victorio Paulón describes his transfer from Coronda Prison, in the province of Santa Fe, to Caseros Prison in April 1979: "Ours was the first transfer of political prisoners. That was when the Inter-American Commission on Human Rights visited, which prompted them to ease the prison system a bit and make a few concessions such as allowing us to receive letters. . . . Caseros was a really bad

CASEROS PRISON

ROW OF PRIVATE CELLS.

prison because it didn't let in any sun. I was completely white when I left there a year and nine months later. We started to receive much more accurate information about what was going on once the repression eased inside. By then the defeat [of the revolutionary goals espoused by left-wing organizations] was clear, and a wave of suicides hit several prisons. But at least in Caseros we had access to the prison yards for two hours every morning and afternoon. Things got done; there were study groups. They had mixed us together from several other prisons. We spent a year and nine months like that until they transferred us to La Plata in November 1980" (see "Plazoletas – Small Squares – 25 de Mayo Freeway," p. 99) [AO.0475].

In September 1979 the Inter-American Commission on Human Rights (IACHR) of the Organization of American States (OAS) arrived in Argentina to investigate human rights violations that had been denounced abroad. The military showed off Caseros as a "model" prison. Prisoners had been brought in from Coronda Prison in the province of Santa Fe, from Sierra Chica and La Plata in the province of Buenos Aires, from Prison Unit 7 in Chaco, and from Rawson Prison in the province of Chubut.

Ernesto Muro describes life in the prison and the visit of the IACHR: "The political prisoners adhered to codes that helped us survive. You could see the contrast with the regular prisoners. The common prisoner ages very quickly; he feels like he's alone against the world. It's different when there is an atmosphere of solidarity that connects people in spite of their differences. We were quite optimistic about the visit from the IACHR because it was our first exposure to the outside world, and we were going to have a chance to spread the word about our situation. So in Caseros we wrote reports about several other prisons, since we had all come from other places. . . . The guys [commission members] passed by the cells, and we handed our reports to them between the bars" [AO.0075].

Jorge Giles, who had been detained in Coronda Prison, described the acts of solidarity that took place: "We were transferred to Buenos Aires when they closed Coronda Prison on the first day of the national strike against the dictatorship [see "*Abrazo* (The Hug), Sculpture in the ATE," p. 109]. It was April 1979. . . . In Caseros a fellow inmate named Flavio was the first one allowed to shop at the prison canteen. We saw him arriving with a cart full of stuff and drop everything in his cell. Using Morse [code], he told me to stretch out my hand, and he gave me a cracker with some cheese. . . . I felt guilty because I thought he was favoring me over the other prisoners. . . . A while later Flavio called the guard and left his cell again with the cart, carrying sandwiches, cheese, and quince paste that he had prepared to share with all of us, cell by cell. He shared everything he had. . . . I got to be quite good friends with Flavio. . . . I never had any visitors in Caseros because they wouldn't let me" [AO.0206].

THE PRISONERS NEVER SAW THE SUN. ALL THE YARDS WERE INDOORS.

THE CASEROS PRISON'S TWO TOWERS.

Other detainees arrived in prison after passing through different Clandestine Detention Centers (CDCs). They were "legalized," meaning that their status as prisoners was publicly acknowledged, and they were placed under the authority of the National Executive Power*. This was the experience of Luis Salinas, who was first held in the Clandestine Detention Center that operated inside the Bureau of Federal Security (see p. 17), and later in Devoto Prison (see p. 199). He was then transferred to Unit 9 in La Plata and later to Caseros: "Trips to court offered a rare opportunity to make contact with people outside the prison and obtain information. Since we had a lot of visitors there, a kind of word-of-mouth news agency quickly developed. It was really efficient. . . . We knew a lot more about what was going on than people on the outside: what the political climate was like in Argentina, and what kind of resistance the military faced. We began to learn about the conflicts within the Church and about the internal divisions within the regime" [AO.0260].

## Experimental block

Many political activists were reunited inside Prison Unit 1 in Caseros after years of isolation. Hernán Invernizzi, who was detained in Magdalena Prison in the province of Buenos Aires until 1981, describes one of these moments, which came after six months of torture:

"Once we were in the cell, we looked out the little window and realized that we had all been placed in cells looking out over Parque Patricios. . . . But we couldn't make sense of where we were or what we were looking at because of the freeways [recently built by the dictatorship]. . . . At that time there were about twenty-two or twenty-three of us, and they took us to an empty prison block on the fourteenth or fifteenth floor. . . . That prison had been built following Foucault's panopticon plan, meaning that each prisoner was always under observation. You couldn't avoid being watched. The cells were laid out in a 'U' shape, all looking toward the outside of the 'U'; they had three walls, and the fourth was all bars. A corridor ran around the 'U' where the guards walked. What happened was that you could never tell where the guard was because you were inside the box, facing the corridor. Anything you did inside the cell you did in front of the guard. But you couldn't see any of the other prisoners, and talking was absolutely forbidden, so you were surrounded by people but unable to communicate with them. There was no sun or fresh air inside. After a few months we all turned a strange shade of greenish grey.

"They brought a select group of prisoners from other cellblocks together here; they had been in an area invisible to us because of the layout of the prison. They were all either very ill or considered security risks. . . . They crammed us all in together and organized an experimental prison block overseen by a specially chosen team of officers and prison guards who were supervised by an

ROOM WHERE PRISONERS RECEIVED VISITORS.

interdisciplinary team including an anthropologist, a social worker, psychologists, doctors, and lawyers. Everything there was different: separate food, a separate routine. The prison block was designed to be as destructive as possible. It lasted six months. Those six months were my worst prison experience, the worst period of my life. During that period a fellow inmate, 'Negrito' Toledo, committed suicide, and two others tried. Two inmates had heart attacks; one who was diabetic went into coma twice; the asthmatic prisoners had the worst asthma attacks I've ever seen; the psychiatric cases got worse, and two new cases appeared. All this took place over a period of six months in a prison block containing fifty people. It was terrible. What was going on in there was so serious that they stopped keeping political prisoners at Caseros after that year. That was when we got into direct contact with human rights organizations, and we circulated a couple of reports. The so-called suicide of 'Negrito' Toledo, a great guy from the Montoneros*, turned out to be the last straw. Officially it was a suicide but really it was murder. Here's what they did to him: they were giving him his proper medication regularly. But one day they started to change the time of day when they would administer it. The next day they would mix up his medications, and the day after that they wouldn't give him any at all. Then they would give it to him again, and then go two days without giving him any. Then they alternated the days. All of this was carefully supervised and recorded in a logbook that was later seized by a judge.

"After that the block was dismantled, and for the first time in my life I was taken to the cellblocks containing ordinary political prisoners. They took all 20 of us who had come from Magdalena and for the first time released us into a block holding 250 fellow political prisoners. We just couldn't stop hugging and kissing each another. We were reunited with people we may not have seen in eight, seven, or nine years, depending on the case. I met up with some old friends. Some of them, we didn't even know if they were alive, or if they'd been disappeared. That was also when we learned what had happened to the organization during our five years in isolation. From the time of the events at Monte Chingolo [December 23, 1975] until 1981 we had been cut off from everything. We were political virgins. That all lasted a month; after that they loaded us onto airplanes and took us to Rawson [Prison]" [AO.0412].

### Unfinished demolition

In late 2004 the planned demolition of the former Caseros Prison was halted. Local residents were concerned about the environmental impact that the building's implosion could have on the neighborhood of Parque Patricios and particularly on the Prof. Juan P. Garrahan Pediatric Hospital, located nearby. Today, the prison has been partially dismantled, and plans are under way to use the land for a new building to house the National Archives (Archivo General de la Nación).

## 114. **Plaza Obispo Enrique Angelelli**

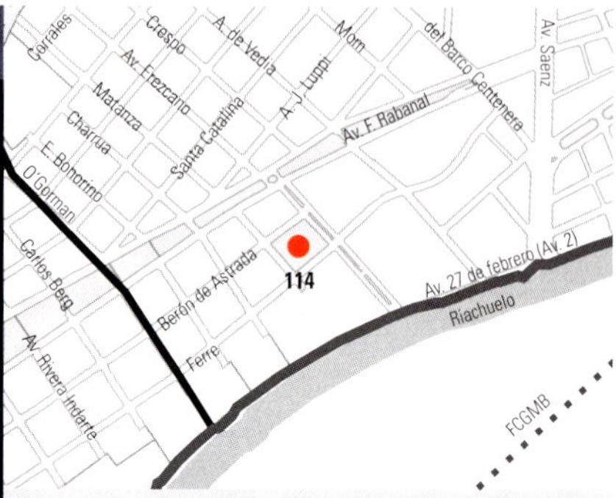


**LOCATION:** BETWEEN FERRÉ, BERÓN DE ESTRADA, AND MATANZA STREETS AND AV. EREZCANO
**TRANSPORTATION:** BUSES: 28, 76, 91, 115, 188.

"I come not to be served, but to serve. To serve everyone without distinction, regardless of social class, way of thinking, or beliefs; just like Jesus, I want to serve our brothers the poor." With these words Monsignor Enrique Angel Angelelli became Bishop of La Rioja in 1968. The bishop was murdered during the last military dictatorship on July 18, 1976. A public square was dedicated in his honor in the neighborhood of Nueva Pompeya on March 22, 2007. Government representatives, local residents, and some of Angelelli's friends took part in this tribute by dedicating a plaque in his memory.

### Bishop of La Rioja

Pope Paul VI appointed Angelelli Bishop of La Rioja on July 3, 1968. The first National Meeting of Priests for the Third World had taken place a few months earlier (see "Cristo Obrero Chapel. Father Carlos Mugica," p. 25), and although Monsignor Angelelli did not take part, he was among the bishops who most enthusiastically supported the movement. That support made him the target of more conservative elements within the Episcopal hierarchy.

Angelelli's friend, Italian priest Arturo Paoli, describes his arrival in La Rioja: "He often said that on that day he started his journey not as a tourist but as a bishop. He got out of the car at the place where the rich paved streets end and the poor mud paths begin. He kneeled and kissed that frontier. . . . I have often thought about Bishop Angelelli's kiss, like the kiss of Saint Francis on the face of the leper. . . . He told me that every fiber of his being cried out to him to turn back toward that rich road that led not only to casinos and comfortable villages but also to his friends, the workers in the neighborhoods of Córdoba.

"He was always visiting those communities on his motorbike, encouraging people to defend their right to work,

to a home, the right to life. Yet he felt that at the point where the paved streets end, there was a leper waiting for him who could not cross that frontier. And that kiss sealed a pact that he never broke in eight years. He began to embody a very unique way of being from La Rioja, not the haughty style of urban elites who refer to the city they administer as 'their city,' as though they're talking about a property they have inherited. He had an earthy temperament, absorbing everything through his pores. It helped him to quickly internalize this fascinating land, with its history and its long-suffering people, more than any other Argentine" (Rice and Torres, 2007).

**The murder**

On August 5, 1976, the daily newspaper *Clarín* published the following announcement: "Monsignor Angelelli has died in an accident. . . . Details of the tragic accident, which left another priest seriously injured, remain unknown. The deceased prelate, who had a powerful personality, belonged to the most progressive sectors within the Church and had been at the center of a great deal of controversy."

According to the morning paper, "The accident occurred when the left rear tire of the car in which he was traveling hit the curb and burst, causing the vehicle to overturn." Angelelli had been on his way back to the capital of La Rioja that day with Father Arturo Pinto. They were returning from the town of Chamical, where they had taken part in a ceremony to honor a pair of priests from the town who had been kidnapped and murdered. The bodies of parish priest Gabriel Longueville and Vicar Carlos de Dios Murias had been discovered in an open field, and the vicar's body had shown signs of torture. Angelelli was investigating the crime. Today these men are known as the Chamical Martyrs.

The *Clarín* article went on: "Monsignor Angelelli's energetic personality had often led to conflicts with provincial and federal authorities. As a direct result of his progressive ideas, Monsignor Angelelli had been locked in a dispute with a group of parishioners from the town of Anillaco in 1973. They rejected the bishop's pastoral line and attacked him severely. Angelelli excommunicated thirteen people, provoking an extremely tense situation in the diocese. Yet Pope Paul XI quickly offered his support to the bishop by sending Vicente Zaspe with the following message: 'I have been sent by Paul VI to inform you that the Holy Father, aware of what has occurred in this diocese, expresses his confidence and compassion toward the bishop. This also signifies that Angelelli is neither a Communist nor a Marxist, but rather a Catholic bishop in absolute communion with the Pope.' The incidents in Anillaco became so violent that the police had to go to great lengths to protect the bishop's personal safety. Angelelli and the priests and nuns who accompanied him were attacked with stones and other objects. A large group of parishioners expelled Angelelli from the parish church because they rejected what they considered to be the bishop's left-wing pastoral line" (*Clarín,* August 5, 1976).

This description of the bishop highlighted suspicions surrounding his death. Fray Antonio Puigjané, a Franciscan priest and a member of the Association of Argentine Missions, described the situation and Angelelli's role differently: "There was already a lot of persecution within the Church in La Rioja even before the coup. . . . Bishop Angelelli asked me to be the parish priest in Anillaco. . . . They received us very well even though we were completely different from the priests who had been there before us. They had never spoken to anyone; they'd just shut themselves away and celebrated Mass in Latin with their backs turned. We showed up there looking really scruffy, wearing jeans and sandals made out of car tires. I visited every house on my first day, and people received me very warmly. . . . It was like that until June 13, 1973, when Menem [Amado, the brother of future president Carlos Saúl Menem] organized a revolt to throw us out. They targeted us and the bishop [Angelelli], who had come to stay in the village for a few days (he was always visiting different villages). I had bumped into Amado Menem a few days earlier, and he had said to me, 'I was wrong about you. You have a different religion. There isn't room here for both of us: it's you or me.' And obviously, he was the one with all the power who was going to stay. . . . On the thirteenth, this man brought in truckloads of drunken men to drive us out. He set up military marches through the town. . . . The bishop had managed to transform the members of the Church into a big family, a great diocese, a great brotherhood, and we had a supportive relationship with the priests in nearby villages. . . . That day they didn't let us hold Mass or the procession, nothing at all. The police were there. They said it was to protect us, but really it was to make sure we didn't do anything. . . . We were never able to set foot in Anillaco again. . . . The town Church was very traditional, very conservative, and they resented Angelelli's arrival. Because from the moment he arrived he sat down to drink *mate* with the poor; he celebrated Christmas under a carob tree instead of inside the Cathedral. They considered this a sin. The bishop was trying to open up a new path for the Church, closer to the Gospel" [AO.0331].

Evidence and suspicions surfaced immediately that Angelelli's death had been a murder. The report by the National Commission on the Disappearance of Persons* (CONADEP, Comisión Nacional sobre la Desaparición de Personas; see "*Nunca Más* Square and Cultural Center," p. 186) read as follows:

"The Bishop was driving a pickup truck, and Father Arturo Pinto, who was accompanying him, recalls that shortly after leaving Chamical they noticed a car following them. The Bishop accelerated, but then another car appeared, and when they reached Punta de los Llanos, both cars closed in on them until they made the truck overturn.

"The pickup truck disappeared and the Bishop's body was left out in the open for six hours. The only injury on his body was at the nape of the neck, which looked like it had been shattered by repeated blows. The folder the Bishop had been carrying was never discovered" (CONADEP, 1984).

In March 1983, a few months before the military gave up power, former Federal Police inspector Rodolfo Peregrino Fernández presented himself to the Argentine Human Rights Commission in Madrid and provided information about the structure of the illegal repression (see "Coordinación Federal," p. 17). The inspector had been an assistant to the Minister of Interior, General Albano Eduardo Hargindeguy.

Peregrino Fernández offered important information about the case of Bishop Angelelli: "A day or two after the incident, the personal papers Bishop Angelelli had been carrying at the time of his death turned up at Government House in a folder sent from the Salta Military Garrison that was addressed to Minister Harguindeguy. The documents were clearly marked 'confidential.' This fact really got the declarant's attention, given that the papers were neither included in the case nor handed over to those close to Monsignor Angelelli; they were instead brought directly to Captain Vaca, who worked at the Ministry of Interior" (Peregrino Fernández, 1983).

**The role of the judiciary**

In 2008 Air Force officers Luis Fernando Estrella, second in command of the Chamical Air Force Base, and Miguel Ricardo Pessetta, a former second lieutenant, were arrested for their role in the kidnappings of the Chamical Martyrs. The prosecutors in charge of the investigation determined that Pessetta had collaborated with Captain Miguel Angel and police officer Juan Carlos Romero in the kidnapping of Fathers Gabriel Longueville and Carlos de Dios Murias. The kidnappers had acted on orders delivered by Vice Commodores Lázaro Aguirre and Luis Estrella and Colonel Osvaldo Pérez Battaglia, who were, in turn, under the authority of Third Army Corps commander General Luciano Benjamín Menéndez. In March 2009 Courtroom B of the Federal Court of Córdoba confirmed that it would prosecute Estrella and retired local police commissioner Domingo Vera for the crimes of unlawful deprivation of liberty, torture, and aggravated homicide. The public trial began in La Rioja in August of 2012.

On April 22, 2009, federal judge Daniel Herrera Piedrabuena of La Rioja ordered an exhumation and autopsy to determine the exact cause of Angelelli's death. He found that Angelelli had been killed in an intentional car collision in retribution for his denunciations of the Chamical murders. The Catholic Church is also pursuing its own investigation after three decades of silence on the issue. Monsignor Carmelo Giaquinta began work on the case two years ago, following a decision by Cardinal Jorge Bergoglio.

Four pivotal trials are currently under way in La Rioja. One is an investigation into the murder of conscript Roberto Villafañe (which brought the 2010 conviction of former sergeant José Rodríguez), and another into the killing of the Chamical Martyrs. Slow progress is being made in the investigations of crimes committed against Bishop Enrique Angelelli and rural leader Wenceslao Pedernera, who was murdered in front of his family on July 25, 1976, by a group of hooded men.

# 115. **Central Aeronautical Hospital**

**LOCATION:** VENTURA DE LA VEGA 3693
**TRANSPORTATION:** BUSES: 42, 46, 76, 150, 188. TRAIN STATION: SÁENZ (BELGRANO LINE).

The terrorist state's repression operated mainly through the practices of forced disappearance and the theft of babies. It depended on coordination between different jurisdictions and institutions, each fulfilling a specific function. In Buenos Aires, as in the rest of the country, a unified repressive apparatus connected the different Clandestine Detention Centers (CDCs), prison units, police stations, security facilities, hospitals, and even the homes of kidnapping victims that were converted into bases of operations. Military repression interconnected with other jurisdictions and activities through this coordination, and illegal activities went on in many places alongside public and legal operations. Normal functions continued while these institutions were being used to hold victims of detention and disappearance.

Prisoners were regularly transferred between these locations and made fleeting appearances in public spaces. The concentration-camp experiences of the Clandestine Detention Centers thus spread into the broader society and the terror embodied in these centers circulated both symbolically and physically through the streets. This "decentralization" of the concentration camps was not accidental. Rather, the dissemination of terror was effective when it was at least partially visible, because repressive practices were aimed not only at the immediate victims but also at the broader society. As Pilar Calveiro explains, "The concentration camp, by its very proximity, its location 'on the other side of the wall,' can exist only within a society that chooses not to see . . . , a society that has disappeared" (Calveiro, 1998).

### The hospital

Located in the neighborhood of Pompeya, the Central Aeronautical

Hospital was one of several hospitals and public institutions that housed the disappeared. The Air Force took prisoners to the hospital who were pregnant or in need of medical attention. In 1977 doctors and nurses at the Aeronautical Hospital treated women who were blindfolded and showed signs of torture; they had been transferred from the Seré Mansion*, a Clandestine Detention Center in the province of Buenos Aires.

Survivor Pilar Calveiro was kidnapped near her home in San Antonio de Padua on May 7, 1977. Three armed men forced her into a Ford Falcon. After a failed escape attempt, she was taken to a house that she later identified as the Seré Mansion. After being interrogated, beaten, and tortured, she was handcuffed and blindfolded and taken to a room on the second floor. She then asked to go to the bathroom and tried to escape through an open window.

"When I fell, I broke my left arm, a bone in my left heel, two or three vertebrae, and some ribs. . . . I received no medical attention from the time I fell and fractured these bones until the end of May. I was left to lie in a corner of the room, later on a mattress, and eventually on my daugher's bed, which they stole from my house. . . . Around May 28th they took me out one night in a car and brought me to a hospital. I was blindfolded, dirty, and battered. There they put a cast on my left arm and leg and on my thorax. I later discovered it was the Central Aeronautical Hospital because they took me to the same place to remove my casts, and *on this one occasion* [she stressed] they left my eyes uncovered" (Urso, 2002).

In another case a former Air Force captain testified to the National Commission on the Disappearance of Persons* (CONADEP, Comisión Nacional sobre la Desaparición de Personas) that he had been illegally arrested at the Aeroparque airport in January 1977 as he arrived from a trip. He was then transferred to the Professional Flight Training Center (CIPRA, Centro de Instrucción Profesional de Aeronáutica), and later moved to the Aeronautical Hospital because of health problems. He was detained there for roughly ten days without his family knowing anything of his whereabouts.

**Decentralizing terror**

Survivors of the Aeronautical Hospital remember the interactions between hospital staff and members of the Armed Forces. Pilar Calveiro recalls that "on the night they put my casts on, they took several X-rays on a table designed for that purpose. . . . The physician operating the machine chatted with the gang [*patota**] completely naturally, obviously aware of what was going on. And the kidnappers were bragging to him about how well they treated us. I was blindfolded the entire time, and the male nurses who were putting on the casts could see this; they could see what horrible shape I was in. I was all battered, covered in sores from the cattle prod [*picana**], and filthy because I'd gone about three weeks without a bath. I was still wearing the clothes I had on when they kidnapped me, and I was blindfolded and guarded by a group of men" (Urso, 2002).

In her account Calveiro explains that she was taken to the hospital one more time from the Navy School of Mechanics (ESMA, Escuela Superior de Mecánica de la Armada; see p. 153), where she was "on loan" (an expression that conveys how the different branches of the security forces would take possession of their detainees). That time she was with Graciela Tauro, who was pregnant and later gave birth in the ESMA (see "Central Military Hospital," p. 77) and who remains disappeared. The doctor removed Pilar's cast and listened to Graciela's chest with a stethoscope. Calveiro recalls that at that moment "he said, 'I'm going to give you a snack so that you leave here with good memories.' And he gave us cookies and milk, which I hadn't tasted since my kidnapping."

THE MAIN ENTRANCE OF THE HOSPITAL.

A SIGN ON THE HOSPITAL GROUNDS READING "ARGENTINE AIR FORCE, MILITARY ZONE."

The doctors and hospital staff worked with these "patients" who were under armed guard and showed signs of torture. They worked with people who had been kidnapped and who described entering the hospital through back doors, who were treated without having to wait or complete any forms. They moved them around the hospital in wheelchairs after clearing the hallways.

This coexistence prevailed in all kinds of social situations, and prisoners were often displayed to the outside world. They were allowed to make phone calls to their families; their captors arranged for them to meet with their young children; they had family visits. All of these activities served to "take the terror out into the streets." The power of the concentration camp thus exposed itself in order to fulfill its fundamental purpose: to spread its terror outward. Society became the "main prisoner" by virtue of what it could see, feel, and sense. Kidnapping operations that took place in the street in broad daylight, torture sessions that were barely muffled with the sounds of the radio, "strange movements": all of these experiences slowly seeped into everyday life until terror embedded itself in the fabric of society.

The terror victimized society as it spread in this way, yet it also secured society's consent to the horror that was taking place: "Society is aware because it is part of the same fabric. Military power uses this social knowledge in order to implicate everyone" (Calveiro, 1998).

## 116. Beatriz Perosio Health Center No. 9

On October 13, 2005, the Human Rights Department of the internal committee of the Association of State Employees (ATE) and the municipal Health Secretariat and Under-secretariat of Human Rights, succeeded in having Health Center No. 9, under the direction of the Argerich Hospital, named for Beatriz Perosio, who was kidnapped on August 8, 1978, and held captive in El Vesubio* Clandestine Detention Center. , representing public employees of the Buenos Aires municipal government,

**LOCATION:** IRALA 1254, LA BOCA

## 117. Plaque in Caminito

A plaque located in Matilde Vara de Anguita Park pays tribute to disappeared political activists from the neighborhood. The plaque was dedicated on the thirtieth anniversary of the last military coup. It reads as follows: "There is too much pain in this world. Though my life may be no more than a grain of sand, I will devote myself to fighting this pain."

**LOCATION:** CORNER OF CAMINITO AND MAGALLANES, LA BOCA

## 118. Olga Agüero – Hugo Raúl Decurger

Olga and Hugo were kidnapped together from their home on April 29, 1977. Olga was twenty-five years old, and Hugo worked for the General Belgrano Railway. Family members, friends, and the Commission of Neighborhoods for Remembrance and Justice placed paving stones in their memory and held a ceremony to pay tribute to them.

**LOCATION:** CORNER OF AV. SAN JUAN AND PIEDRAS, CONSTITUCION

## 119. Faculty of Social Sciences, UBA

Father Carlos Mugica was honored in 2007, thirty-four years after his murder, by the Board of Governors of the Faculty of Social Sciences of the University of Buenos Aires. The board chose to dedicate lecture hall no. 107 in the Constitución campus building in his name and to place a plaque there in his memory. It recognized Father Mugica's organizing work in the city's shantytowns as a sign of his commitment to social justice.

**LOCATION:** SANTIAGO DEL ESTERO 1029, CONSTITUCION

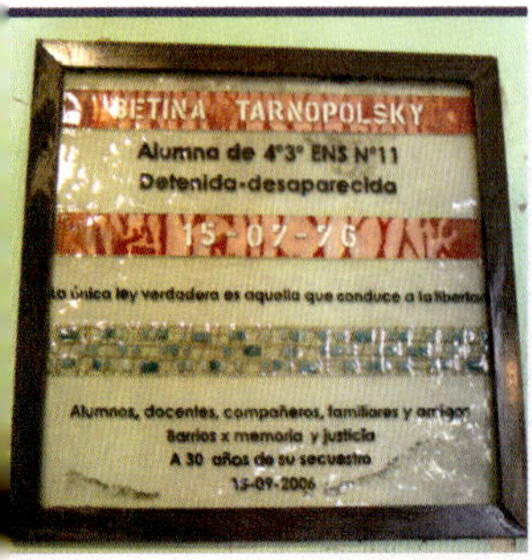


## 120. **Betina Tarnopolsky**

Betina was sixteen years old when she was kidnapped along with her parents, one of her brothers, and her sister-in-law. On September 15, 2006, Dr. Ricardo Levene School No. 11 held a tribute ceremony in her honor involving teachers, students, former schoolmates, family members, friends, and the Commission of Neighborhoods for Remembrance and Justice. The students participated in workshops on state terrorism and listened to talks by Betina's friends and family members.

**LOCATION:** DEAN FUNES 1821, PARQUE PATRICIOS

## 121. **Edith Vilma de León**

Two plaques were unveiled at Argentine Aeronautical School No. 7 on October 9, 2007, to honor former teacher Edith Vilma de León. Former students, family members, and schoolmates dedicated one. The other was put up by unions of education workers (UTE and CTERA) and the Buenos Aires office of Argentine Workers' Central (CTA). The ceremony took place after a series of classroom debates culminating in a musical tribute to the former teacher performed by the school choir.

**LOCATION:** QUILMES 473/79, NUEVA POMPEYA

## 122. **Tribute to Disappeared Galicians**

On October 5, 2007, the Federation of Galician Associations of the Argentine Republic commemorated the disappeared Galicians who fell victim to state terrorism. Events included the inauguration of an exhibit paying tribute to the twenty-one disappeared Galicians and the unveiling of a piece of ceramic art at the entrance to the federation's headquarters. Family members, friends, and human rights organizations participated in the ceremony.

**LOCATION:** CHACABUCO 955, SAN TELMO

## 123. **Adelina Noemí Gargiulo**

A group of Adelina's friends petitioned the Buenos Aires city government for permission to hold a ceremony honoring Adelina in Plaza Dorrego, where she used to have a craft stall. Their request was granted on December 10, 2003, and the tribute ceremony took place on July 7, 2007, thirty-one years after she disappeared. Participants included the Association of Artisans, Craftworkers, and Artists of Plaza Dorrego, Adelina's daughter Camila, and other family members.

**LOCATION:** CORNER OF HUMBERTO I AND DEFENSA, SAN TELMO

## 124. **Faculty of Engineering, UBA**

In September 1984 the Faculty of Engineering's Student Union paid tribute to detained and disappeared students with a bronze plaque. It bears the following inscription: ". . . so that human rights may never again be violated in our country, so that we never forget. The guilty must be punished for the repression unleashed within this institution of learning and for our fellow students who were murdered, detained, disappeared, and tortured."

On November 27, 1996, the Faculty's Permanent Commission for the Reconstruction of Memory hung an acrylic plaque bearing the following inscription: "For our fellow students who were murdered or disappeared: you will always be with us!" A Day of Remembrance was established on November 26, 2000, and another plaque was dedicated with the inscription, "The justice system remains indebted to the people."

The victims were also remembered in fourteen works of art. A Remington typewriter was placed at the site as a symbol of the struggle against arms sales: ". . . why should we remain quiet, when you continue to rise up and rule? Why, when the famous Remington Company continues to supply you and your people with rifles to shoot, while it supplies people like us with nothing but typewriters? This Remington will not be silent as long as you somehow manage to hold onto your power."

**LOCATION:** AV. PASEO COLON 850, SAN TELMO

## 125. **Paloma Alonso – Pablo Faimberg – Mario Clar – Sergio Clar**

Paving stones dedicated to the memories of Paloma, Pablo, Mario, and Sergio were laid by neighbors, family members, residents of San Telmo, and the Commission of Neighborhoods for Remembrance and Justice.

**LOCATION:** CORNER OF DEFENSA AND CARLOS CALVO, SAN TELMO

## 126. **Mural at Av. San Juan and Defensa**

On March 23, 2002, a group of visual artists painted a mural on the side of the Pablo C. Ducrós Hicken Film Museum, an initiative of the Plaza Dorrego Community Assembly. With materials supplied by neighborhood residents and shopkeepers, they expressed the assembly's ideas and opinions. The building was demolished when the museum moved in late 2009. By court order the mural was reproduced in the new Buenos Aires Museum of Modern Art, inaugurated in 2010 on the same block.

**LOCATION:** CORNER OF AV. SAN JUAN AND DEFENSA, SAN TELMO

## 127. **Plazoleta Rodolfo Walsh**

This small square was created in 1990 and remodeled in 2005 as part of a program organized by the Culture Secretariat of the City of Buenos Aires. The work involved restoring the mural and sculpture representing Walsh. These had been created in 1997, twenty-five years after the Trelew Massacre*, by the organization known as H.I.J.O.S.* (Children for Identity and Justice Opposed to Forgetting and Silence). The square also contains extracts from Walsh's "Open Letter to the Military Junta," written on March 24, 1977 (see p. 96).

**LOCATION:** CORNER OF PERU AND CHILE, SAN TELMO

## 128. **Disappeared Workers**

On March 23, 2005, leaders of the CGT (General Confederation of Labor) and government representatives (Carlos Kunkel, General Undersecretary to the President, and Eduardo Luis Duhalde, Human Rights Secretary) placed a floral offering and unveiled a commemorative plaque on the Monument of Labor to pay tribute to detained and disappeared workers.

**LOCATION:** AV. PASEO COLON 1250, SAN TELMO

## 129. **Buenos Aires Federation of Graphic Workers**

A plaque was dedicated at the entrance to the federation headquarters, next to a list of names and dates of disappearance. It bears an inscription honoring disappeared graphic workers: ". . . We reiterate our demand: justice and life imprisonment for those who are guilty. . . ." The ceremony took place on November 13, 1986.

**LOCATION:** AV. PASEO COLON 731, SAN TELMO

## 130. **CGT – Azopardo**

A plaque in the headquarters of the General Confederation of Labor recalls the first strike to take place under the dictatorship, in 1979 (see p. 109). The plaque reads as follows: "Today, just like yesterday, we hold the same unswerving commitment to defend freedom and democracy through social justice. Argentine Labor Movement."

**LOCATION:** AZOPARDO 802, SAN TELMO

# SECTOR 5

BELGRANO, COGHLAN, COLEGIALES, NÚÑEZ, AND SAAVEDRA

# 131. **Navy School of Mechanics (ESMA)**

### Location

The ESMA (Argentine Navy School of Mechanics), one of Argentina's largest Clandestine Detention Centers (CDCs), is located on Avenida del Libertador near the riverfront on the north side of Buenos Aires,. Originally designed for the technical training and accommodation of naval petty officers, it maintained its normal operations during the dictatorship alongside its function as a Clandestine Detention Center. It is estimated that some five thousand people were detained here; most remain disappeared to this day.

Several features combined to make the ESMA a symbol of illegal repression and state terrorism. It was one of the first Clandestine Detention Centers to be identified; Rodolfo Walsh mentioned it in his "Open Letter to the Military Junta" (Carta abierta a la Junta Militar) in March 1977 (see "Corner of San Juan and Entre Ríos," p. 96). The large numbers of prisoners and the widespread circulation of survivors' testimonies reinforced the site's symbolic power. Finally, the ESMA's monumental size and architectural design, as well as its location on one of the city's main avenues, accentuated the contrast between its original educational mission and its function as a facility dedicated to systematic torture and extermination.

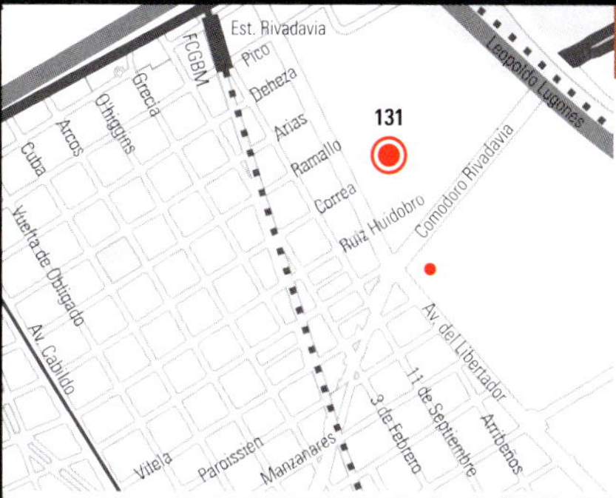


**LOCATION:** AV. DEL LIBERTADOR 8151
**TRANSPORTATION:** BUSES: 15, 28, 29, 117, 130. TRAIN STATION: RIVADAVIA (MITRE LINE).

Buenos Aires City Council transferred this seventeen-hectare property to the Naval Ministry in 1924 for the establishment of a military training center. Its boundaries are marked by Avenida Libertador, Avenida

OFFICERS' CLUB.

Comodoro Martín Rivadavia, and Avenida Leopoldo Lugones and by the grounds of the Raggio Technical Schools. The ESMA is located just a few blocks away from one of the city's largest soccer stadiums, the Club Atlético River Plate.

The ESMA's operations have been reconstructed with the help of survivors' testimonies, particularly those obtained through the National Commission on the Disappearance of Persons* (CONADEP, Comisión Nacional sobre la Desaparición de Personas) and the Trial of the Military Juntas* in 1985. The facilities were used mainly by Special Task Group* 3.3.2, by aeronautical commandos, by the Argentine Coast Guard (Prefectura Naval Argentina), and by other police and military groups who took prisoners there after they were detained and disappeared.

The entire ESMA premises were used for repressive, illegal, and clandestine activities, though most prisoners were held and tortured in the Officers' Club; hooded prisoners were often moved between the club and other areas on the property. Some were forced to work in the print shop or other workshops; others were moved to the medical treatment area run by ESMA personnel. Jorge Torres, who began his studies in the School of Mechanics in 1974, testified at the Trial of the Military Juntas that "everybody could see" the Special Task Groups' movements within the ESMA, including officers, petty officers, and students.

**Operations**

The Special Task Groups (Grupos de Tareas) were responsible for illegal kidnappings. One group, the *patota** ("gang"), performed the kidnappings; they dressed in civilian clothes and carried false identification. Another group was charged with obtaining information through torture. The Special Task Group based at the ESMA conducted operations throughout the city, in the province of Buenos Aires, in other provinces, and even abroad. As Pilar Calveiro (1998) has explained, the Clandestine Detention Centers were designed to erase the prisoners' humanity. They functioned within a repressive structure organized as a "machine to torture, extract information, terrorize, and kill." This structure sought to exterminate not only revolutionary movements and guerrilla organizations, but also their individual members and sympathizers. Kidnapping and interrogation under torture were fundamental to this plan.

**Captivity**

The Clandestine Detention Center operated mainly in the Officers' Club, where kidnapping victims were detained and tortured in specially prepared rooms. Some members of the Special Task Group actually lived and planned their operations in the same building. Such was the case of Captain Rubén Jacinto Chamorro, who lived with his family on the building's ground floor when he was Director of the ESMA.

During the ESMA's eight years of operation as a Clandestine Detention Center, the Special Task Groups entered and exited the premises through different access points. Cars entered and approached the Officers' Club, where handcuffed and hooded prisoners were moved to the basement located under the building's central wing. Once inside, they suffered repeated torture sessions at the hands of ESMA personnel who sought information to be used to plan further kidnappings. Prisoners were then taken to *capucha* ("hood"), an L-shaped room located in the fourth-floor attic that stretched across one entire wing of the building and half of its central section. They were kept handcuffed and shackled on mattresses, with black masks (known in the concentration camp as *tabiques*, or "walls") covering their eyes and hoods over their heads that were tied at the

CENTRAL SECTION OR BUILDING WITH FOUR COLUMNS.

GUIDED TOUR FOR SECONDARY STUDENTS IN *CAPUCHA*.

neck. They were forced to lie down and remain silent. Many of the prisoners spent long periods of time like this, not all of them even aware they were at the ESMA.

When *capucha* was filled to capacity, some prisoners were kept in a third-floor room called *capuchita* ("little hood").

**Torture**

Most prisoners inside the Officers' Club moved between *capucha* or *capuchita* and the basement located under El Dorado, where the Special Task Group planned its operations. At different moments, the basement served as darkroom, infirmary, drafting room, canteen, and as a workshop where documents were forged. Yet the area dedicated to torture remained the same: between three and five rooms were specially equipped for the extraction of information under torture.

"Torture is a unique experience," explains Cristina Aldini, an ESMA survivor. "It cannot be compared to any other life experience. I carry the memory of torture inscribed in all of my senses. I say this because other people's experience is different. Some remember it as if they had watched from a distance as it happened to someone else. I remember it both these ways, and I've even dreamt about it. For me, the terrible thing about torture is that a supposed human being is standing in front of you, inflicting the worst possible suffering on another person in order to take away what is most precious to him or her. For me this extreme, primal experience is the essence of torture." Aldini contrasts this dehumanizing practice with the personally enriching experience of political activism; while she remembers her activism as "infinitely" rewarding, "torture is the exact opposite. It is like being thrown into the void, a space of nothingness where one human being is committing the worst possible acts against another" [AO.0072].

As Pilar Calveiro has observed (1998), torture served two purposes. First, it was used to obtain information from kidnapping victims in order to speed up the illegal detentions and multiply the disappearances. Second, it served to "break" the prisoners, to "destroy" their identities and make them vulnerable to the Clandestine Detention Center's conditions of absolute submission. The terror apparatus used relentless torture to create subjects who were fearful, distrustful, broken, submissive, and authoritarian. This process of de-subjectification forced prisoners to relinquish information to the repressive apparatus and then left them dehumanized, blinded, and immobilized, to await their extermination. The routinized and bureaucratic nature of these tasks reinforced the prisoners' objectification, while the hoods used to cover their faces dehumanized them in the eyes of their torturers.

## "Transfers"

So-called death flights*, in which kidnapping victims were sedated and dropped alive from military aircraft into the Río de la Plata, became one of the ESMA's most emblematic practices.

These flights were fundamental to the crime of "disappearance" because they denied victims a grave to signal their absence. In Western traditions, burial—whether real or symbolic—is crucial to the mourning process; it represents an unmistakable sign that the person once formed part of the human community.

The river returned the bodies of a handful of victims, like those kidnapped from the Santa Cruz Church (see "Santa Cruz Church," p. 89), who were identified many years later by the Argentine Forensic Anthropology Team* (EEAF, Equipo Argentino de Antropología Forense). Yet the vast majority of the bodies sank into the riverbed's boggy soil. This is why certain points along the riverbank, such as the current Park of Memory (Parque de la Memoria, p. 162,) have become memorial sites for many of the victims' families.

## Survivors

It remains unclear why a small number of people were left alive out of the thousands of disappeared. The military's arbitrary power limited victims' resistance strategies while reinforcing the torturers' sense of themselves as gods, lords, and masters over life and death. That power offered no "reasoning" behind its choice of survivors, leaving victims with the guilt of not knowing by what criteria some were disappeared while others were left—at least temporarily—in that limbo between life and death.

Some prisoners were kept alive to work for the repressive apparatus or to serve as "bait" to draw out other activists the special task forces wanted to kidnap (*chupar*, or "suck," according to the military's slang).

Alfredo "Mantecol" Ayala describes what daily life was like: "The first few months I spent in the ESMA were really difficult: the first torture sessions, the first times they took me out. I was hardly ever at the ESMA at first because they took me out every day on 'outings' or to meetings they'd set up to 'suck'

BASEMENT STAIRWAY.

THE BASEMENT.

(kidnap) fellow activists. Once I spent the whole night riding the number 60 bus between Constitución and Tigre; other times I spent the whole day with them in the train station in José León Suárez. They took me around San Isidro, to the theater, all over the place. I don't think they expected me to sing [*cantar*, or "snitch"], but they wanted to see who would approach me. Then they'd take me back to the ESMA, and I'd have to stay there while my fellow militants arrived after being kidnapped; they wanted to watch their reactions. The worst torture for me was when they showed me off to the new prisoners and told them, 'You'll be fine if you behave. Look at 'Mantecol.' He's alright here; he's already starting a new life.' They'd say, 'You'll suffer a bit, but then you'll be just like him.' And that hurt a lot because it made me an accomplice to something against my will. I think lots of the other activists felt the same way. And sometimes I'd just lose my mind; I'd go into the bathroom and smash my head against the wall" (AO.0418).

The boundaries of the Clandestine Detention Centers were blurred. Many of the disappeared were "detained" in plain sight during the early years of the dictatorship. Later on, some even did administrative work in government offices using false names, kept under surveillance by the security forces working alongside them.

Within the ESMA, some prisoners were forced to work in maintenance and logistics tasks as part of the so-called rehabilitation process, while others were forced to provide political and media analysis to support the political goals of the ESMA's top commander, General Emilio Massera.

Beginning in early 1977, Massera sought to exploit the detained activists' skills and political and cultural expertise in order to promote his own leadership ambitions within the armed forces and project an image of himself as the chief architect of national policy.

According to Cristina Aldini, the rehabilitation process "put us through a series of experiences that were somehow supposed to make us give up our beliefs, our habits, and all the values that sustained our political activism. The process took different forms. They might let a prisoner live if he or she demonstrated less overt resistance and had qualities that could serve Massera's goals. But then again, these weren't the only considerations that determined survival because a lot of the people put through this 'rehabilitation process' weren't political ideologues within their organizations. Many of us were very young and inexperienced. But there you go, that's just how random it was. What were the criteria? Sometimes they were just totally arbitrary. Some people had to do specific tasks, including basic maintenance work. Some worked in *la perrada* [slang for "the group that works like dogs"] doing jobs like painting, manual labor, or office work like typing and photocopying. I did those kinds of things. Others worked in the darkroom or forged documents. And there were also more skilled jobs like analyzing and filing press clippings, doing translation work, that sort of thing. . . . If I had to choose an image to capture the relationship I had with the repressors, I would say I always felt like I was standing high up on a ledge, in a permanent state of alert. I think I've never been able to completely relax, not even after all these years" [AO.0072].

In 1979 renovations were made to the Officers' Club in anticipation of the arrival of the Inter-American Commission on Human Rights (IACHR), which was visiting Argentina to investigate overseas reports about state terrorism acts. All traces of illegal detention were removed, and the prisoners were moved to an island in the Tigre delta called El Silencio (The Silence). There they were held in a house belonging to the Catholic Church, which functioned as a Clandestine Detention Center for the duration of the IACHR visit. The Officers' Club underwent several other renovations as well. Offices were built on the fourth floor opposite *capucha* and near the storeroom that housed goods stolen during kidnapping raids. Prisoners performed forced labor behind glass panels that earned the space the nickname "fishbowl." At other moments the basement was renovated to accommodate a darkroom, a room for forging documents, and a soundproof room called the egg carton (huevera) used for video and sound recording. A cafeteria was enlarged, and the torture rooms were redesigned.

These renovations were executed by a group of prisoners organized into a labor gang under the leadership of another detainee who had worked as a master builder. The gang was known as *la perrada* ("the group that works like dogs"), a variation of the rural term *la peonada* ("a gang of unskilled laborers"). Alfredo Ayala, an activist in the Peronist Shantytown Movement* (Movimiento Villero Peronista; see "Cristo Obrero Chapel. Father Carlos Mugica," p. 25), was forced to work on these projects: "You couldn't show any feelings there. You really had to watch yourself. If you laughed too much, it was taken as a sign that you'd switched sides; if you were really down, it was seen as a sign of resistance; and if you showed any anger they took you down a notch. I saw guys sent to *capucha* because they were depressed. . . . Feet shackled, hands cuffed, hooded, left without food for three or four days, lying there without a bath, just because they didn't seem to be adapting well. You really had to keep yourself in check. . . . For lots of us it was a victory just to stay alive for a few more seconds. . . . . When I wasn't hammering, I was organizing photographs. They would bring boxes and boxes of photos to be sorted by category: parties, neighborhoods, families, etc." [AO.0418].

**Clandestine maternity ward**

Besides operating as a military institution and a Clandestine Detention Center, the ESMA contained a clandestine maternity ward. Pregnant women kidnapped by the institution's Special Task Groups or transferred from other detention centers were brought there to give birth, assisted by other female prisoners and by

*CAPUCHITA.*

PARKING LOT FOR CARS USED TO TRANSPORT THE DISAPPEARED.

medical personnel assigned to the ESMA. Women were transferred to the Naval Hospital in the case of complications.

Martha Alvarez describes her experience: "I was kept in *capucha* until October, when they moved me to one of the rooms they called *camarotes* ["berths"] on the other side of *capucha*. I spent my whole pregnancy there. . . . They opened an infirmary in the basement later on to accommodate all the pregnant women; there was another prisoner who was pregnant at the same time as me, and our babies were going to be born down there. They took me to the infirmary when my contractions began, but there were complications, so they decided to move me to the Naval Hospital during the night. My son was born at dawn. They took me back to the ESMA right away, and the next day they brought my baby back too" [AO.0502].

In most cases babies were taken from their mothers soon after birth and handed over to naval officers, members of the other security forces, or their associates. Some were taken back to the ESMA to spend their first few months with their mothers; in extremely rare cases they were turned over to their extended families.

The systematic abduction of minors involved not only children born in captivity, but also those kidnapped along with their parents. These children's identities were changed, and some were placed in institutions and adopted in good faith by families who knew nothing about their backgrounds or their parents' identity (see "Central Military Hospital," p. 77).

**Euphemisms**

State terrorism also functioned discursively, using a wide variety of euphemisms to avoid mentioning the brutality it was committing. As Rodolfo Walsh pointed out in his "Open Letter to the Military Junta," written a year after the coup: "What you call good decisions are errors, what you recognize as errors are crimes, and what you fail to mention are catastrophes" (see "Corner of San Juan and Entre Ríos," p. 96).

Pilar Calveiro (1998) has examined state terror's impact on language in her research on the ways power spread outward from the Clandestine Detention Centers to affect the broader society. The dictatorship expressed itself through euphemisms used in the camps. Systematic murders were called "transfers" (*traslados*). Torturers referred to the electric cattle prod (*picana*) used in torture sessions as the "machine" (*máquina*). The forced labor area was called the "fish-bowl" (*pecera*). Prisoners told they would be going on "outings" (*paseos*) were really taken out to facilitate further kidnappings. The area of the cells was called the *capucha* ("hood") in reference to the hoods prisoners were forced to wear over their heads.

The language used within the camp extended outward, and the broader society became an accomplice to the exercise of repression by adopting words that "stated without naming." Examples include the use of the term "disappeared" rather than "illegally detained." Another was the vague term "something" used in the common expression "they must have done something" in reference to victims of disappearance. This use of language helped to justify thousands of disappearances.

**The ESMA today**

The ESMA facilities remained under Navy control after the return to democracy. In early 1988 the Navy School of Mechanics moved to Puerto Belgrano, and the government of President Carlos Menem sought to demolish the building. Yet the courts prevented this demolition on the grounds that the site contained legal evidence. In June 2000 Buenos Aires City Council unanimously approved a law revoking the Navy's original land grant and legislated that the buildings would eventually house a Museum of Memory (Museo de la Memoria). In March 2004 then-President Nestor Kirchner evicted the military institutions and ordered the premises returned to the city.

The eviction was completed by September 30, 2007. Two months later, on November 20, an inter-jurisdictional body was established to plan the museum project. It included human rights organizations; an advisory council of former ESMA prisoners; the National Memory Archive (Archivo Nacional de la Memoria), representing the federal government; and the Space for Memory Institute (Instituto Espacio por la Memoria), representing the Buenos Aires city government.

Today, the ESMA grounds are home to a large number of human rights and cultural institutions, including the Space for Memory Institute (Instituto Espacio para la Memoria); the Haroldo Conti Cultural Center (Centro Cultural Haroldo Conti); the National Memory Archive (Archivo Nacional de la Memoria); the Nuestros Hijos Cultural Center of the Mothers of the Plaza de Mayo Association (Centro Cultural Nuestros Hijos de la Asociación Madres de Plaza de Mayo); the Family Members of Those Disappeared for Political Reasons Space (Espacio Familiares de Desaparecidos y Detenidos por razones Políticas); the Our Children, Lives, and Hope House of the Mothers of the Plaza de Mayo – Founding Line (Casa Nuestros Hijos, Vida y Esperanza de Madres de Plaza de Mayo – Línea Fundadora), which offers musical training; the Activist House (Casa de la Militancia) run by H.I.J.O.S., the association representing the children of the disappeared, which provides training to activists and educational projects relating to memory; the Identity House (Casa por la Identidad) of the Abuelas de Plaza de Mayo, dedicated to cultural and educational projects; the Latin American Initiative for the Identification of Persons (Iniciativa Latinoamericana para la identificación de personas) run by the Argentine Forensic Anthropology Team (EAAF), the National Memory Archive, and the Federal Ministry of Health; the Patrick Rice Center (Espacio Patrick Rice), dedicated to ecumenical understanding; the Institute for Human Rights Policy of MERCOSUR (Instituto de Políticas Públicas en Derechos Humanos); the UNESCO-sponsored International Center for the Promotion of Human Rights (Centro Internacional para la promoción de los Derechos Humanos); and the broadcasting offices of the Encuentro television channel, the children's channel Paka-Paka, and the online educational resource "Educ.ar," all run by the federal Ministry of Education, Science, and Technology.

Guided tours of the premises, including the Officers' Club with its four imposing columns, have been offered since 2007. Plans are in place to create a permanent exhibition in this building.

## 132. **Park of Memory**



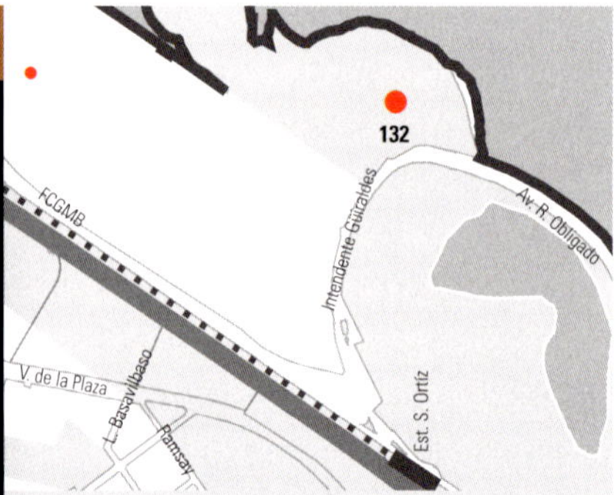


**LOCATION:** AV. COSTANERA RAFAEL OBLIGADO AND CIUDAD UNIVERSITARIA
**TRANSPORTATION:** BUSES: 28, 33, 37, 42, 107, 160. TRAIN STATION: SCALABRINI ORTÍZ (BELGRANO LINE).

The Monument to the Victims of State Terrorism was inaugurated in the Parque de la Memoria (Park of Memory) on November 7, 2007. Hundreds of people in attendance walked together around its four walls looking for the names of their loved ones among the thousands inscribed there. They located, touched, and cried over these names, and left flowers or messages between the plaques. Then they walked along the processional path to the pier, where they cast flowers into the river. This ceremony, which had begun years earlier as an ecumenical act to remember the disappeared along that stretch of riverbank, now struck a different tone.

### The initiative

Plans for the Park of Memory had begun ten years earlier in 1997 when human rights organizations had first approached city authorities asking them to create a monument.

Their initiative marked a turning point in recent Argentine efforts to construct collective memory. The 1996 commemoration of the coup's twentieth anniversary had prompted an outpouring of memory work, as tributes and cultural events dedicated to the disappeared became more and more frequent. The Park of Memory project emerged from this context, bringing together ideas that have informed more recent efforts to transform former Clandestine Detention Centers into remembrance sites.

The Monument was the first commemorative site in the city to bear witness to the dictatorship's actions. Its design, scale, and location near

MONUMENT TO THE VICTIMS OF STATE TERRORISM.

FLOWERS THROWN INTO THE RIVER TO REMEMBER THE DISAPPEARED.

SCULPTURE BY ROBERTO AIZEMBERG.

the river all contribute to its enormous symbolic importance. In 1998 Buenos Aires's first autonomous city government approved Law 46, which set aside fourteen hectares for the Parque de la Memoria and for the installation of the Monument and a sculpture garden. Alberto Varas won the design competition. The Pro-Monument Commission (CPM, Comisión Pro-Monumento) was established to oversee the project, with representation from the executive and legislative powers, the University of Buenos Aires, and ten human rights organizations. In 2009 a new law created the Council for the Management of the Park and Monument to guarantee the park's proper maintenance.

Believing that art could be an important tool for the cultivation of memory, the CPM organized an international art competition that received 665 entries designed by artists from forty-four countries. Eight of the seventeen chosen works are already in place.

An information center was also built to promote art, research, and public activities to represent the life stories of the victims named on the Monument.

**The Monument**

The Río de la Plata holds deep significance, because its waters became the final resting place for many victims of disappearance. Testimonies from camp survivors and research conducted by human rights groups and and family members of the victims all point to the "death flights"* as the Armed Forces' main strategy for erasing the traces of their crimes. Victims were thrown from airplanes into the river so that their bodies would never be found.

The Monument symbolizes a wound running between the coast and the river. Its four large walls contain thirty thousand plaques of porphyry stone from Patagonia to represent the estimate of thirty thousand victims usually cited by the human rights movement. The porphyry, a stone native to Argentina, contains variations in color and seams that represent the victims' unique and individual identities.

The names appear alphabetically and chronologically by date of disappearance or death. The height of the plaques allows visitors to run a hand over the inscriptions and touch the names of friends or loved ones. This experience of the engravings powerfully symbolizes resistance to state terrorism's efforts to deny the existence of the disappeared.

Law 46 established that the Monument's list of names should match the one drawn up by the National Commission on the Disappearance of Persons* (CONADEP, Comisión Nacional sobre la Desaparición de Personas). After rigorous corroboration, 8,727 names were inscribed on the Monument. The choice of names remains unfinished and open to new requests, and has provoked painful yet important debates that are fundamental to the project's development.

**Debates**

Controversy accompanied the project from the beginning. Human rights organizations and the victims' family members proposed that this heritage site represent society's fundamental shared values. Some groups in favor of the military objected to the naming of victims on these grounds, arguing that such recognition was divisive because it implied a condemnation of the actions undertaken by the armed forces.

Two human rights organizations also objected during the placing of the Monument's cornerstone, declaring the tribute inadequate because the naming of individual victims diluted the notion of collective identity. They also questioned the city government's role in the project.

Further controversy arose in 1999 around the statement read out at the cornerstone's unveiling: "Here shall stand the Monument paying tribute to the victims of state terrorism and to the ideals of freedom, solidarity, and justice for which they lived and fought." This wording raised the question of who should be counted as a "victim" and have their names inscribed on the Monument. It was finally decided that it should bear the names of "those detained and disappeared, and those who were murdered or died while fighting for Argentina" between 1969 and 1983, regardless of nationality. Also included were the names of Argentine citizens kidnapped and murdered outside the country as part of Operation Condor, the program through which the Southern Cone military regimes coordinated their repressive operations.

Other controversies surrounded the Monument's scale and cost during the difficult years of construction, when the country was facing problems of widespread poverty and financial crisis. Regardless of one's position in these debates, the project's magnitude has undeniably strained the city's already overstretched maintenance and operational capacity.

The main challenge, however, is to ensure that the park serves its dual function as both a powerful site of denunciation and a natural greenspace for reflection and relaxation. Some victims' family members, including Daniel Tarnopolsky, believe that "it is very important that this park exist and remain open to the public. . . . It's located on the waterfront [Costanera] in an area near the food stands [*carritos*], a place where people go fishing, and where people will be able to walk, look around, and learn" [AO.564].

Daniel raises the most difficult issue facing the park: how to encourage people to adopt the space as their own in heart, mind, and consciousness, how to make it part of a lived experience.

In any case, the Monument was completed just as human rights trials reopened after years of struggle. In order for this space to foster collective memory within this new context, it must remain open and dynamic enough to accommodate a variety of uses and interpretations.

# 133. **Ricardo Marcos Zucker Jr. Grandstand**

**LOCATION:** AV. COMODORO RIVADAVIA 1450
**TRANSPORTATION:** BUSES: 15, 28, 29, 130.
TRAIN STATION: NÚÑEZ (MITRE LINE).

The grandstand known as La Techada is reserved for fans of the Defensores de Belgrano soccer club and is also a commemorative site dedicated to a loyal "Defe" fan who was disappeared during the last military dictatorship. Ricardo Marcos Zucker represents countless young people who responded to injustice by choosing a life of political activism.

This unprecedented initiative came from a member of the club's management committee. It marked the first tribute to a disappeared fan in Argentina, a country where soccer is king. The soccer world's other commemorative sites—stadium boxes, seating areas, and balconies—have all been dedicated to coaches, players, or sports journalists.

Ricardo Zucker began as a student activist, rising to join the four-person leadership committee of the Union of Secondary School Students* (UES, Unión de Estudiantes Secundarios) by 1974, when fellow UES activist Eduardo Beckerman was gunned down by the Triple A* (Argentine Anticommunist Alliance; see "Automotores Orletti," p. 220). Zucker was a coffin bearer at Beckerman's funeral alongside fellow leaders Claudio Slemenson, Cristian Caretti (see p. 81), and Isaac Dricas. The daily newspaper *Noticias* carried a front-page photo of them holding up their hands in a V sign, a gesture that meant "Viva Perón" (Long Live Perón). More deaths followed. Slemenson was kidnapped in Tucumán in October 1975. The following year, Caretti was captured and Dricas swallowed a cyanide pill when he was caught in a *pinza** ("pincer") operation.

Ricardo Zucker's sister María Cristina Zucker recalls that "he was already involved in the Montonero* organization" as a high-profile political militant by 1974. By then he was so

exposed "that he decided to set aside his activism and return to his other passion: soccer" [AO.0369].

Yet politics would ultimately define his destiny. He was kidnapped first in March 1977, and then again in 1980. "He lived with my mother," recalls his sister. "They showed up very early in the morning, at six o'clock. It was a big gang [*patota**] of about six or seven armed men" who told his mother they were members of an antidrug squad. "My mother was on her knees telling them that her son had never taken drugs, but they took him away." He was held illegally for forty-six days in an undetermined Clandestine Detention Center.

After his release Zucker went into exile to Brazil and then Madrid, where he stayed in contact with the Montoneros*. In 1980, convinced of the dictatorship's imminent collapse, he decided to return to Argentina to take part in the Montonero Counteroffensive*.

Yet the military had discovered the Montoneros' weapons cache in a warehouse on the outskirts of Buenos Aires, working on intelligence information obtained through the torture of a captured Montonero militant. "They found the equipment . . . and they stationed themselves there to wait, in Olivos," recounts Cristina Zucker.

Former Special Task Group* member Sergeant Nelson Ramón González stated in a 1997 television interview that the orders for Ricardo Marcos Zucker's murder had come from Cristino Nicolaides, then chief of the Military Education and Training Command Unit at the Campo de Mayo* military base.

In 2005 the Argentine Supreme Court overturned the laws that had halted judicial proceedings for the crimes of the dictatorship in the 1980s: the Law of Due Obedience* (Ley de Obediencia Debida) and the Full Stop Law* (Ley de Punto Final). New cases were brought forward relating to the repression, first against police personnel, but then against military leaders. General Nicolaides, former Commander in Chief of the Argentine Army, was one of the first to be convicted. In 2007 he was sentenced to twenty-five years in prison for six crimes, including Zucker's murder. The judge ruled that these crimes should be categorized as crimes against humanity.

# 134. **Miguel Sánchez Sports Track**



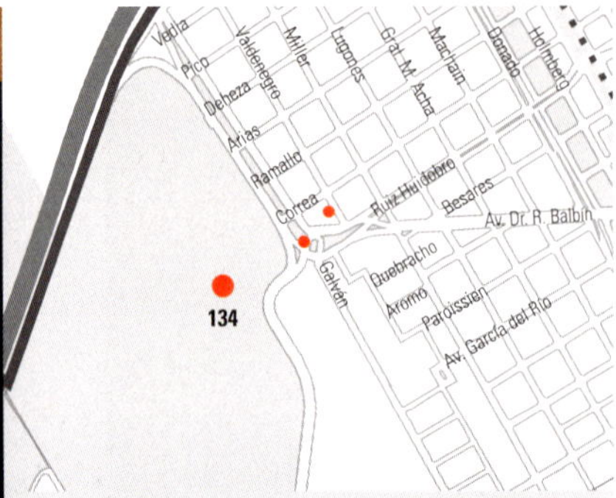


**LOCATION:** PARQUE SARMIENTO, AV. DR. RICARDO BALBÍN 4750
**TRANSPORTATION:** BUSES: 21, 28, 41, 67, 110.

Runner Miguel Sánchez was among the athletes disappeared during the last military dictatorship. The annual Miguel Races honor his memory in different cities in Argentina (Buenos Aires, San Miguel de Tucumán, Bariloche, Necochea, and Berazategui) and around the world (including Rome and Havana). In 2004 the athletic track at Parque Sarmiento, a seventy-hectare sports facility run by the City of Buenos Aires, was rededicated in his name.

Miguel Sánchez has symbolized athletes victimized by state terrorism since Italian journalist Valerio Piccione first learned of his case during a 1998 visit to Argentina and developed it into a book. Piccione organized the first Corsa di Miguel (Miguel Race) in Rome two years later. Three hundred and fifty people ran through the streets wearing t-shirts bearing Sánchez's photo and the poem "For You, Athlete" (*Para vos atleta*), which he had published in São Paulo's *La Gaceta* just days before his disappearance. The Argentine Sports Secretariat organized the first Miguel Race in Buenos Aires in March 2001. Participation has grown since then, and the race has become the first major event of the Buenos Aires running calendar. In 2009 over 15,000 people took part in the Buenos Aires race, and thousands more turned out to honor Miguel in other cities.

Miguel Venancio Sánchez was the youngest of ten children born into a poor family in the province of Tucumán. At seventeen he migrated to Buenos Aires with his family and found a job painting houses. He also played soccer at the Gimnasia y Esgrima de la Plata soccer club until forced to give it up when he found a job as an office assistant in the headquarters of the Banco Provincia.

His job didn't keep him away from sports, though, and he soon developed a passion for running. He represented the bank in several races and was invited to join the Independiente de Avellaneda Club. Miguel also ran in international races, and was in fact disappeared on his return from one of these trips.

He had traveled to Brazil to run in the December 31st San Silvestre Race through the streets of São Paulo. His coach, Osvaldo Suárez, had won the race three times. Miguel headed home through Uruguay to run in another race and finally arrived in Argentina on January 6, 1978. He was kidnapped from his home two days later in an operation probably ordered through Operation Condor, the coordinated policy of repression that linked the military governments of the Southern Cone countries in the 1970s.

"He'll be right back," the kidnappers told his family as they forced him, blindfolded, into a gray Ford Falcon. Yet Roadrunner (Correcaminos), as his friends liked to call him, never returned. His family waited ten years to clean out his room, where they had lovingly kept his fifty trophies and thirty-six medals.

The events of that night remained a mystery for years until journalist and lawyer Pablo Llonto turned up a clue. Survivor Alfredo Manzo recalled that he had encountered a young Chilean man who had just run a marathon in Brazil while he was being detained inside the Clandestine Detention Center known as El Vesubio*. Llonto reasoned that "the Chilean man wasn't actually Chilean. Miguel Sánchez was from Tucumán, but [Manzo] likely assumed from his accent that he was Chilean" (AO.0432). Although Manzo never learned the man's name, the dates he gave for the kidnapping and race coincide with Miguel's. Llonto managed to interview the former director of El Vesubio, Major Pedro Alberto Durán Sáenz, and inquire about the runner held there in 1978. Durán Sáenz responded that he was no longer running the Center by that date and, when pressed for information about his successor, he replied, "Those kinds of memories become blurred when you look back."

Miguel had been active as a community organizer in the Peronist Youth Movement* (Juventud Peronista), working in poor areas within his neighborhood of Berazategui. His sister Elvira recalls, "Miguel couldn't stand to see the social and economic conditions in which some people found themselves. He had a lot of empathy for other people, and he was proud to come from a poor family" (*Página/12,* March 30, 2003). A mural in his honor stands just a few blocks from his home, where he was kidnapped on August 8, 1978. It reads, "Let us run even harder today, thirty years later, so we don't forget those who are no longer with us."

# 135. **Mothers of the White Scarf Plaza**

**LOCATION:** AV. DR. RICARDO BALBÍN, AV. PARQUE ROBERTO GOYENECHE AND AV. GARCÍA DEL RÍO
**TRANSPORTATION:** BUSES: 29, 41, 67, 71, 93, 110, 130. TRAIN STATION: L. M. SAAVEDRA (MITRE LINE).

In 1996 a group of residents from the neighborhood of Saavedra took over the empty space left by the abandoned Highway 3 project and transformed it into a plaza using all recycled materials. They named the space the Plaza Madres del Pañuelo Blanco in reference to the headscarves worn by the Madres de Plaza de Mayo. Neighbors built a seesaw from poles discarded by the cable television companies, and made tables out of the cable spools left by the telephone companies. In 2008 Buenos Aires City Council officially designated this space Plaza Madres del Pañuelo Blanco.

### The diaper as symbol

The white headscarves worn by the Madres de Plaza de Mayo (see "Plaza de Mayo," p. 3) have become one of the key symbols in the fight against state terrorism in Argentina. When the Madres began to organize, they realized they needed greater public exposure to strengthen their demands that the military government release information about the whereabouts of their children.

They decided to take part in the yearly Catholic pilgrimage to the Basilica of Luján, one of the few events that continued to bring thousands of people together during the dictatorship. To keep sight of each other during the procession, they decided to cover their heads with a white diaper, an everyday domestic item typically associated with motherhood. In time they exchanged these for white headscarves and, in the process, transformed a practical gesture into a symbolic one. The Madres now use the headscarf as a symbol

MURAL IN THE MOTHERS OF THE WHITE SCARF PLAZA.

of identity in public ceremonies. White headscarves have also been painted on the stones around the central Pyramid in the Plaza de Mayo, where the Madres have marched weekly every Thursday since they began to meet in April 1977.

The headscarf makes the resistance efforts of victims and their family members visible. The figure of the mother with her diaper/headscarf came to symbolize the forced absence of her children. By identifying themselves with motherhood, a value undisputed even by official ideology, the Madres transformed women's place within politics and the meaning of motherhood itself. Each Madre's headscarf carries the embroidered name of the child she is seeking.

In the 1990s headscarves were also used by the organization representing the children of the disappeared, H.I.J.O.S.* (the acronym, a play on the Spanish word for "children," stands for Children for Identity and Justice Opposed to Forgetting and Silence). Many H.I.J.O.S. members wore headscarves around their necks during public demonstrations and shaming protests (*escraches**) in front of the homes of known repressors and torturers.

### The AU3

The Plaza's location is particularly significant. In 1977 the military government expropriated over eight hundred homes to build the AU3, one in a series of new freeways proposed in the Urban Freeway Plan (Plan de Autopistas Urbanas) designed by architect Guillermo Laura and partially implemented by the city government controlled by Brigadier Osvaldo Cacciatore. Others included the 25 de Mayo freeway (see p. 99), the Avenida 9 de Julio, and the Perito Moreno highway.

Expropriations for the AU3 began as soon as the plan was adopted, and demolition began at the project's north end. Then it was suddenly abandoned and, gradually, the expropriated homes were taken over by squatters.

For more than thirty years the neighborhoods of Saavedra, Coghlan, and Villa Urquiza have shared the scar of these demolitions, the wound left by an act of power that robbed so many families of their homes. The people who live there now say they "live on the AU3." This incongruous image of countless homes living out their existence on an imaginary freeway exemplifies a particular idea of progress, one oblivious to human lives.

## 136. Bet-el Temple

A plaque honoring disappeared Jews was unveiled in this temple on March 24, 2001, following an initiative by Rabbi Daniel Goldman. Daniel Filmus, then-Minister of Education for the City of Buenos Aires, attended the ceremony with members of the temple's congregation.

**LOCATION:** SUCRE 3338, BELGRANO

## 137. University Campus, UBA

In 1983 students and professors of the Faculty of Architecture, Design, and Urbanism (FADU) of the University of Buenos Aires (UBA) created a commemorative flag bearing the photographs and names of disappeared Faculty members. On May 31, 2005, the Faculty opened up files pertaining to disappeared students, alumni, and professors to assist with the design of a new flag to replace the original.

The Faculty of Exact and Natural Sciences organized several activities to mark the coup's thirtieth anniversary, including a roundtable discussion about the dictatorship's impact on the institution, and a ceremony to unveil a plaque dedicated to the thirty thousand victims of disappearance and to those who maintain the fight for human rights.

A plaque was dedicated on September 23, 2005 in the third-floor biology laboratories. The event was organized by the Student Union by Pablo Spinella, son of former student Miguel Spinella, who disappeared along with Daniel Bendersky. In 1996 the Student Union had created a mural in Pavilion II bearing the names of all the disappeared students, professors, and staff.

**LOCATION:** INTENDENTE GUIRALDES 2160, NUÑEZ

## 138. Tribute to Athletes in the CENARD

At the National Center for High Performance Athletics (CENARD, Centro Nacional de Alto Rendimiento Deportivo), two plaques honor detained and disappeared athletes: Miguel Sánchez (see p. 168), an affiliated athlete kidnapped on January 3, 1978, and Daniel Shapira, a tennis player disappeared on April 7, 1977.

**LOCATION:** CRISOLOGO LARRALDE 1050, NUÑEZ

## 139. José Alfredo Madrid

In late 2006 the Félix de Azara School hung a plaque and photograph honoring Madrid, a teacher kidnapped and disappeared on February 3, 1977. The event finalized a student project about state terrorism that had been initiated in response to Buenos Aires City Council Law 547 (see "Disappeared Teachers Remembered in Their Schools," p. 204), passed in 2001.

**LOCATION:** JOSE P. TAMPORINI 3948, COGHLAN

## 140. Tribute by Municipal District 12

On December 15, 2006, municipal authorities in District 12, representing Saavedra, Coghlan, Villa Urquiza, and Villa Pueyrredón, joined with neighborhood and human rights organizations to replace a plaque originally installed in 1981 by the military's appointed mayor, Gen. Osvaldo Cacciatore in Sarmiento. The new plaque, installed along with a panel listing the names of disappeared residents, reads, "Our comrades join us to defend history from oblivion."

**LOCATION:** PARQUE SARMIENTO, ENTER ON AV. R. BALBÍN, SAAVEDRA.

## 141. Colegiales Club

Damián Cabandié was kidnapped on November 23, 1977. A few hours later a Special Task Group* seized Alicia Alfonsín, who was five months pregnant at the time; she gave birth in the ESMA. Their son Juan recovered his identity in early 2004 (see p. 77). Alicia and Damián had first met in the Colegiales Club, where a plaque was hung to remember them.

**LOCATION:** TEODORO GARCIA 2860, COLEGIALES

# SECTOR 6

AGRONOMÍA, CHACARITA, PARQUE CHAS, PATERNAL, VILLA CRESPO, VILLA PUEYRREDÓN, VILLA ORTÚZAR, AND VILLA URQUIZA

# 142. **San Patricio Church – Pallottine Martyrs' Passage**

San Patricio Church contains a monument honoring the Pallottine Martyrs, five members of the Pallottine Society who were murdered by the dictatorship on July 4, 1976. The sculpture, completed in September 2005, is titled *El Camino de los Palotinos* (The Pallottines' Way). Buenos Aires City Council hung a plaque in the Church honoring these men in 2006, on the thirtieth anniversary of their deaths. A nearby passage running between Estomba and Plaza Streets was also named Mártires Palotinos (Pallottine martyrs).

**LOCATION:** CHURCH – ESTOMBA 1942; PASSAGE – BETWEEN ESTOMBA AND PLAZA
**TRANSPORTATION:** BUSES: 76, 113, 114, 133. TRAIN STATION: L. M. DRAGO (MITRE LINE).

### The early hours of July 4

A Special Task Group* entered the Parochial House of San Patricio Church around one a.m. on Sunday, July 4, 1976, and murdered Fathers Alfredo Leaden, Pedro Eduardo Dufau, and Alfredo José Kelly and seminarians Salvador Barbeito Doval and Emilio José Barletti. The killers took the five men out of their bedrooms and led them to a windowless room, where they shot them from behind and left their bodies to bleed onto the red carpet.

The next morning two young men named Luis Pinasco and Guillermo Silva reported to Pallottine priest Father Efraín Suedo Luque that they had seen two cars parked outside the Parochial House the night before. They had been accompanied by a third young man, Julio Víctor Martínez, son of an officer appointed by the dictatorship to direct the provincial government of Neuquén. Martínez had reported the men to Police Precinct No. 37 because he suspected they were planning an attack on his home, though he had to make several requests before the police would take his statement. Eventually Officer Miguel Angel Romano visited the church and spoke with the men in the suspicious cars. He then warned Pedro Alvarez, the security

DETAIL OF THE COMMEMORATIVE SCULPTURES.

guard stationed at Martínez's house, not to go into the street if he heard shots because they were going to "trash the home of some lefties [*zurdos*]." Pinasco and Silva reported that around two a.m. armed men got out of the cars and went inside the Parochial House. The murderers later emerged and made a quick escape in their cars.

At around 7:30 a.m., sixteen-year-old church organist Rolando Savino discovered the bodies of the five Pallottines. Some parishioners had been waiting at the church doors to go in for Mass; when they rang the bell and no one answered, Savino climbed through an open window. He opened the door for the people waiting outside and went upstairs to look for the priests.

A clipping from the comic strip "Mafalda" had been left on the body of Salvador Barbeito, depicting the comic's main character pointing at a police truncheon and saying, "This is the little ideology-bashing stick." The men's faces had been beaten beyond recognition, and the killers had written, "To avenge our partners killed in the explosion at Federal Security. We shall triumph. Long live Argentina" (see "Coordinación Federal," p. 17). According to several reports, they also left a message on the carpet reading, "These 'lefties' died because they were indoctrinating innocent minds and were members of the MSTM [Movement of Priests for the Third World – Movimiento de Sacerdotes del Tercer Mundo]" (Seisdedos, 1996).

Two days earlier the Montonero guerrillas had placed a bomb in the dining hall of what was then known as the Bureau of Federal Security (Superintendencia de Seguridad Federal), a police administration office that also functioned as a Clandestine Detention Center (CDC); twenty-one people had died. The first note left with the bodies made reference to this event.

On Monday morning the daily *La Nación* printed an official report of these events that blamed leftist organizations for the killings at the church: "Subversive elements cowardly murdered the priests and seminarians. This thuggish crime was committed on the premises of the San Patricio Church, proving that its perpetrators are not only unpatriotic but Godless" (*La Nación,* July 5, 1976).

**The Pallottine martyrs**

The Pallottine community had founded its church in the growing neighborhood of Belgrano in the late 1920s to meet the needs of English-speaking Catholics living in the area. The parish church was dedicated to Saint Patrick (San Patricio), Apostle of Ireland.

**Father Alfredo Leaden**

Father Leaden was born in Buenos Aires on May 23, 1919. In 1932 he helped to found the Pallottine Preparatory School in Rawson, in the province of Chubut. He completed his novitiate and studied philosophy in Thurles, Ireland, and then began his theological studies in Rome, completing them in Argentina at the Jesuit-run Colegio Máximo de San Miguel. He was ordained in 1942. Father Rodolfo Capalozza recalls him as a man interested in youth issues and sympathetic to the texts that rallied young people in the 1960s and 1970s.

**Father Pedro Eduardo Dufau**

Father Dufau was born on October 13, 1908, in Mercedes, a town in the province of Buenos Aires. His grandmother raised him when he was orphaned, and when she in turn died he began his studies at San Patricio School. He completed his novitiate in Thurles, Ireland, and studied philosophy, going on to study

theology at the Gregorian University in Rome. He was ordained in 1933 and in 1958 was transferred to the Parish of San Patricio, where he worked as rector and parish priest. He founded the San Vicente Pallotti Institute, the school adjoining the Church. He also worked on-call as a volunteer in the Emergency Priest Services.

Father Dufau's sermon for that day's Mass was discovered after the murders. It contained the following words: "We would have no need for prophets if humans did not need to change. Yet as soon as the Prophet begins to condemn individual and social sins, his job becomes more difficult and more unpleasant. And people who will do anything to avoid listening routinely take such prophets out of circulation by locking them up and killing them" (San Patricio Parish Church and Human Rights Office of the City of Buenos Aires, 2001).

**Father Alfredo José Kelly**

Father Kelly was born on May 5, 1933, in Suipacha, a town in the province of Buenos Aires. He entered the Pallottine congregation in Mercedes as a teenager. He studied at Rawson, in the province of Chubut, and completed his novitiate in the province of Buenos Aires at San Antonio de Areco. He completed his postsecondary studies at the Colegio Máximo de San Miguel and the Gregorian University of Rome, then returned to Buenos Aires; he was ordained in 1957 in the San Patricio Church of Mercedes. Father Kelly served as Educational Director in the San Patricio Church in Belgrano and worked closely with the youth pastoral team.

**Salvador Barbeito Doval**

Salvador Barbeito Doval was born on September 1, 1946, in Pontevedra, Spain, and emigrated to Buenos Aires with his family at the age of three. He completed his early seminary studies in the Archidiocese of Buenos Aires, where he also studied philosophy and theology, and then went on to complete his theological and educational training in the Governing Board of Catholic Education. He worked as a tutor and catechist in the Bethania and San Vicente Pallotti schools in Belgrano and then taught psychology, philosophy, and catechism in the Santa Brígida and Santa Unión schools. He entered the Pallottine congregation in Belgrano in 1975.

**Emilio José Barletti**

Emilio José Barletti was born in San Antonio de Areco, in the province of Buenos Aires, on November 22, 1952. He studied law and social sciences at the University of Buenos Aires and was a student in the Catholic Apostolate Society in the San Patricio congregation in Belgrano. He took part in the Movement for Renewal and Change (Movimiento Renovación y Cambio) led by Raúl Alfonsín, president of Argentina in 1983–1989. Barletti joined the Peronist Youth Movement* (JP, Juventud Peronista) during the years of Juan Domingo Perón's return to Argentina. He worked in poor neighborhoods and edited the publication *17 de Noviembre*.

**The monument**

Built in September 2005, the monument titled *El Camino de los Palotinos* contains five figures made of stone blocks that evoke the murdered priests and seminarians. For Roberto Frangella, one of the architects behind the work, these sculptures represent the men's spiritual figures more than their earthly images. The work, installed in a small square with an entrance ramp and a tree, invites visitors to enact their own symbolic pilgrimage.

PALLOTTINE MARTYRS STREET

### The judicial inquiry

Within days the military junta was forced to admit that their own forces had been involved in the murders. Yet the inquiry was suspended after Judge Guillermo Rivarola failed to identify the killers after investigating through 1976 and 1977.

Judge Néstor Blondi was assigned to the case in 1984, after the return to democracy. Testimony from several witnesses implicated the Navy School of Mechanics (ESMA; see p. 153). Former naval serviceman Miguel Angel Balbi told the court his friend Claudio Vallejos admitted to taking part in the Pallottine murders along with Antonio Pernías, Lieutenant Aristegui, and the noncommissioned officer Cubalo. ESMA survivor Graciela Daleo also testified that Pernías had often boasted about his role in the priests' murders.

More questionable testimony came from Miguel Angel Romano, the police officer who had visited the church a few hours before the murders in response to Julio Víctor Martínez's statement at the police station. Romano told Judge Rivarola that when he had checked the parked cars, he had found only one man who claimed to be waiting for a woman. In May 1986 then–Public Prosecutor Aníbal Ibarra ordered that Romano be indicted for perjury. He also called for the prosecution of former Precinct 37 Police Chief Rafael Fensoro, who had held Martínez's report for 3 days before filing it. Judge Blondi dismissed both these charges when defense lawyers invoked the statute of limitations.

### The journalistic investigation

In 1989 journalist Eduardo Kimel published one of the most comprehensive investigations into the case in *La masacre de San Patricio* (The San Patricio massacre). Judge Rivarola sued Kimel in 1991 for slander and libel. In 1995 Judge Angela Braidot sentenced him to a one-year suspended sentence and ordered him to pay 20,000 pesos in damages. One year later Division VI of the National Court of Appeals overturned this decision, though the original sentence was reinstated in 1998 when Kimel lost a Supreme Court appeal launched by Rivarola.

In December 2000 Kimel, along with the Center for Legal and Social Studies (CELS) and the Center for Justice and International Law (CEJIL), brought the Argentine government before the Inter-American Commission on Human Rights (IACHR). The commission recognized their claim in 2006 and ordered the government of Argentina to appear before the Inter-American Court for breaching articles relating to judicial guarantees and freedom of expression. The government accepted responsibility for the case under the presidency of Néstor Kirchner.

# 143. **Roberto Santoro Cultural Center**

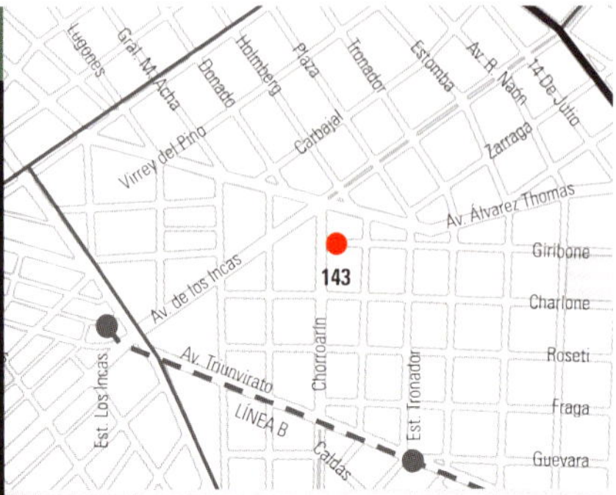


**LOCATION:** GIRIBONE 1961
**TRANSPORTATION:** BUSES: 71, 80, 87, 113, 127, 133. SUBWAY STATION: TRONADOR (B LINE).

"The president . . . speaks of freedom and democracy. . . . They are distributing leaflets about preventing subversive activities in the schools. The president says he rejects an indulgent press. The Ford factory in Pacheco, which employs 4,800 workers, closes for five weeks. . . . Bishops talk of peace and pray. [The author Jorge Luis] Borges declares that literature and art are forms of amusement. . . . [Yet] the fact remains that our companions are still imprisoned, and we need you to give us a hand, to show us a gesture of solidarity. . . . In any case, we're still optimistic. This has only just begun. Right now we have to fight, and the future is ours" (Extract from Roberto Santoro's "Carta de denuncia" (Letter of denunciation) to the Confederation of Latin American Writers).

### Culture worker

Roberto Santoro was born in Buenos Aires on April 17, 1939. He was kidnapped from his workplace, the Fray Luis Beltrán National Technical School No. 25, on June 1, 1977. Roberto worked as a painter, market vendor, tutor, printer, street peddler, journalist, and poet; he viewed poetry as a tool for change, liberation, and political struggle. This vision inspired him to launch and direct a number of cultural projects such as the publishing house and magazine that both bore the name *El Barrilete* (The kite). Santoro wanted to use publishing as a vehicle for social protest, and these initiatives brought together many young journalists and writers. "Amateur" publishers printed Santoro's poems as well as those of Carlos Patiño, Francisco Chiroleu, Carlos Higa (also disappeared), and Alberto Costa (who was exiled in Spain); artist friends provided the illustrations for these works. This artisanal publishing was part of a broader cultural effort to challenge the dictatorship's hegemonic discourse, which was founded on misinformation and the impoverishment of ideas.

Roberto gave a speech in April 1964 at an event sponsored by the National Alliance of Intellectuals: "We have only ourselves to blame if culture is the privilege of the few, because we have spent our lives fighting each other. . . . We believe that the Alliance of Intellectuals must bring together members from associations of visual artists, writers, musicians, and theater and film professionals. It should coordinate a broad cultural plan in which each guild directs its actions toward the advancement of culture, in the interests of the majority of people. Nothing more."

In the mid-1970s Roberto set out to challenge the leadership of the Argentine Writers' Society (SADE, Sociedad Argentina de Escritores). He and Alberto Costa invited writers renowned for their literary accomplishments and their commitment to democracy to join in a powerful collective action. The only way for the Writers' Guild to achieve its goal of overturning the SADE leadership was to present a candidate for election; writer David Viñas ran for the position of secretary. Though their efforts were unsuccessful, these writers formed a group committed to addressing social issues through their literary texts, joining literature to social critique.

Describing Roberto's organizing work, his sister Emilia Santoro recalls that "he always referred to writers and poets as culture workers. This was why he always tried to bring literary works to broader audiences, not only to a select few. He wanted literature to be available to the masses, so that even people with no resources could somehow access culture. . . . Since the people who control the media are not going to facilitate change, we have to keep fighting with our pens and words" [AO.0029].

Santoro denounced the dictatorship's atrocities to an audience outside the country in June 1976. He presented his signed "Letter of Denunciation" (Carta de denuncia) before the Confederation of Latin American Writers, with head offices in Mexico City. In it he demanded that the military publish the names of prisoners and provide information about beatings and threats suffered by writers and journalists.

## Cultural Center

The Roberto Santoro Cultural Center was inaugurated on April 28, 2000. Sculptor and painter Pedro Costa, Santoro's friend and fellow activist, designed the plaque bearing his name. The Cultural Center shares a building with the Cecilia Estrada de Cano Special Needs School for the Arts No. 18, and the school has deepened its community ties since the Center opened.

The return to democracy brought the rebirth of cultural centers throughout Buenos Aires in the 1980s, though many closed their doors again in the following decade. After 2000, the city's Department of Culture revitalized many of these spaces through its Neighborhood Culture (Cultura en Barrios) program and proposed that each center should have its own unique name. The Roberto Santoro Cultural Center was named for the neighborhood's own poet and honors him by working to preserve memory and popular culture.

# 144. **Faculty of Agronomy – Agronomía Neighborhood**

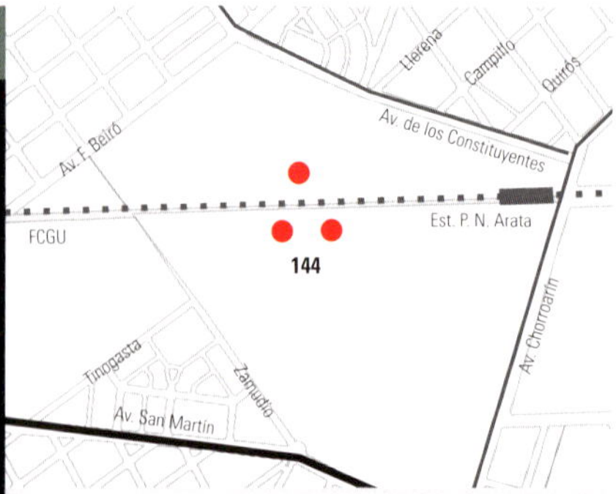


**LOCATION:** AV. SAN MARTÍN 4453
**TRANSPORTATION:** BUSES: 47, 57, 78, 105, 133, 134, 146. TRAIN STATION: ARATA (URQUIZA LINE).

The University of Buenos Aires Faculty of Agronomy is located on thirty hectares within Buenos Aires city limits, adjacent to the residential neighborhood known as Agronomía. The Commission of Parks and Green Spaces (Comisión de Parques y Paseos) first designated this area as parkland in 1893 because of its extremely fertile soil. The original plan called for the construction of a greenspace far outside the city center on an area of 80 to 100 hectares, though an executive order from 1901 assigned 185 hectares to the project, thirty of which were set aside for the future Faculty. This space, originally intended as an "agronomy farm," evolved into the Agronomy and Veterinary Institute in 1904, and then the Agronomy and Veterinary Faculty of the University of Buenos Aires in 1909.

The Faculty became a hub for the surrounding area as it attracted infrastructural improvements such as paved streets and a train station. Houses gradually appeared nearby, and the neighborhood known as Agronomía was officially founded on September 25, 1904.

## Enacting memory

The neighborhood and university communities have collaborated on several commemorative sites within the grounds of the Faculty. The Bosque de los Derechos Humanos (Human Rights Forest) was created in 1997, twenty-one years after the military coup, by the Student Union's Human Rights Commission. Its goal was to foster consciousness and keep alive the hope for justice.

In 2004 Buenos Aires City Council honored disappeared agronomy students by designating a plaque to

HUMAN RIGHTS WOOD

TRIBUTES IN FRONT OF THE FACULTY OF AGRONOMY.

commemorate the students as well as the entire period during which the military imposed its own appointed administrators on the Faculty.

Other memorial sites were inaugurated in 2004 on the neighborhood's one-hundredth anniversary. A time capsule was buried as part of a long day of celebrations. It contained a copy of the *Nunca Más* report (see "Nunca Más Square and Cultural Center," p. 186) and messages written by local students and by the neighborhood's Centenary Commission; these objects were to be preserved until the community's next major anniversary, on September 25, 2054. The Agronomy and Veterinary Faculty collaborated with the Historical Studies Committee of the neighborhoods of Agronomía and Parque Chas to organize this event. Another activity involved the planting of one hundred trees surrounding the plaque honoring disappeared students. Teachers and students from local schools adopted the trees and took part in the ceremony. A plaque created by the Centenary Commission and the Roberto Santoro Cultural Center (see "Roberto Santoro Cultural Center," p. 182) was also dedicated in honor of disappeared residents from the neighborhood.

A memorial ceremony was held on March 24, 2006, thirty years after the coup, to commemorate disappeared agronomy graduates. Two plaques were dedicated: one honoring students, and another paying tribute to two agricultural engineers disappeared in 1977. María Marta Badano and José Oreste Sorzana were also remembered for their political and social commitment. María Marta had been active in the Faculty first as a member of the student union and later as an instructor.

# 145. **Nunca Más Square and Cultural Center**



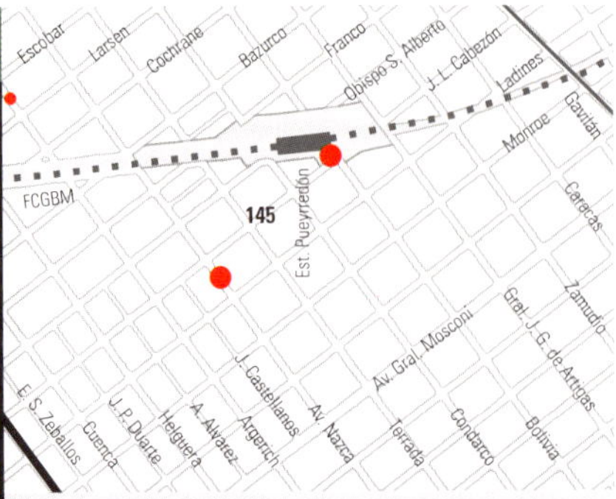


**LOCATION:** CULTURAL CENTER – AV. NAZCA 5099; PLAZA – BOLIVIA & J. L. CABEZÓN **TRANSPORTATION:** BUSES: 107, 110, 127, 169, 175. TRAIN STATION: PUEYRREDÓN (MITRE LINE).

### The Villa Pueyrredón Assembly

In March 2002 the residents of Villa Pueyrredón designated the area next to Pueyrredón Station (on the Mitre rail line), at the intersection of Cabezón and Bolivia Streets, as Nunca Más Square. They finally won official recognition for the name in April 2011, after years of petitions to city government. Buenos Aires City Council officially adopted the plaza's new name that day, rescinding the original name imposed by Brigadier Osvaldo Cacciatore during his time as mayor; Plaza Teniente General Eduardo Lonardi had commemorated the officer who led the military coup against Juan Domingo Perón's second presidential term in 1955.

In December 2001 a catastrophic banking crisis provoked major social and political unrest in Argentina; local residents throughout Buenos Aires organized neighborhood assemblies to propose community solutions to the problems that arose during those dramatic days. The members of the Villa Pueyrredón Assembly decided to rename the square where they held their meetings, as a first step toward mending the community's broken social bonds. This policy of neighborhood commemoration would be repeated in other neighborhoods. The Assembly launched an investigation into cases of disappearance that had affected the community. It assembled a list of detained and disappeared residents and dedicated a plaque in the square in their honor.

One year later the assembly inaugurated the Nunca Más Cultural Center at the corner of Nazca and Cabezón Streets. This institution hosts a variety of community activities. One member of the assembly, Ximena Rattoni, defines the Cultural Center's

NUNCA MÁS SQUARE.

work in the following terms: "We try to focus most of our efforts on issues facing the community today, even though we're always doing things to foster remembrance. We try to combine both kinds of work because it would not be very useful if we spent all our time paying tribute to the past. In our commemorative work we try to create spaces to foster remembrance and reflection. Because if we can't reflect, if we can't draw on the positive to transform the negative, then we are going to keep tripping over the same stones or falling into the same traps. . . . For us, remembrance takes place in the present moment."

**Nunca Más (Never again)**

The name chosen for the square and cultural center refers to one of the most important books in recent Argentine history. *Nunca Más* was the title given to the report published by the National Commission on the Disappearance of Persons* (CONADEP, Comisión Nacional Sobre la Desaparición de Personas), which was established by President Raúl Alfonsín a few days after he took office in December 1983. The title *Nunca Más* was quickly taken up as a slogan by a wide range of social actors to express both their repudiation of state terrorism and their expectations for their fledgling democracy. The book detailed both the methods and the scope of state terrorism. It was translated into several languages, and its Argentine and foreign editions have sold over half a million copies.

Victims' family members and human rights organizations conducted the first investigations into the whereabouts of the disappeared and the workings of state terrorism. The state took over this task after the return to democracy with the creation of the CONADEP. Human rights organizations called for the creation of a bicameral commission that would function through the National Congress and judge the dictatorship through political channels. Yet President Alfonsín instead decided to appoint a commission made up of high-profile public figures. He decreed the founding of the CONADEP on December 15, 11983, and named writer Ernesto Sábato as its director. The commission requested copies of the human rights organizations' archival documents and research materials.

The CONADEP made public its preliminary conclusions on a television program featuring participation and firsthand testimony by several survivors of the Clandestine Detention Centers. The program's title, *Nunca Más*, was quickly adopted as a slogan by the broader society and chosen as the title of the final published report. Although several people have tried to take credit for the title, its origins can be traced to a monument in the Dachau concentration camp in Munich, Germany, where a similar phrase appears in several different languages.

The CONADEP filed its report on August 6, 1984. It received testimony about 8,960 cases of disappearance and proved that 340 buildings had been used as Clandestine Detention Centers.

Seventy thousand people came out in public support when Ernesto Sábato presented the report to President Raúl Alfonsín at the Casa Rosada (government house). Many demonstrators then marched to the Federal Courts to demand that the justice system prosecute those implicated in the crimes.

The military had published its own "Final Report of the Military Junta Regarding the War on Subversion and Terrorism" (Documento final de la Junta Militar sobre la guerra contra la subversion y el terrorismo) on April 28, 1983, shortly before giving up power. It discredited the reports of disappearance and concluded that the military's actions would be judged only by "divine justice" (Crenzel 2008). Along with this report the military passed a Law of National Pacification, known as the "self-amnesty law," by which it hoped to prevent the prosecution of those responsible for state terrorism. This law was later repealed and declared unconstitutional by the Alfonsín government.

At first Alfonsín's government suggested human rights violators should be tried through Military Tribunals in order to avoid undermining the integrity of military institutions. Yet the tribunals' inaction quickly made it clear that justice could never be achieved through these channels. Eventually pressure from human rights organizations and the broader society prompted the government to transfer the trials to the federal justice system. Human rights interests argued that the traditional practice by which military personnel were subject only to military tribunals did not apply in cases of crimes against humanity. The investigation carried out by the CONADEP was then used by the Federal Tribunals as evidence in the Trial of the Military Juntas.*

Public Prosecutor Julio Strassera made the following observations in his closing statement at the trial: "We, the Argentine people, have tried to achieve peace by forgetting the past, but we have failed; we have already spoken of past amnesties that were unsuccessful. We have tried to achieve peace through violence and the extermination of our opponents, but we have failed; I am referring to the period we have just described. The current trial and the sentence that I am proposing make it our responsibility to build a peace based on memory, not forgetting. Justice, not violence. This is the opportunity before us, and it may be our last. With these considerations in mind, I hereby charge the defendants with the crimes that have been described, and I request that in the final ruling they receive the following sentences: Jorge Rafael Videla: life imprisonment . . . ; Emilio Eduardo Massera: life imprisonment . . . ; Orlando Ramón Agosti: life imprisonment . . . ; Roberto Eduardo Viola: life imprisonment; Armando Lamruchini: life imprisonment; Leopoldo Fortunato Galtieri: fifteen years imprisonment; Omar Rubén Graffiña: fifteen years imprisonment; Jorge Isaac Anaya: twelve years imprisonment; Basilio Lami Dozo: ten years imprisonment. . . . Your Honors: I explicitly decline any claims to originality in my choice of closing words. I wish to close this statement with a phrase that is not my own, because it already belongs to the Argentine people. Your Honors: Nunca Más."

Over time the CONADEP report became the principal source of information about the mechanisms and scope of state terrorism. Its original publication prompted a great deal of controversy, in particular because of Alfonsín's decision not to include the names of Armed Forces and Security Forces personnel accused of committing human rights crimes. Alfonsín resisted pressure from human rights organizations to publish these names because he feared a military backlash. In later years civil society groups working on issues relating to state terrorism began to question the explanatory framework laid out by Ernesto Sábato in the prologue of *Nunca Más.* Many critics see in this prologue the foundational ideas behind what came to be called the theory of the two demons ("teoría de los dos demonios"). With little evidence and no historical analysis, this prologue laid out a narrative that depicted civil society as the defenseless bystander caught in the crossfire between the guerrilla movements and the Armed Forces. To a certain extent, then, military pressure during the early transition to democracy influenced the way the book's prologue framed the analysis in *Nunca Más.*

Cordoban philosopher Héctor Schmucler has proposed a more responsible interpretation of the country's recent past that rejects the very idea of demons:

"When we speak of demons—regardless of whether or not there is a theory—we find ourselves with a serious problem, though it may not be the problem identified by the human rights groups, no matter how justified their criticisms and indignation. The problem of demonization does not stem from the

NUNCA MÁS CULTURAL CENTER.

TRIBUTE TO THE DISAPPEARED FROM VILLA PUEYRREDÓN.

comparison between the guerrillas and the repressive forces, for example; that is not the problem. Neither is the idea that the repressive forces were the sole demons. The problem is that if they were demons, we would consider them blameless. Demons can't be anything but demons, which means they're not responsible for being demons. Yet if we are responsible, if each and every one of us is responsible for our own actions, if there is any meaning behind the violence that engulfed us for years, thirty or forty years ago, then it is because that violence was committed by human beings. And that is why they can be held responsible" (Schmucler, 2007).

# 146. **Grafa Murals**

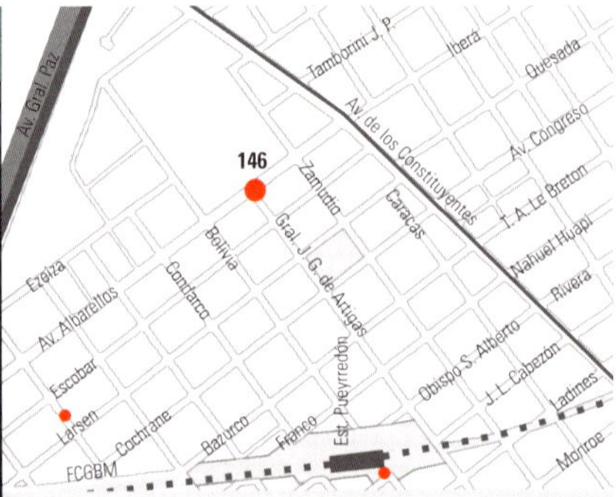


**LOCATION**: AV. ALBARELLOS BETWEEN 2400 AND 2600
**TRANSPORTATION:** BUSES: 110, 111, 127, 140, 169, 175. TRAIN STATION: PUEYRREDÓN (MITRE LINE).

On October 23, 2000, forty-eight murals were inaugurated in the neighborhood of Villa Pueyrredón to commemorate the Grafa factory's importance to the neighborhood's development. Originally known as Textil Sudamericana, the company at one time employed seven thousand workers. The murals were painted on the former factory's walls by students and teachers from schools in District No. 16; the History and Culture Committee of Villa Pueyrredón and the Historical Institute of the City of Buenos Aires contributed documents and photographs. Many local residents, including former Grafa workers, also shared their own memories, descriptions, and anecdotes. One mural pays tribute to the shop-floor union delegates of the Grafa factory who were detained and disappeared during the last military dictatorship.

In June and July 1975 Grafa workers took part in protests against the economic policies put forward by Celestino Rodrigo, then Finance Minister in the government of Isabel Perón. Rodrigo had won his appointment thanks to pressure from José López Rega, Isabel's notorious adviser and leader of the right-wing paramilitary group known as the Argentine Anticommunist Alliance (see "Coordinación Federal," p. 17).

Rodrigo took office on June 2, 1975, and, two days later, announced a brutal policy of financial adjustments that came to be known as the Rodrigazo. These harsh reforms mirrored similar policies implemented in neighboring countries such as Chile; they signaled a new economic era marked by the concentration of wealth and the loss of historic labor gains. This moment signaled the end of decades of welfare state policies that, in April 1975, held the

MURAL CREATED BY SIXTH-GRADE STUDENTS FROM A NEIGHBORHOOD SCHOOL.

unemployment rate at 3.2 percent, an astonishing figure compared with the high unemployment of subsequent decades. Isabel Perón's government was paving the way for the neoliberal policies that would later be installed by the military government and its Finance Minister, José Alfredo Martínez de Hoz.

The Grafa workers participated in these protests that occurred just a few months before the coup. On June 4 Rodrigo announced increases of 100 percent to the exchange rate and public prices. U.S. dollar exchange rates jumped by 80 to 160 percent. Energy bills went up by 75 percent, gasoline by 181 percent, and other public utilities by between 40 and 75 percent. Train fares increased by 80 to 120 percent, and a bus ticket went from 1 peso to 1.50. Wages increased only 45 percent in the face of these price hikes, which meant a significant decrease in purchasing power.

This situation provoked a swift and powerful response from the labor movement, culminating in national strikes on July 7 and 8. Workers demanded that real wages be restored and called for the resignation of López Rega and Rodrigo. The mass protests against the Rodrigazo were exceptional for at least two reasons: they were the first national strikes against a Peronist government, and they were organized in spite of the resistance of trade union leaders, who had rejected the first strike calls that emerged from hundreds of factories between June 2 and 27. The union leadership distanced themselves from the protests until July, when pressure from their own rank-and-file membership forced them to join.

Shop-floor union commissions and elected delegates ignored their leaders' instructions to disband the protests and relied on a different type of organizing network to defend workers and their struggles. Inter-factory coordinating committees had been formed in 1973, connecting workers in different factories and cutting across the divisions between traditional trade union branches. Several different political organizations took part in the committees including the Peronist Workers Youth Movement* (JTP, Juventud Trabajadora Peronista), Grassroots Peronism* (Peronismo de Base), the Workers' Revolutionary Party* (Partido Revolucionario de los Trabajadores), Worker Politics* (Política Obrera), the Communist Party*, and the Revolutionary Communist Party (Partido Comunista Revolucionario). They promoted economic demands, pressured for greater union democracy, and challenged the trade union bureaucracy that controlled the Sixty-Two Organizations (the Peronist movement's block of loyal unions) and the General Confederation of Labor (CGT, Confederación General del Trabajo). They also denounced the murders of activists by the right-wing paramilitary organization known as the Triple A* (Argentine Anticommunist Alliance; see "Coordinación Federal," p. 17).

On July 3 large numbers of demonstrating workers in the city of La Plata clashed openly with police in front of the CGT's temporary headquarters in the Construction Workers' Union of Argentina (UOCRA, Unión Obrera de la Construcción de la República Argentina). The demonstrators included over two thousand employees of the Río Santiago Shipyards and companies such as Siap, Ofa, In-deco, Swift, Petroquímica Mosconi, Cochoflex, and Kaiser Aluminio as well as public employees from the justice system and the municipal government. They had assembled to demand that their leaders grant them the right to strike indefinitely. Meanwhile, far away, at the entrance to the Grafa factory in Villa Pueyrredón, the Federal Police Infantry Corps surprised workers from the morning shift as they were gathering to march to the Plaza de Mayo (see "Plaza de Mayo," p. 3). The police also dispersed activists and arrested ten workers in the neighborhood of Caballito and broke up a group of activists in the neighborhood of Mataderos.

MURAL CREATED BY THE UNION OF EDUCATION WORKERS.

MURAL FOR THE DISAPPEARED OF GRAFA.

Under pressure from the mounting conflicts, the CGT called a forty-eight-hour strike four days later, on July 7 and 8, and the government finally gave in to the workers' demands. Yet eight months after the protests the military government would use systematic state terror to put an end to the welfare state and implement neoliberal economic and political policies, imposing a new economic model whose basic principles would remain in place for the next three decades.

As one sign of this new economic climate, Walmart opened a store on the grounds of the former Grafa factory in the mid-1990s. This corporation currently faces 1,400 charges of violating child labor laws. In November 2005 a Norwegian ethics committee that investigated Walmart's activities in the United States, Canada, Nicaragua, El Salvador, Honduras, and Indonesia, among other countries, concluded that Walmart "systematically violates its employees' human and labor rights, . . . systematically employs minors in hazardous working conditions, discriminates against women, and does not compensate employees for overtime" (cited in "Noruega vende por razones éticas títulos de Freeport y de Wal-Mart," *El País,* June 7, 2006).

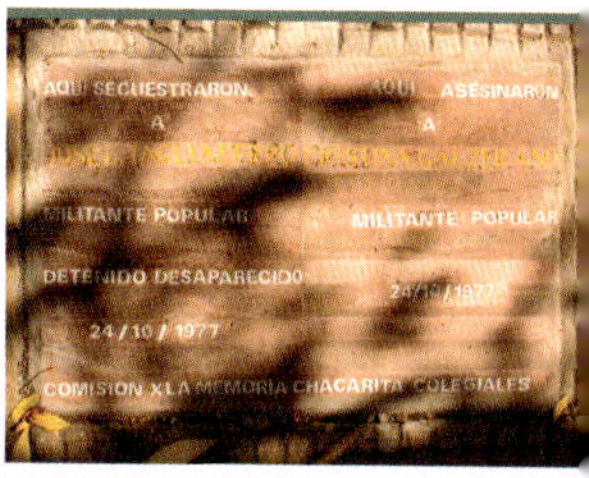


## 147. José Luis Tagliaferro – Cristina Galzerano

On October 27, 2007, residents of the neighborhoods of Chacarita and Colegiales joined with this couple's family members to dedicate a paving stone in their memory. Cristina was murdered at the entrance to her home, while José Luis was kidnapped and taken away alive. At that time they lived with Cristina's six-year-old son Esteban.

**LOCATION:** LEIVA 3972, CHACARITA

## 148. Roberto Santoro Square

In 1996 a small square (*plazoleta*) in the neighborhood of Chacarita was named after the poet Roberto Santoro, and two commemorative plaques were dedicated containing biographical information. Roberto had written, "If this fury called hope should escape, if it should one day leave us, I will crucify love and, after burying my brothers, I will take the tramway of death and lock my heart away in a square" (see p. 193).

**LOCATION:** AV. FOREST AND TEODORO GARCIA, CHACARITA

## 149. Esther Ballestrino de Careaga

Esther Ballestrino de Careaga had sought exile in Argentina as an opponent of the Alfredo Stroessner dictatorship in Paraguay. She married Paraguayan exile Raymundo Careaga, and they had three daughters. She began working with families of the disappeared when security forces kidnapped her son-in-law and her youngest daughter, Ana María, who was three months pregnant. Esther did not stop searching for the others even after her daughter was released. She was kidnapped on December 8, 1977 (see p. 99).

**LOCATION:** CORNER OF GANDARA AND BAUNESS, PARQUE CHAS

## 150. La Muralla Cultural Center

On February 17, 2006, a mural about the military dictatorship was painted in the La Muralla Cultural Center, the first in a series of neighborhood murals painted around the city. This project was undertaken by members of the Communist Party, the Youth Federation of the neighborhood of La Paternal, the group Culture in Movement (Cultura en Movimiento, from Chile and Argentina), and the Jorge Calvo Mural School Brigade.

**LOCATION:** ADOLFO DICKMAN 1361, PATERNAL

## 151. Tributes in the Avenida San Martín

On June 3, 2006, the Commission of Neighborhoods for Remembrance and Justice of the neighborhoods of La Paternal and Villa Mitre, along with the Association of Fans of Argentinos Juniors for Remembrance (Hinchas de Argentinos Juniors x la Memoria) placed paving stones in memory of Guillermo Moralli, Ernesto Szerszewicz, Néstor Sanmartino, Héctor Moreira, and Américo Marchetti (see p. 209).

**LOCATION:** AT THE INTERSECTION OF AV. SAN MARTIN WITH DONATO ALVAREZ, NICASIO OROÑO, AND J. B. JUSTO, PATERNAL

## 152. José Eduardo Feldman

"Here studied José Feldman, a grassroots activist disappeared by the forces of state terrorism on August 6, 1977." The paving stone honoring Feldman is located in front of Commercial School No. 20. José studied law and played minor league soccer for the Argentinos Juniors Club. A paving stone was dedicated to Gregorio Nachman the same day, during celebrations marking the neighborhood's 102nd anniversary.

**LOCATION:** NICASIO OROÑO 2131, PATERNAL

## 153. Gregorio Nachman

Theater actor and director Gregorio Nachman was kidnapped on June 19, 1976. Along with the paving stone placed in his memory, a hall in the Auditorium Theater in Mar del Plata bears his name. June 19 was established as the Day of Mar Del Plata Theater to remember him and Luis Conti, an actor who disappeared along with him (see p. 69).

**LOCATION:** CORNER OF AV. SAN MARTIN AND PAYSANDU, PATERNAL

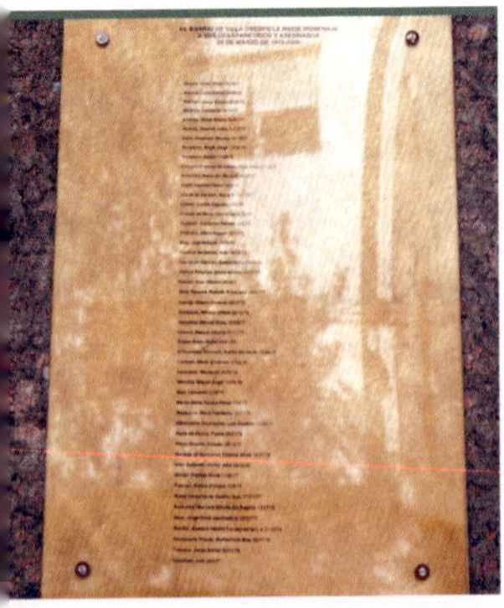

## 154. Tribute in the Neighborhood of Villa Crespo

A plaque was dedicated on March 29, 2006, to honor neighborhood residents who had been detained and disappeared. Family members, neighbors, friends, and fellow activists took part in the event. Local residents were invited to join a committee formed that day to investigate, defend, and pay tribute to the ideals and political struggles of those who had been disappeared.

**LOCATION:** CORNER OF AV. SCALABRINI ORTIZ AND DRAGO, VILLA CRESPO

## 155. Alicia D'Ambra – Cristina Navajas – Manuela Santucho

Alicia D'Ambra was first detained in 1975, although she managed to escape. She was kidnapped on July 12, 1976, and her brother Carlos was disappeared on November 20th. On April 16, 2005, the town of Alta Gracia in Córdoba gave their names to the street where they were born. Cristina, wife of Julio Santucho, was 2 months pregnant when kidnapped. Her son may have been born in captivity in early 1977. Manuela was seen in the Automotores Orletti CDC (see p. 220).

**LOCATION:** WARNES 735, VILLA CRESPO.

## 156. Scholem Aleijem School and the Zionist Youth Movement

On March 25, 2008, a plaque was hung to honor disappeared former students of the Scholem Aleijem School, along with the painting *Por la noche* (At night) by artist Nora Patrich. This event was organized by the school, the World Alumni Association, the Jewish–Argentine Mutual Association (AMIA), and the Association for the Families of Jews Disappeared in Argentina (AFDJA, Asociación de Familiares de Desaparecidos Judíos en la Argentina).

**LOCATION:** GURRUCHAGA 338, VILLA CRESPO

## 157. Horacio Elbert

A paving stone honoring Horacio Elbert was dedicated at the corner of his house as part of the Seventh Neighborhood Festival of Resistance. Activities followed in the nearby square, including performances by street musicians and dancers (*murgas*), a community meal (*olla popular*), and demands that disappeared witness Jorge Julio López be discovered alive (see p. 105) and that police and military personnel who had participated in the repression be imprisoned.

**LOCATION:** CORNER OF LUIS VIALE AND AV. SAN MARTIN, VILLA CRESPO

## 158. Mónica Goldstein

Sociologist and sculptor Mónica Goldstein was kidnapped on October 6, 1976, by a group of men who injured her and took her away in a car. Her husband and son later discovered that their apartment had been ransacked. A paving stone was dedicated in her memory on April 5, 2008; in attendance were Mónica's friends, her brother, her husband, and her son (who had traveled from Mexico especially for the occasion).

**LOCATION:** AV. CORRIENTES 4779, VILLA CRESPO.

## 159. **Father Pablo Gazzarri**

A plaque was dedicated in Plaza Esteban Echeverría on November 27, 2002 to commemorate Father Pablo Gazzarri. This event took place twenty-six years after his forced disappearance, with official recognition from Buenos Aires city government. The plaque reads, "In honor of Father Pablo María Gazzarri (Born 19/09/1944. Detained and disappeared on 27/11/1976). For his work on behalf of the poorest of the poor."

**LOCATION:** BAUNESS AND NAHUEL HUAPI, VILLA URQUIZA

## 160. **Rodolfo Walsh School No. 1**

School No. 1 had no identifying name until school administrators invited students, teachers, and parents to vote on one. They chose the name Rodolfo Walsh (see p. 96), and City Council approved the designation through Ordinance 52040/CJD/97. "He shall be remembered for more than just his death," reads the inscription beneath his name.

**LOCATION:** ARGERICH 5651, VILLA PUEYRREDON

# SECTOR 7

MONTE CASTRO, VILLA DEL PARQUE, VILLA DEVOTO, VILLA GENERAL MITRE, VILLA REAL, AND VILLA SANTA RITA

# 161. **Female Political Prisoners in Devoto Prison**

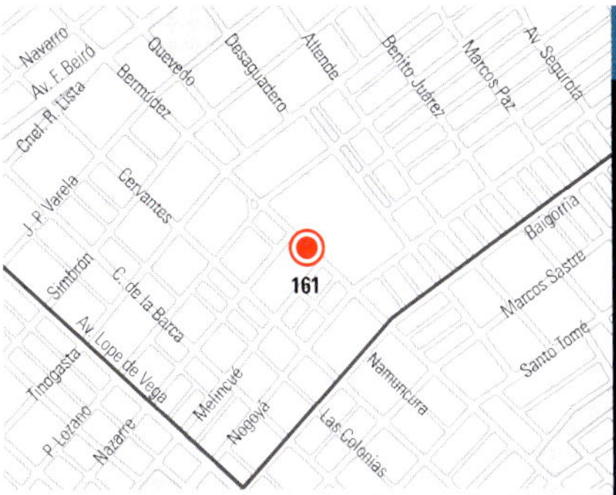


**LOCATION:** BERMUDEZ 2651
**TRANSPORTATION:** BUSES: 25, 47, 53, 85, 107, 109, 124.

The number of political prisoners in the Devoto Prison doubled after the military coup of 1976, and abuse inside the prison increased. By the middle of that year roughly three hundred prisoners were being held there for political reasons. By the end of the dictatorship's first year the number of political prisoners throughout the country had risen to over five thousand.

From 1975 on, political prisoners in Devoto were jailed under a system of maximum security that included tight restrictions on visiting hours, use of the yard, and access to published materials. Women imprisoned for political reasons were classified according to three categories: G1 denoted those viewed as unredeemable; G2 identified those considered capable of rehabilitation; G3 referred to women who were allowed some privileges. The different classifications determined the women's rights to spend leisure time in the prison yard, receive visitors, and buy specific items from the prison canteen.

Most of the eleven thousand political prisoners detained during the dictatorship were held under decree of the National Executive Power*, a form of official government detention without charge. Most remained in prison for seven years, the maximum period allowed by law.

### After the coup

The living conditions in Devoto were unhealthy. The building was infested with cockroaches and other bugs, mosquitoes, lice, and rats; the food, referred to as *tumba* ("grave"), usually consisted of rice or noodle stew swimming in fat. Prisoners often had to turn down meals no matter how hungry they were because the food served to them was rotten.

DEVOTO PRISON TODAY.

Conditions worsened in the weeks leading up to the coup. Acts of cruelty became more commonplace, aggravating the existing problem of overcrowding. The authors of the book *Nosotras, presas políticas* (We, female political prisoners) recall "the prison doctors who, when presented with a case of pneumonia or bronchitis, would conduct a gynecological examination, as well as the dentist who smoked and drank *yerba mate* while she pulled out teeth instead of offering treatment. There was also the case of the prison guard who refused a pair of twins their first visit with their mother because they were crying" (*Obra colectiva,* 2006).

**Women's prison**

During the dictatorship the prison held over twelve hundred female political prisoners informally accused of being "terrorist criminals" or "subversive criminals." The women were held without charge, legal counsel, or any formal legal proceedings. They were political activists, including some members of armed movements, who had been fighting for a fundamental transformation of society.

Political prisoners were kept separate from common prisoners. Most of them lived in the "blocks": prison floors containing twenty-two cells, each measuring less than 9 feet by 7½. Four prisoners were forced to share this small space for seventeen hours each day, using it as bedroom, eating area, and bathroom.

Most of the women had been illegally detained and tortured before entering Devoto. According to survivors, "After those experiences, arrival at the prison was like a happy ending to a horrific sequence of events. It meant you had surfaced in a legal, institutional context where you were more likely to survive." Arriving at the prison after days or weeks of secret detention, the women could shower, sleep in a bed, drink hot *mate,* communicate with family members, and, most importantly, "see the friendly faces of the women who were already there" (*Obra colectiva,* 2006).

There was still no guarantee of survival, however. Many women, like Teresa Di Martino, were disappeared after their release. In the book *Nosotras, presas políticas,* Cristina Torres recalls how Teresa feared for her life and resisted release. She had already been imprisoned inside the network of Clandestine Detention Centers and had been deeply scarred by the extreme torture she had endured. She often said she couldn't believe she had been legalized. Teresa was last seen in the Clandestine Detention Center known as El Vesubio* by a survivor who heard her being interrogated and tortured (*Obra colectiva,* 2006).

Political prisoners were constantly moved around to deepen their sense of uprootedness and isolation; sometimes their final destination was not another prison but death. The report by the National Commission on the Disappearance of Persons* (CONADEP, Comisión Nacional sobre la Desaparición de Personas) records the cases of 157 political prisoners added to the list of the disappeared after the Executive Power had ordered their release. Another twenty cases have been identified of prisoners disappeared after a judge had ordered their release from detention under National Executive Order. There were orders to shoot prisoners, sometimes even inside the prisons. As explained in *Nunca Más* (CONADEP, 1984), "If the authorities had decided they were to die, they would be riddled with bullets in an 'attempted escape' or gunned down in an 'armed confrontation.' "

These prisoners would later be listed as having died "in combat" or through the application of the "law of flight," by which authorities simulated an attempted escape because the law permitted them to shoot a fleeing prisoner in the back. The Margarita Belén massacre is one example of this kind of deliberate cover-up

VISITORS' ENTRANCE ON BERMÚDEZ STREET.

of summary executions. On December 12, 1976, seven political prisoners were moved from the maximum-security prison known as Regional Unit No. 7, in Resistencia, to the local city hall. They were severely tortured along with other political prisoners held there. A military commission appeared in the early morning hours of December 13 and presented a prisoner transfer order, a simulated transfer intended to cover up the prisoners' summary execution. This event, now known as the Margarita Belén massacre, left twenty-two dead, five of whom have yet to be identified.

**Mothers' cell block**

Pregnant women and women with small children were held separately in Block 49; the entire sixty-five-by-thirty-foot space served as kitchen, bathroom, bedroom, and library. The prisoners staged a hunger strike in 1975 to demand improved conditions; at that time, sixty-seven women and twelve nursing babies were living in the block.

"We cooked. We kept really busy all day, giving classes, holding political discussions, keeping up our military training," recalls Diana Cruces, who was detained at the very beginning of her pregnancy (Paleo, 2004). Before the coup, infants were allowed to stay with their mothers until the age of two; afterwards, the period was cut to six months.

Diana Cruces recalls, "They took me to the Sardá maternity clinic, where all the other women had given birth, but there was no room there. We went to the Ramos Mejía Hospital, but it was also full. They finally left me at the Rawson Hospital." Members of the security forces stayed in the room as the women went through labor. "They took me to the labor room. I went in with a doctor, nurses, and a group of armed infantrymen. The doctor asked them to leave the operating room because I was about to give birth. The soldiers refused, and the doctor got into an argument with them because he wouldn't attend to a patient with them in the room. Finally I said, 'Doctor, please hurry, the baby's coming.' "

The babies endured the same prison conditions as their mothers, remaining locked up twenty-two hours a day. The women received no extra milk for them, and they had no way to sterilize bottles or warm up milk.

### The showcase prison

Devoto Prison's different sections were spread out over the grounds, which measured four city blocks. These included areas for body searches, education, security, medical and spiritual assistance, and legal affairs, as well as the hospital. The prison was presentable enough to be shown to visiting international human rights organizations and thus served to hide the crimes being committed in the Clandestine Detention Centers. "We used to call it the 'showcase prison' because of these features of legality and public display" (*Obra colectiva,* 2006).

The day before the Inter-American Commission on Human Rights (IACHR) arrived in mid-1979, female prisoners under the age of eighteen were moved and isolated from the other prisoners in Devoto so the commission members would not see them. The prison priest, who the prisoners nicknamed San Fachón (St. Fascist), visited them regularly during this period of separation, trying to convince them to sign a statement of repentance in return for a "promise" of freedom.

Authorities also moved older women and those who were very ill so that the members of the IACHR would not see them being detained under such harsh conditions. Prison conditions nevertheless included humiliating body searches for both the female prisoners and their visitors, confinement for fourteen hours a day, and solitary confinement for serious breaches of discipline.

### Information and communication within the prison

Taking advantage of the prison's location in the middle of the city, women used the *jarreo* (an action whose name derives from the Spanish word for jug) to draw attention to their situation. They would bang their metal water jugs on the floor to attract the attention of neighbors when they were being taken away to an unknown destination.

The punishment cells were called *chanchos* ("pigs"); here women lost access to privileges such as mail, visiting hours, and use of the prison yard. Women were prevented from building relationships through the *calesita* ("carousel"), which referred to the periodic rotation of cells. The same tactic was used for rotations between prisons; a prisoner might be moved from one end of the country to the other so as to confuse family members seeking information about her whereabouts.

A pane of glass separated visitors from prisoners to prevent direct contact. Letters, books, and newspapers were censored as they entered the prison, though the prisoners developed alternative methods of communication to get around these obstacles. One was the *caramelo* ("candy"), a message written in tiny letters on cigarette paper. Prisoners used it to communicate with each other and to transmit information between the prison and the outside world through family members.

**Today**

Recently, former political prisoners have conducted a series of visit to prisons around the country, including an event at Devoto to honor "those who resisted and died behind bars." At the last minute, the Federal Penitentiary Service withdrew permission for the visitors to enter Devoto, arguing that it might be too stressful for the current prisoners.

The event was instead staged outside the prison's entrance on September 12, 2008. A plaque was placed in memory of three deceased political prisoners from Devoto, including Teresa di Martino, Alicia Pais, who died inside the prison because of a lack of medical attention, and Mario Abel Amaya, member of congress, defense lawyer representing political prisoners, and activist in the Radical Party. Amaya was transferred to the Central Penitentiary Hospital in Devoto from Rawson Prison, arriving in very poor health because of torture. Former senator Hipólito Solari Irigoyen was detained at the same time; he saw Amaya in Rawson Prison for the last time: "His head was split open, he was bruised from the beatings, and he spoke with difficulty. He managed to tell me, 'I'm in really bad shape'" ("Recuerdo de Mario Abel Amaya," *La Nación,* September 30, 2001). He was moved in this condition over fourteen hundred kilometers and died shortly after being admitted to the Penitentiary Hospital in October 1976. Amaya was being detained under Executive Order, accused of "ties to subversive activities."

# 162. **Disappeared Teachers Remembered in Their Schools**

Buenos Aires City Council passed a law in 2001 that committed the city government to compiling a list of all the students, teachers, and educational staff from every education level who were victims of state terror. To date, the names of 108 educators have been registered. Many schools in the city formally remember teachers who were disappeared.

### 162a. Américo Jorge Marchetti

ABEL AYERZA SCHOOL NO. 23
AV. SALVADOR MARIA DEL CARRIL 3650
VILLA DEVOTO

"Since the day after his disappearance I can remember hearing the whispered comments made by other teachers in the school's courtyard. When we asked what had happened to the teacher who didn't come any more, they told us he was on leave. I think they knew what had happened to him from the day of his disappearance; I'm not sure. But people said they'd taken him away in a car from a neighborhood park, and supposedly several students had seen it happen" [FMA]. This is the account left by one of Marchetti's former students.

On August 16, 2005, a plaque was unveiled in the Abel Ayerza School to remember Américo Jorge Marchetti. His wife Marta Kleinberg participated in the ceremony along with family members and former colleagues and students from the school.

Américo was thirty-three years old when he was kidnapped in public in August 1976. He was later seen in the Clandestine Detention Center known as Coordinación Federal (see p. 17). He also appears in the mural to disappeared fans at the Argentinos Juniors soccer stadium (see p. 209).

ABEL AYERZA SCHOOL, WHERE TEACHER AMÉRICO JORGE MARCHETTI IS REMEMBERED.

PLAQUES IN HONOR OF TEACHER JORGE LUIS CHINETTI, KIDNAPPED AT THE ENTRANCE TO THE SCHOOL.

TEACHER PATRICIA PALACÍN IS REMEMBERED IN RUÍZ DE LOS LLANOS SCHOOL.

### 162b. Jorge Luis Chinetti

ROBERTO M. ORTIZ SCHOOL NO. 24
BAHIA BLANCA 2535. VILLA DEVOTO

Jorge Luis "El Chino" Chinetti was a gym teacher. He was detained in broad daylight near the school by a group of armed plainclothes men, as he was leaving after classes ended. His family received an anonymous call in 1978 informing them that he was being held in the ESMA (Navy School of Mechanics; see p. 153), though no witnesses have come forward to confirm this information.

Jorge was twenty-seven years old at the time, and his daughter was just a few months old. In 2005 a plaque was dedicated to his memory at the school where he was working at the time of his disappearance on August 16, 1978. Participants in the ceremony included education authorities from the City of Buenos Aires and representatives from human rights organizations and the Confederation of Education Workers of the Argentine Republic (CTERA). Jorge's wife, Alicia Ocariz, spoke a few words in his memory when the plaque was unveiled. A poem was read in his memory, and a children's choir performed.

### 162c. Patricia Palacín

R. RUIZ DE LOS LLANOS SCHOOL NO. 4
AV. F. BEIRO 4548. VILLA DEVOTO

On Tuesday, April 5, 2005, a ceremony was held to remember teacher and school psychologist Patricia Palacín and her husband, Roberto Toranzo, who was an electronics technician, an engineering student at the University of Buenos Aires, and an employee of a metalworking company. Patricia was twenty-five years old and three months pregnant at the time of her kidnapping on April 5, 1978. Her husband was abducted on the same day, and both remain disappeared.

The ceremony was organized by friends of Patricia and Roberto and by Roberto's brother, Francisco. Participants included representatives of the Buenos Aires city government's Education Secretariat and Under-Secretariat of Human Rights, the Union of Education Workers (UTE, Unión de Trabajadores de la Educacion), the Abuelas de Plaza de Mayo, and administrators from School No. 4 and from School Districts 16 and 17.

Family members, friends, and the Abuelas de Plaza de Mayo continue to search for Patricia's and Roberto's child (see "Dr. Cosme Argerich Central Military Hospital," p. 77).

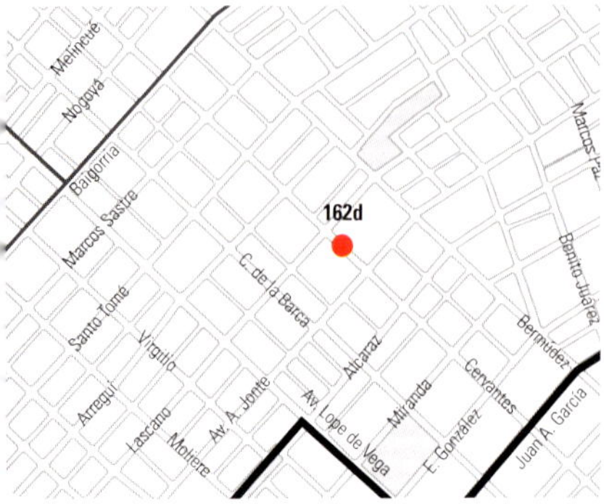

TRIBUTE TO TEACHER MIGUEL ANDRÉS DEL VALLE.

## 162d. Miguel Andrés del Valle

ALEJANDRO AGUADO SCHOOL NO. 2
CERVANTES 1911. MONTE CASTRO

Miguel Andrés del Valle was born in the town of Miramar in the province of Buenos Aires on February 16, 1949; he lived in the neighborhood of Flores in Buenos Aires. He completed his teacher training in 1966 at Mariano Acosta School and went on to teach in a number of schools, including Alejandro Aguado School No. 2.

Miguel was a union organizer and activist in the revolutionary movement known as ERP (Ejército Revolucionario del Pueblo, or People's Revolutionary Army*). He met his wife, Mónica Pites, through his political activism, and they had two children named Ana and Santiago. Miguel and Mónica were abducted together on May 12, 1976; their burned bodies were discovered in El Palomar, in the province of Buenos Aires, on June 19 of that year; both bodies had bullet wounds in the back of the head.

A plaque was unveiled in their honor on May 12, 2006, in a ceremony organized by the Human Rights Coordinating Office of the city government's Ministry of Education. This ceremony closed a series of activities involving sixth- and seventh-grade students, including workshops and talks by Miguel's children, Ana and Santiago del Valle.

## 162e. María del Carmen Di Blasi

REPUBLICA DE MEXICO SCHOOL NO. 7
JUAN AGUSTIN GARCIA 2755. VILLA GENERAL MITRE

María del Carmen Di Blasi was born on July 5, 1944. She taught in a number of schools in School District 17; the last was the República de México School, where she taught a fourth-grade class. She had two children, Mariana and Pablo.

María del Carmen and her partner were kidnapped by a Special Task Group* that burst into their home on the night of July 5, 1978. She was thirty-four years old.

The República de México School held a ceremony in María del Carmen's honor on Tuesday, July 4, 2006; the ceremony was organized by the Buenos Aires Ministry of Education's Coordinating Committee on Human Rights. María del Carmen's children attended, along with teachers and students. During the ceremony a commemorative plaque was unveiled, and students in the fourth, fifth, and

TRIBUTE TO TEACHER MARÍA DEL CARMEN DI BLASI.

sixth grades put the finishing touches on a major project they had been working on. Students participated in workshops about state terrorism using materials developed especially by the Ministry of Education; they also had an opportunity to speak with members of Di Blasi's family.

## CTERA

The Confederation of Education Workers (CTERA) is working on a project to collect information and reconstruct the life histories of teachers and students across the country who were victims of state terror. The list includes more than six hundred names.

CTERA was formed in September 1973 as the first national union to represent teachers. From the beginning, the union joined its demands to those of the broader labor movement, identifying itself with other radical unions. The unions within CTERA faced difficulties during the government of Isabel Perón (1974–1976), which saw the strengthening of the orthodox Peronist labor movement (see *Abrazo*. Sculpture in the ATE," p. 109). As repression increased around 1975, its member unions came under attack, and its leaders were threatened by the right-wing paramilitary organization known as the Triple A* (Argentine Anticommunist Alliance; see "Coordinación Federal," p. 17). Despite this repressive climate, the CTERA played a leading role in the creation of the Permanent Assembly for Human Rights (APDH, Asamblea Permanente por los Derechos Humanos).

CTERA held what would be its final Confederal Conference in March 1976. Isauro Arancibia, one of the confederation's founding members, was murdered along with his brother Arturo in the main office of his union in Tucumán early on the morning of the coup. Over time, more than six hundred teachers who had been active in political, social, or union organizations were disappeared, jailed, or forced into exile. The military government took over many of the grassroots CTERA unions; most of the confederation's unions ceased their activities in the face of persecution.

The few remaining members of the CTERA's National Executive Board devoted themselves almost exclusively to managing claims of habeas corpus* and assisting members who had been detained. A typical case was that of Alfredo Bravo, Secretary General of CTERA and joint president of the Permanent Assembly for Human Rights. He was kidnapped from the school where he worked and tortured in September 1977. International outcry and public interviews with the Minister of Interior led to his being "legalized," and in mid-1978 he was granted supervised release.

On the occasion of the visit to Argentina by the Inter-American Commission on Human Rights (IACHR) in 1979, CTERA presented the commission with a list of teachers who had been disappeared, detained, or fired.

Labor organizing increased and strengthened after the return to democracy. During the Alfonsín and Menem presidencies, CTERA headed the teachers' struggle and thereby won legitimacy as the national trade union representing education workers. In the 1990s the organization strongly opposed government policies that undermined education, particularly the Federal Law of Education, which, among other things, absolved the state of its responsibility to maintain the education system.

CTERA is currently the largest teachers' union and one of the largest labor organizations in the country. It numbers some 234,000 members, or 45 percent of Argentina's teachers. It is affiliated with the Argentine Workers' Federation (CTA, Central de Trabajadores Argentinos), an organization it helped to found. It devotes itself to the defense of public education, an institution that is fundamental to social equality.

# 163. **Mural in the Argentinos Juniors Soccer Stadium**

"We at Argentinos Juniors believe that our participation in this event is very important because those of us involved in sport, and especially soccer, are deeply indebted to Argentine society. Sport was used to whitewash the image of the military dictatorship, to distract people from their real problems and from what was happening in the country during those years. So our involvement in this event also serves as a kind of self-reflection on the attitudes displayed by soccer clubs during the dictatorship." Carlos Russo, a member of the Board of Directors of Argentinos Juniors made these comments during a ceremony held on March 25, 2006, to inaugurate the mural painted on one of the walls of the Diego Armando Maradona Stadium.

**LOCATION:** GAVILAN 2151
**TRANSPORTATION:** BUSES: 63, 109, 113, 133, 135.

The mural pays tribute to Argentine Juniors fans who were detained and disappeared during the last military dictatorship and to all victims of state terrorism. It was painted by the artist Sebastián Maissa following an initiative launched by the Commission for Remembrance and Justice of the Neighborhoods of La Paternal and Villa Mitre. Local residents helped with the work, as did participants in the Informal Education workshops (Talleres de Educación No Formal) given by the city's Ministry of Education. The mural is located beside Visitor Entrance No. 4 on Boyacá Street. It bears the names of Horacio Héctor Moreira, disappeared in the Navy School of Mechanics (ESMA; see p. 153); Américo Jorge Marchetti, who was taken to the Clandestine Detention Center known as Coordinación Federal (see p. 17); Néstor Julio Sanmartino, a worker in the former city yard who was disappeared in 1977 (see p. 231); Guillermo "Willy" Moralli and Ernesto "Jaio" Szerszewicz, both taken to the El Vesubio* detention center by security forces under the order of General Guillermo Suárez Mason.

MURAL IN THE ARGENTINOS JUNIORS STADIUM ON BOYACÁ STREET.

Suárez Mason was commander of the First Military Corps from 1976

THE MURAL WAS CREATED TO MARK THE THIRTIETH ANNIVERSARY OF THE COUP.

to 1980. He oversaw several Clandestine Detention Centers, among them Automotores Orletti (see p. 220), Pozo de Banfield*, La Cacha*, and El Olimpo. Suárez Mason was both a supporter and an honorary member of Argentinos Juniors, a privilege he held until it was revoked in 1999, subsequent to an initiative launched by other club supporters. Other soccer clubs similarly honored figures within the repressive forces.

The dictatorship chose two stadiums in the city of Buenos Aires to host two of the most important games in the World Cup of 1978. One was River Plate's Estadio Monumental. It was completely renovated; old grandstands were refurbished, and a whole new seating area was built. Entrances were modernized, and the stadium was equipped with an electronic screen, towers, and high-tech lighting. The state assumed the full burden of this expensive project, which involved many irregularities in estimated costs and execution. In return, the River Plate club gave honorary lifetime memberships to several members of the First Military Junta: Emilio Eduardo Massera, Jorge Rafael Videla, and Orlando Ramón Agosti. These honors remained in place until 1997, fourteen years after the return to democracy.

The "Monumental" project also had an impact on the neighborhood surrounding the stadium. The Bajo Belgrano shantytown was forcibly eradicated in order to "beautify" the area, which would be seen by foreign journalists and tourists; the same thing would occur later in precarious neighborhoods in Retiro and Colegiales (see "Cristo Obrero Chapel. Father Carlos Mugica," p. 25). In 1980 the Municipal Housing Commission celebrated this eviction in its *Blue Book* (*Libro Azul*), calling it the "first great expulsion" of a shantytown located near "landscaped areas, lakes, a municipal golf course, private clubs, the riding clubs, etc., . . . in one of the capital city's best neighborhoods." The first few blocks were "swept away" in record time on March 11, 1978. It took just over two months to finish the job and "recover 7.2 hectares of prized land that can be dedicated to a social and urban planning program befitting Buenos Aires's status as a 'Great City' of cosmopolitan extension." The "cleared" land was soon earmarked for a special housing development registered as "U23" in the Urban Planning Code that had been approved a year before the World Cup. In subsequent years poor residents were forced out of the area, and high-end apartment buildings and luxury homes were built to house the wealthy.

The World Cup, a mass sporting event used by the military to foster national unity and political legitimacy, brought with it the mass expulsion of thousands of city residents. One year later, in 1979, director Sergio Renán titled his film about the event *La fiesta de todos* (Everyone's party).

## 164. **The Disappeared of La Paternal**

On June 10, 2007, a paving stone was placed in Plaza Roque Sáenz Peña to remember the neighborhood's disappeared. The day's events included a festival, music, and games. Organizers also replaced a damaged paving stone that day that had been dedicated earlier to those killed in the police repression of December 19 and 20, 2001.

**LOCATION:** CORNER OF AV. JUAN B. JUSTO AND BOYACA, VILLA GRAL. MITRE

## 165. **Kleber Mauricio Silva Iribarnegaray**

"Mauricio Silva Iribarnegaray, Uruguayan Salesian priest and street sweeper, was kidnapped from this site on July 14, 1977." Neighborhood residents, former co-workers, and fellow activists took part in the ceremony dedicating a paving stone in his memory. Mauricio was a priest from the Uruguayan Salesian Congregation; he worked as a city street sweeper in the former city yard of Floresta.

**LOCATION:** CORNER OF MARGARINO CERVANTES AND TERRERO, VILLA GRAL MITRE

# SECTOR 8

CABALLITO, FLORES, FLORESTA, PARQUE CHACABUCO, AND VÉLEZ SARSFIELD

# 166. **El Olimpo**



Welcome to the Olympus of the gods," announced the mural that greeted prisoners when they arrived at the torture chamber, which was known as the "operating room" (*quirófano*). The Clandestine Detention Center known as El Olimpo functioned in a building at the corner of Ramón Falcón and Lacarra Streets from August 1978 through February 1979. Roughly five hundred people were detained there after being kidnapped as part of the military junta's plan of repression.

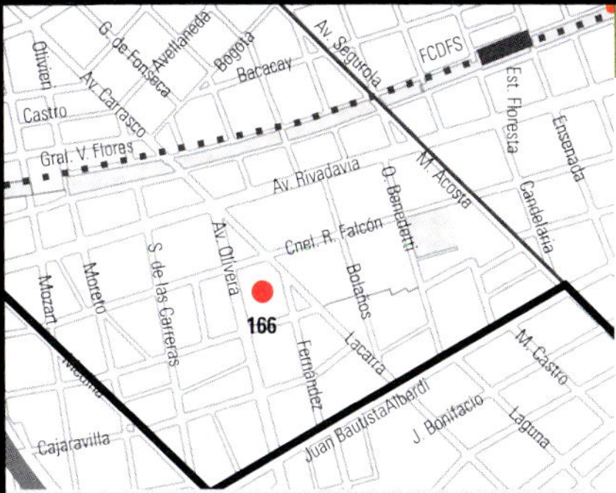


**LOCATION:** COLONEL R. FALCON AND LACARRA STREETS
**TRANSPORTATION:** BUSES: 1, 2, 5, 36, 46, 49, 63, 86, 88, 92, 96, 107, 113, 114, 136, 153, 163, 182.
TRAIN: FLORESTA STATION (SARMIENTO LINE).

## The site's history

The site known as El Olimpo was originally a tramway station; its trams carried passengers and cargo from the nearby meat-processing plants and slaughterhouses. The building became a bus station when the city's tramways stopped operating in the 1960s and was later transferred to the Transport Department. In 1976 it was acquired by the Federal Police to replace the Club Atlético detention center (see p. 129), which was to be demolished to make way for construction of the 25 de Mayo Freeway.

In fact, the Club Atlético continued to function from mid-1976 through early 1979; although it changed name and location, it maintained the same prisoners, guards, and interrogators. Originally called Atlético or Club Atlético, it began operating in 1976 in the basement of the Argentine Federal Police Supplies Department, at the corner of Avenida Paseo Colón and Cochabamba Street. The premises were temporarily evacuated in December 1977, and the prisoners were transferred to the detention center

ISOLATION SECTOR.

CORNER OF RAMÓN FALCÓN AND LACARRA STREETS.

known as El Banco*, in the province of Buenos Aires, while construction was under way on El Olimpo.

**Transfer from El Banco**

"We were transferred to El Olimpo between August 16 and 18. I recognized people who had been in El Banco because they moved all of us from there." Susana Caride was kidnapped on July 26, 1978. She describes the transfer: "They came in trucks. They had to make several trips because they took all the furniture, even the dog. They moved us in groups, hands cuffed and feet shackled, lined up like sardines with all the furniture and the cupboards" [AO.0058].

Omar Eduardo Torres worked as a guard in the Campo de Mayo* military detachment. In his testimony he observed: "When the soccer World Cup ended, around thirty of us who had been guarding the stadium were called to Campo de Mayo. The Second Commanding Officer, whose nom de guerre was Cortez, told us about a special mission that would earn us some extra money. We were supposed to let our hair grow long, grow beards, and use nicknames. He later ordered us to go to the corner of Lacarra and Falcón Streets during the first few days of July 1978. When we went in, we saw that personnel from the Federal Penitentiary Service were finishing construction on the area that was to house the prisoners. I often saw members of the "gang" [*patota**], the ones who carried out the kidnappings, carrying stolen goods from the houses they'd raided in their cars. There was also a warehouse where they kept the booty. We were in charge of the camp's internal security. We weren't allowed to have any contact with the prisoners, although sometimes we let them out to use the bathroom. The inside of El Olimpo was like a prison. At the entrance to the guard station there was a book where they registered whenever prisoners entered or left. They also marked down the prisoners' cells, the numbers assigned to them in place of their names, and the reason for their detention" (CONADEP, 1984).

**Description**

The premises of El Olimpo covered a whole city block. When the site operated as a Clandestine Detention Center, access was through a steel gate; a two-story building was on the left. The officers' club was on the second floor, and

GRAFFITI DRAWN WHEN THE POLICE STILL OCCUPIED EL OLIMPO.

BRICKED-IN BALCONY ACROSS FROM THE CLANDESTINE DETENTION CENTER.

the ground floor contained a series of rooms, one of which had a telephone that prisoners were forced to use to call their families and tell them not to file a report or a writ of habeas corpus*. Each detainee was assigned a letter and number here too. Rebeca Sacolsky, who survived imprisonment at El Olimpo and El Banco, recalls that she was told, "You're not a name anymore, you're P63, and that is what you will call yourself whenever you are speaking to the authorities" [AO.0064].

The center was built in a large parking lot. Susana Caride recalls, "It was designed to hold more people. One side was used as a garage, and they built a concrete structure on the other side with the *tubos* ("tubes," or small cells), the kitchen, the solitary confinement cells, and the torture chamber. It was bigger than El Banco" [AO.0058].

Ironically, the solitary confinement area stood closest to the street. Although its big arched windows were mainly bricked up, they remained open at the top, making it possible to hear what was going on inside and outside. Rebeca Sacolsky heard "a newspaper delivery man passing by every day" through those windows. Every afternoon she heard him "call out the names of the newspapers" [AO.0064].

The illegal detention center's operation so close to residential neighbors reveals how terror spread through the everyday reality of the broader society (see "ESMA," p. 153). Today, a bricked-up balcony on a home directly across the street remains as a metaphor for this coexistence. Those held at El Olimpo knew that terror made them invisible, even though it was obvious what was going on inside. Of her experience inside the concentration camp, Susana Caride observes: "It's like being dead even though you're still alive, like you're in a burial niche. You don't exist for those outside, and they don't exist for you" [AO.0058]. The repressive apparatus sought to spread terror beyond the physical space of the Clandestine Detention Centers and touch society as a whole. Yet to achieve this goal, the concentration camps could not be made fully invisible; some vague and ambiguous information had to leak out into society through the use of certain euphemisms. The prisoners' isolation within the Clandestine Detention Centers was thus deepened by the isolation that affected every member of a society blindfolded by terror to avoid seeing what it already knew. The concentration camps' power spread further each time society averted its eyes to deny what was happening, and the violence underpinning the dictatorship's project reshaped social ties by spreading this embodied terror to each and every individual.

### Kidnapping victims: The case of Poblete

Chilean José Liborio Poblete had been active in Christian organizations since he was a teenager. At sixteen he lost both legs when he was run over by a train. He decided to travel to Buenos Aires to seek treatment, and there he helped to form the Peronist Front for the Disabled (Frente de Lisiados Peronistas). He met Gertrudis Hlaczik through his activist work, and together they had a daughter; all three were kidnapped in 1978 and taken to El Olimpo. Several prisoners, including Susana Caride, witnessed the repressors' particular cruelty toward Poblete: "They would make him walk on his stumps. They would lift him and throw him to the floor. They treated him brutally" [AO.0058].

The couple's daughter, Claudia Victoria, was illegally appropriated by a lieutenant colonel, and it took two decades for her to rediscover her biological roots following a long investigation by the Abuelas de Plaza de Mayo (Grandmothers of the Plaza de Mayo; see "Central Military Hospital," p. 77).

The so-called impunity laws (the Full Stop Law* and Due Obedience Law*) in force from 1987 closed off all legal recourse for the dictatorship's crimes. In 2000, however, the Center for Legal and Social Studies (Centro de Estudios Legales y Sociales) petitioned the court to nullify these laws; at the same time, it asked the court to investigate and try those responsible for the crimes committed against Poblete and Hlaczik.

The federal courts annulled the impunity laws in 2001 and began legal proceedings in the case. The judge argued that the crimes committed against the couple had been part of a systematic plan of repression enacted by an unelected government. He considered them crimes against humanity, which precluded any exemption from criminal responsibility because of "due obedience." In 2005 the Supreme Court declared the impunity laws unconstitutional on the grounds that they violated international human rights law; this decision removed the obstacles to justice that had been in place for twenty years.

A historic conclusion was reached in August 2006. The repressor Julio Simón was sentenced to twenty-five years in prison for multiple crimes against Poblete and Hlaczik: unlawful deprivation of liberty, the torture they suffered in El Olimpo, and the appropriation of their daughter, Claudia Victoria. This marked the first sentencing in a trial for crimes against humanity since the overturning of the impunity laws; in fact, the sentence formed part of the legal proceedings that struck those laws down.

### The end of El Olimpo

Though it remains unclear why El Olimpo was dismantled in February 1979, two hypotheses have been put forward. One attributes the closure to disagreements within the First Army Corps, which oversaw the center. The other suggests the center was closed to preclude an inspection by the Inter-American Commission on Human Rights, which intended to visit places that had been identified as Clandestine Detention Centers by survivors outside the country.

The Automotive Department of the Federal Police used the El Olimpo site after the prisoners were evacuated.

"CARLOS FUENTEALBA" PUBLIC LIBRARY.

The first *escraches** (shaming protests against those who had participated in the repression and torture) took place in 1996 to draw attention to El Olimpo's past. Neighborhood activists, survivors, and human rights organizations began to hold marches along the ten blocks between El Olimpo and the former detention center known as Automotores Orletti. They aimed to reveal the horrific history of this site that stood in the heart of the neighborhood. They also sought to evict the Federal Police from the premises and recover what was left of El Olimpo to convert it into a site of remembrance.

The police finally left the premises in 2005, and a Work and Consensus Committee (Mesa de Trabajo y Consenso) was founded by residents long active in promoting historical remembrance at the site. With offices on the premises of El Olimpo, this committee fosters memory work through projects such as Neighborhood Memories (Memorias de Vecindad), which has collected interviews with local residents about their experience of living near the Clandestine Detention Center.

Current activities include guided tours, arts and crafts workshops, and permanent exhibits. The site also houses the La Bemba community radio station and the Carlos Fuentealba Community Library, where visitors can access books including many that were once banned by the dictatorship. Area schools also conduct workshops about state terrorism and human rights. They encourage students to make connections between past and present, touching on contemporary human rights issues such as problems of police brutality. The goal is for students to reflect upon the possibility of change and the ways to safeguard society against authoritarianism.

## 167. **Automotores Orletti**

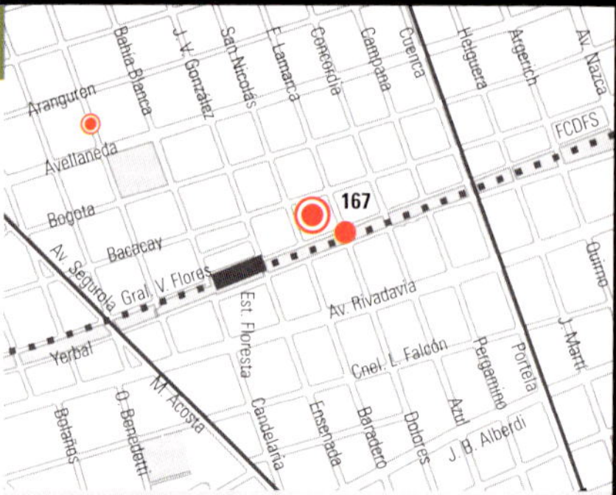


**LOCATION:** VENANCIO FLORES 3519/21
**TRANSPORTATION:** BUSES: 1, 2, 5, 25, 36, 49, 55, 63, 85, 88, 92, 99, 104, 113, 126, 136, 153, 163, 172, 180. TRAIN: FLORESTA STATION (SARMIENTO LINE).

Operation Condor, the plan that coordinated the repressive efforts of several South American dictatorships, was run out of an innocent-looking location: a car repair shop. Some three hundred people are estimated to have passed through this building that was between a family home and a school, in the midst of an ordinary neighborhood. Survivors recognized the location by the noise of the train that passes in front of the building and the voices of children playing at the school.

### Description

The center operated from May to November 1976 under a series of military nicknames: El Jardín ("the garden"), El Taller ("the workshop") and La cueva de Flores ("the Flores cave"). When it was rented by the State Intelligence Agency (SIDE, Secretaría de Inteligencia de Estado), its sign read Automotores Cortell, in reference to the owner's name. Yet it came to be known as Automotores Orletti (Orletti car repair), perhaps through a clerical error.

Vehicles carrying prisoners entered through a metal garage door that was opened from the inside when kidnappers radioed ahead with the command Operación Sesamo (Operation Sesame). They entered a large room divided by a curtain, behind which the prisoners were kept on the concrete floor, which survivors remembered as cold, dirty, and greasy. The floor was strewn with vehicles and chassis, some even belonging to the victims. Sometimes the guards ran the engines to suffocate the prisoners or to drown out the sounds and screams of those who were being tortured.

Many witnesses and investigations have demonstrated that the military derived special sadistic pleasure from kidnapping and torturing family

THE FORMER CLANDESTINE DETENTION CENTER VIEWED FROM THE TRAIN.

members together. In Automotores Orletti this spiteful practice was applied to Carlos and Manuela Santucho, the brother and sister of guerrilla leader Mario Roberto Santucho, who headed the PRT–ERP* (Workers' Revolutionary Party – People's Revolutionary Army). Survivor Enrique Rodríguez Larreta has described what happened to them inside Automotores Orletti.

Prisoners were hung from a hook and submerged into a two-hundred-liter water tank that stood in the middle of the room. The soldiers forced the prisoners to watch as they killed Carlos Santucho by submerging him repeatedly while his sister read aloud the newspaper article about her brother Roberto Santucho's murder that same day.

A stairway on the right side of the garage led to five rooms on the upper floor, each of which had a specific function: interrogations, torture, or detention. After the military abandoned the building, the owner had to take down the cardboard and styrofoam sheets that covered the walls, no doubt placed there to muffle the noise and avoid alerting the neighbors. Another large room held the office of Aníbal Gordon, head of operations at Orletti. Actor Marta Bianchi recalls entering after she was kidnapped while leaving the theater: "They took off my blindfold. There was a large desk in front of me; it was an office. Behind the desk was a flag, an enormous portrait of Hitler, one of Rosas, and one of Colonel Villar" [AO.0467].

The repressors used another room for meetings. Members of a team that inspected the room in 2006 saw "Triple A"* written on the wall next to several small holes. Witnesses recall that the captors used a photo of Che Guevara as a dartboard on that wall.

**Operation Condor**

The Clandestine Detention Centers functioned not only as jails but also as bases of operations for planning kidnappings. Orletti was the Buenos Aires office of Operation Condor, the coordinated plan of repression that linked the intelligence services of Argentina, Chile, Uruguay, Brazil, Paraguay, and Bolivia. Many foreign victims were held here for this reason. Operation Condor was implicated in the kidnapping from Bolivia of Argentine Graciela Rutilo Artes and her daughter Carla, who was a Bolivian citizen. Graciela and Carla were handed over to Argentine authorities on the northern border of Argentina, between Villazón and La Quiaca, and then transferred to Orletti. The girl was illegally appropriated by Eduardo Ruffo, one of the center's directors. In 1983 the Abuelas de Plaza de Mayo found the child still living with Ruffo, who was a fugitive. She recovered her identity in 1985; her mother remains disappeared (see "Central Military Hospital," p. 77).

Most prisoners at Orletti were Uruguayans, who were often brought in groups after their kidnappings. Others included Chileans, Bolivians, Paraguayans, Brazilians, and Cubans. Some were murdered, others transferred to Uruguay or released. One couple managed to escape, though most prisoners remain disappeared to this day.

**Repressors: Triple A and SIDE**

Orletti was under the command of General Otto Paladino, then head of the State Intelligence Agency (SIDE, Secretaría de Inteligencia del Estado). He worked in conjunction with the Army and the Uruguayan military. Paladino ordered the establishment of this operations base, which he called OT 18. Several witnesses who recognized him in a lineup have testified to having seen him at Orletti.

WRITING FOUND ON THE CENTER'S WALLS.

STAIRWAY TO THE INTERROGATION, TORTURE, AND HOLDING CELLS.

The center reported to SIDE's Tactical Operations Department under the command of Néstor Horacio Guillamondegui, who was then an Air Commodore of the Argentine Air Force. Now retired, Guillamondegui has been charged with unlawful deprivation of liberty and torture in the cases of fifty-two people held captive while he led the Tactical Operations Department.

The head of operations at Orletti was Aníbal Gordon, a former member of the Triple A (Argentine Anticommunist Alliance) and an unofficial agent of the SIDE. The official agents in charge of the center were Eduardo Ruffo, alias Zapato ("Shoe") or Capitán ("Captain"), and Juan Rodríguez. Ruffo has been charged with sixty-five cases of kidnapping and torture. He was invited to return to work at the SIDE by its then-Director Hugo Anzorreguy during the presidency of Carlos Menem.

Ruffo and Rodríguez reported to Eduardo Cabanillas, who, in spite of his actions during the dictatorship, ascended to the rank of general and head of the Second Army Corps well after the transition to democracy. He was charged in 2006 in the legal proceedings into crimes committed by the First Army Corps, including the murder of Marcelo Gelman, son of poet Juan Gelman.

Others complicit in human rights violations at this center included intelligence agents Honorio Martínez Ruiz and Raúl Guglielminetti, who managed to reinvent himself after the democratic transition by working as a bodyguard to President Raúl Alfonsín.

Cabanillas was sentenced to life in prison on March 31, 2011 after being convicted of five counts of homicide and twenty-nine counts of unlawful confinement. The judge also imposed prison sentences of twenty-five years for former intelligence agents Horacio Martínez Ruiz and Eduardo Ruffo and twenty years for Raúl Gulielminetti, former member of Army Intelligence Batallion 601.

**Spoils of war**

War booty was especially important in this center. Nearly everyone kidnapped also had their personal belongings plundered; army trucks carted away furniture, jewelry, money, and anything of value. Some prisoners witnessed arguments between Uruguayan and Argentine agents over how they should split the stolen goods. Actor Marta Bianchi's testimony highlights the kidnappers' greed: "They sat us down someplace, and they took my jewelry and my purse. They started questioning me about how much I had paid for my ring, my watch, my coat" [AO.0467].

**Chaos**

Orletti was far more chaotic than other detention centers because there was no clear chain of command below Gordon, which might account for the successful escape of one Uruguayan couple who stole weapons from their distracted guards to defend themselves. The center's closure is attributed to this escape.

In another example of chaos, the agents working inside Orletti left intelligence documents behind when they vacated the center; the papers were found stuffed into gunshot holes in the wall during a legal inspection of the premises in July 2006. They reveal intelligence work dating from before the military coup about people considered political or ideological opponents of the military. From their date of production and their contents, it is clear that victims were targeted for kidnappings and disappearance even before March 1976, when state institutions were already being used for illegal repression.

Further evidence from Orletti points to the actions of the Triple A* and the fact that members of this paramilitary organization continued to work in the repressive apparatus after the coup. For example, Luis Brandoni and Marta Bianchi were kidnapped together as they were leaving the theater. Aníbal Gordon interrogated them at Orletti about why they had left Argentina in 1975. "Because the Triple A threatened us," answered Marta. Gordon asked, "Then why did you come back?" They replied that as Argentines they had every right to live in their own country, to which Gordon responded, "You left because of the Triple A and then you came back because you didn't give a shit about the Triple A. Now it's our turn to screw you over." They were eventually released, but only after being warned: "No more 'bolshie' plays or Jewish friends" [AO.0467].

**Today**

The site known as Automotores Orletti resumed its role as a car repair shop in the 1990s. In 2006 the Buenos Aires City Council declared it to be of "public interest" and "subject to expropriation" in order to guarantee its preservation and its incorporation into the city's historical memory. In July 2008 Judge Gallardo ordered the building's expropriation; it was transferred to the Space of Memory Institute (Instituto Espacio por la Memoria). In 2011 a federal law declared Automotores Orletti and all other Clandestine Detention Centers that operated until December 10, 1983, "Sites of Memory" in order to "guarantee their preservation for the purposes of judicial investigation as well as the preservation of memory" (law 26.691).

The courts recently ordered the arrest of several agents who worked at Automotores Orletti as part of the mega-trial into severe human rights violations committed by the First Army Corps. This trial became possible when the Law of Due Obedience* and the Full Stop Law* were annulled by the courts. The defendants in this case include Argentine and Uruguayan military officers, former SIDE agents, and members of the Triple A.

# 168. **Doctor Dámaso Centeno Military Social Institute**

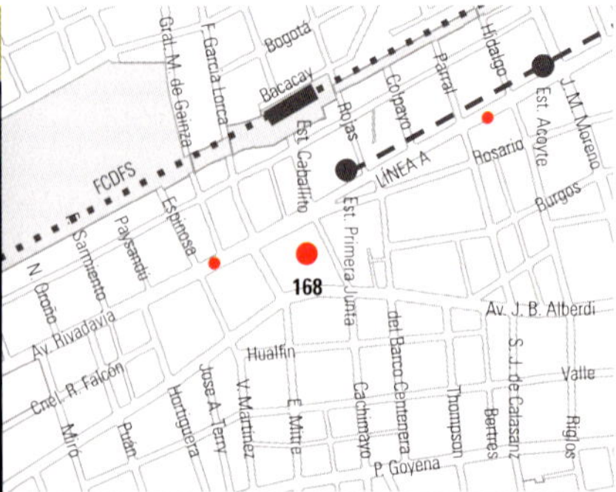


**LOCATION:** CACHIMAYO 55
**TRANSPORTATION:** BUSES: 1, 2, 5, 25, 26, 36, 42, 49, 53, 55, 85, 86, 88, 103, 104, 132, 136, 141, 153, 163, 180. SUBWAY: PRIMERA JUNTA STATION (A LINE). TRAIN: CABALLITO STATION (SARMIENTO LINE).

Former students of the Doctor Dámaso Military Social Institute held a ceremony on October 11, 2006, to unveil a plaque to remember detained and disappeared students from the school. Located in the neighborhood of Caballito, the institute is run by the Army, and the tribute generated controversy within the school community. A retired colonel in charge of the Institute at the time opposed the event; he resigned his position when the Minister of Defense declared his support. Other former students sent threatening messages to try to keep the tribute from going ahead.

Argentine Minister of Defense Nilda Garré and Chief of the Army General Staff General Roberto Bendini both attended. Some 150 former students participated in the event, which honored eight disappeared students: Eduardo Giorello, kidnapped in September 1977; Alejandro Capobianco, kidnapped in March 1978; Juan Eduardo Estévez, kidnapped in May 1977; Juan Carlos Cubas, kidnapped in April 1977; María Luz Vega and Sergio Nocera, both kidnapped in March 1977. During preparations, the organizers identified two more disappeared students who had attended the institute but whose names had not been added to the plaque: Eduardo Vega, brother of María Luz, and Alejandro Almeida, kidnapped in June 1975.

The Dámaso Centeno Institute is run by the Army's Department of Basic Education, though it is now open to anyone. Founded in the early twentieth century as a home for orphans from military families, in 1947 it

DÁMASO CENTENO MILITARY SOCIAL INSTITUTE, AV. RIVADAVIA 5550.

PLAQUE WITH THE NAMES OF DISAPPEARED FORMER STUDENTS.

became the School for Military Orphans (Colegio de Huérfanos Militares). Though it was reserved for the children of Army personnel for most of its history, they now make up only 22 percent of students.

The former students who paid tribute to their disappeared schoolmates used anecdotes and song to evoke the years they spent together in the classroom.

In mid-1973 Juan Eduardo Estévez, Alejandro Capobianco, Eduardo Giorello, Julio Fernández, Daniel Fuksman, Oscar Bisceglia, and Carlos Estévez published one of the many magazines that circulated in public parks where young people got together. They called it *Descomprimiéndonos* ("Taking the lid off ourselves"), in reference to the album *Desatormentándonos* ("Untormenting ourselves") by the band Pescado Rabioso, led by singer Luis Alberto Spinetta. Released in 1972, the album's lyrics called into question the inherited lifestyles and cultural values of earlier generations.

These young men channeled their rebellion into Argentine rock as a way of resisting the military school's conservative environment, and the commemoration ceremony included songs by the classic Argentine rock bands Almendra and Vox Dei. It also featured the song "Aprendizaje" (Learning) by Sui Generis, the band founded by Charly García and Nito Mestre when they met in the late 1960s in the Institute's classrooms. Within the period's tumultuous context of cultural, social, and political changes, Sui Generis sang, "Aprendí a ser formal y cortés/cortándome el pelo una vez por més/y si me aplazó la formalidad/es que nunca me gustó la sociedad" (I learned to be formal and polite/cutting my hair once a month/and if I failed at formality/it's because I never liked high society).

# 169. **House on Franklin Street**

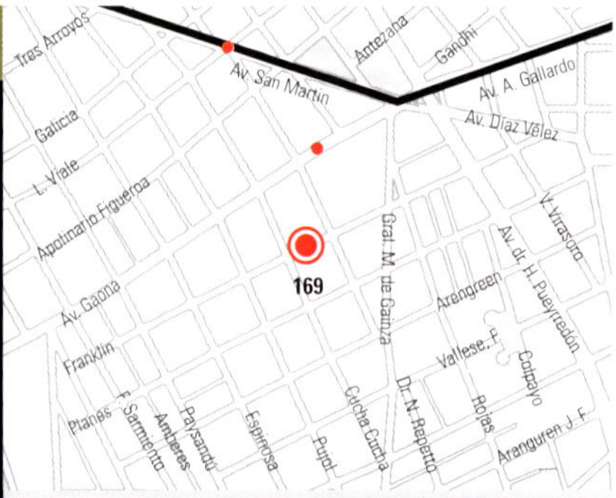


**LOCATION:** FRANKLIN 943
**TRANSPORTATION:** BUSES: 24, 52, 57, 76, 92, 99, 105, 110, 124, 135, 146.

The house located at 943 Franklin Street, which operated as a Clandestine Detention Center during the dictatorship, looks dazzling today, renovated and freshly painted. Sergio Bufano, detained in this house in July 1976, remembers it instead as "an old, dilapidated house" [AO.0067].

Little is known about this house that once operated as a detention and torture center surrounded by family homes in the middle of a middle-class neighborhood, because no other survivors have left testimonies.

Bufano was kidnapped along with Guillermina Santamaría Woods, a fellow activist from the Communist Organization for Workers' Power (OCPO, Organización Comunista Poder Obrero). The Special Task Group* that kidnapped them acted in broad daylight, exercising the public impunity that served to spread terror throughout the society as a whole.

Though Sergio Bufano managed to escape, Guillermina Santamaría Woods remains disappeared. Nicknamed Lotti, she was a teacher and a psychology student at the University of Buenos Aires; she was also pregnant.

### The escape

Bufano took advantage of a moment when he was left alone and managed to escape from his captors a few hours after his kidnapping. The house may have been abandoned as a detention center after this escape, which would account for the lack of information about other survivors.

For Pilar Calveiro, physical escape exists on a continuum with many other methods used by prisoners to resist their conditions of detention: "There were many ways to escape the apparatus of the concentration camp besides physical escape" (Calveiro,

1998). All were rooted in a refusal to follow the detention center's rules and in an assertion of the detainee's individual identity. Prisoners used these resistance methods to preserve their dignity, undermine discipline, and transgress the camps' rules, thereby sabotaging the logic and operation of the bureaucratic machinery.

Prisoners used laughter to assert their humanity; they deceived their captors and conspired with other detainees in order to rebuild the bonds of solidarity and ease their sense of extreme isolation. They even committed suicide, taking away the repressive forces' power to decide on life and death. All these were forms of resistance, ways of "escaping" the logic and goals behind the concentration camps' power.

Other prisoners besides Sergio Bufano managed to escape physically (see "Automotores Orletti," p. 220). Some seized on a momentary opportunity and decided to escape in spite of the intense security in the camps and their own limited and fragmented information about where they were being held. One of the biggest such escapes took place at the detention center known as the Seré Mansion* in the suburban municipality of Morón, in the province of Buenos Aires. Claudio Tamburrini, Guillermo Fernández, Carlos García, and Daniel Rusomano escaped, completely naked, by overcoming the camp's own psychological mechanisms. They stopped seeing their situation as completely hopeless. Instead, they exploited any flaw in the detention center's operation to gather every shred of information that could help them break the barrier of isolation and suspicion and rebuild the bonds of solidarity with their fellow prisoners.

## 170. Faculty of Philosophy and Letters, UBA

### Rodolfo Walsh lecture hall

In 1997 a plaque was dedicated to Rodolfo Walsh in lecture hall 250 of the Faculty of Philosophy and Letters at the University of Buenos Aires. Walsh was a writer, journalist, translator, and collections consultant. As an activist in the Montonero* revolutionary movement, he founded the Clandestine News Agency (ANCLA, Agencia de Noticias Clandestina) in 1976. He worked in a variety of genres, including detective fiction, investigative journalism, and testimonial. His best-known works include *Operación Masacre* (Operation massacre) and *Quién Mató a Rosendo* (Who killed Rosendo?) (see p. 96).

### Perla Waserman lecture hall

A plaque was dedicated on May 12, 2000, to Perla Waserman, a member of the Madres de Plaza de Mayo (Mothers of the Plaza de Mayo) who was completing her studies in history at the time of her death. She had a long history of antifascist political activism and joined the Madres after her daughter Susana was kidnapped. The sign bearing the name of the lecture hall was removed in 2007, leading to an investigation.

### Patricia Tosi plaque

Patricia Tosi was a history student and member of the Student Union of the Faculty of Philosophy and Letters. She also worked at the National Grain Board (Junta Nacional de Granos). She was kidnapped on June 17, 1975. A group of family members, fellow political activists, and work and study companions joined to pay tribute to her with a plaque that reads, "Our greatest tribute is to follow the example of her struggle."

### Mural for students and alumni

In 1995 the Student Union led an initiative to dedicate a plaque bearing the names of ninety-nine former students who had been disappeared, though it was taken down shortly after the dedication. Students and family members of the victims joined together to repudiate this action by painting a mural in lecture room 108, which was completed on May 18, 2000.

**LOCATION:** PUAN 480, CABALLITO.

## 171. Estanislao Severo Zeballos Advanced Normal School No. 4

Paving stones were laid on September 26, 2008, to pay tribute to students Leticia Akselman, Cristina Arrillaga, Beatriz Carbonell, M. Irene Cortés, M. Cristina García, M. Gabriela Juárez, Hilda Leikis, Hebe Mascia Silvana Parirle, Mabel Pasut, Alicia Raboy, Irma Rago, Noemí Ramos, and Rosalba Vensentini and to the teachers Nélida Ardito and Blanca E. de Tarnopolsky.

**LOCATION:** AV. RIVADAVIA 4950, CABALLITO

## 172. Magdalena "Malena" Gallardo

A paving stone was laid on June 6, 2007 to pay tribute to Malena, who was kidnapped early on the morning of July 8, 1976. Her boyfriend, Alejandro Goldar Parodi, was last seen that same night after he dropped her off at home and headed to the cinema with Juan Marín, Hugo Tosso, and Pablo Dubcovsky. All five remain disappeared.

**LOCATION:** AV. ACOYTE 512, CABALLITO

## 173. María Claudia Falcone

The Commission of Neighborhoods for Remembrance and Justice of Almagro-Balvanera and the educational community of School No. 7 laid a paving stone in tribute to María Claudia Falcone on September 20, 2007. Students marched in Yatay Street and held a *siluetazo* (silhouette protest) in Malabia Street (see p. 81). Claudia and a group of fellow students petitioning for student bus fares were kidnapped on a night remembered in Argentina as *La noche de los lápices* (The night of the pencils).

**LOCATION:** YERBAL 25, CABALLITO.

## 174. Luis Carlos Arcuschin

The Commission of Neighborhoods for Remembrance and Justice of Almagro and Balvanera paid tribute to Luis Carlos Arcuschin by laying a paving stone in front of the house where he lived. Participants in the event included his niece, friends, and fellow students from the Hipólito Vieytes school.

**LOCATION:** NEUQUEN 1109, CABALLITO

## 175. **Faculty of Social Sciences, UBA**

Two plaques commemorate disappeared Faculty members. One, dedicated by Buenos Aires City Council, honors Silvio Frondizi; the other pays tribute to teachers, administrative staff, alumni, and students who fell victim to state terrorism.

A plaque on the ground floor recognizes the "teachers, graduates, and students of Sociology from the University of Buenos Aires and other universities in Buenos Aires who were murdered and disappeared under the military dictatorship." It also bears the victims' names.

The auditorium is named for Roberto Eugenio Carri, a sociologist, essayist, professor, and journalist. Roberto and his partner Ana María Caruso were kidnapped together from their home in Hurlingham, in the province of Buenos Aires.

**LOCATION:** PARQUE CENTENARIO CAMPUS, 841 RAMOS MEJIA, CABALLITO.

## 176. **Primera Junta National School No. 17**

On September 14, 2007, a plaque was dedicated to disappeared graduates of National School No. 17: Diego Jacinto Fernando Beigbeder, Jorge Miguel Name, Ricardo Alfredo Nicotera, Sergio Tarnopolsky, Luis Tossi, and Ernesto Urfeig. Friends who had graduated with Luis Tossi had placed a bronze plaque in his memory in April 2005.

**LOCATION:** AV. RIVADAVIA 5161, CABALLITO.

## 177. **Marianist School of Buenos Aires**

An event was held on June 15, 2007, to remember eleven former students from the school who were disappeared. A ceramic mural was unveiled honoring Virginia Monzani, Teresita Scianca, Alejandro Almeida, Carlos Andisco, Eduardo "Lasty" Biancalana, Fernando Degregorio, Daniel Rodolfo Grieco, Germán "Chango" Kuhn, Luis Fernando Kuhn, and Guillermo Adrián Kuhn.

**LOCATION:** AV. RIVADAVIA 5625, CABALLITO

### 178. **Dr. Teodoro Alvarez Hospital**

"Those who leave a trace do not disappear" ("No desaparece quien deja huella") reads the plaque placed at the entrance to the hospital on March 24, 2002. Hospital employees launched this initiative to remember Pedro Fernández and Oscar Furman, doctors disappeared between 1976 and 1977. Family members, friends, and colleagues gathered for the ceremony to honor their work at the hospital.

**LOCATION:** DR. F. J. ARANGUREN 2701, FLORES

### 179. **Collective Mural Project**

On March 25 and 26, 2006, friends from the Flores Sur Social and Cultural Center joined with neighbors, members of the Filete Colectivo muralist group, and the Herederos de la Locura *murga* (street performance troupe) to create a mural honoring disappeared residents from the neighborhood. In the days leading up to the event, large posters were hung on the façades of houses where those being honored once lived.

**LOCATION:** AV. VARELA 1301, FLORES.

### 180. **Roberto Luis Cristina**

School No. 8, where Roberto Luis Cristina once worked, hosted a day of events honoring his memory on November 23, 2007. Students and community members took part in the ceremony, which saw the dedication of a paving stone, a plaque, and a photograph in his honor. Also present were his daughter María, his sister, and Jorge Watts, a fellow activist and survivor of El Vesubio* Clandestine Detention Center. The students asked questions about Roberto's story and about the events of that period.

**LOCATION:** AV. VARELA 358, FLORES.

### 181. **Floresta City Yard**

Local residents recovered this site, which is now used as a community center housing cultural and social activities. It was inaugurated on May 1, 2005, along with a mural paying tribute to three workers from the yard who were disappeared in 1977. Local residents, friends, and members of the Flores Sur Social and Cultural Center painted a mural in their honor.

**LOCATION:** CORNER OF AV. GAONA AND GUALEGUAYCHU, FLORESTA

## 182. María del Carmen Perciavati – Daniel Manzotti

María del Carmen and Daniel were kidnapped from their home on August 24, 1977 along with María del Carmen's father, Esteban Perciavati, who was released three days later. The Floresta neighborhood assembly dedicated paving stones in their memory on August 25, 2007, with their children Ana and Ernesto in attendance.

**LOCATION:** CARRASCO 845, VELEZ SARSFIELD.

## 183. Ángela María Aieta de Gullo

Twenty-five years after her kidnapping, Angela María Aieta de Gullo's family and friends joined with representatives of government and human rights organizations to place a plaque in her memory. Her loved ones honored her again on the thirtieth anniversary of her kidnapping by placing a plaque in front of her home (see p. 99).

**LOCATION:** CACHIMAYO 1940, PARQUE CHACABUCO

# SECTOR **9**

LINIERS, MATADEROS, PARQUE AVELLANEDA, VERSALLES, VILLA LUGANO, VILLA LURO, VILLA RIACHUELO, AND VILLA SOLDATI

# 184. **Human Rights Walk**

**LOCATION:** PARQUE INDOAMERICANO, AV. ESCALADA AND AV. CASTANARES
**TRANSPORTATION:** BUSES: 36, 47, 50, 56, 86, 101, 114, 143, 193.

"Where should we put the flowers?" asked Vera Jarach at the inauguration of the Paseo de los Derechos Humanos (Human Rights Walk). "We've thrown them into the river so many times. This place is going to bring together many generations for a long time to come," she said in front of the grove of trees dedicated to disappeared students from the Buenos Aires National School, a group that included her own daughter Franca Jarach.

The "Fundación Memoria Histórica y Social Argentina" (Argentine Foundation for Historical and Social Memory) was founded on November 18, 1987, by family members of victims disappeared by the last military dictatorship. It was one of the earliest institutions to recognize the importance of memory as a foundation of democratic society and has worked tirelessly since its origins to promote awareness of human rights issues. It organized a documentation center early on and promoted interdisciplinary research into state terrorism and its effects by offering grants and subsidies, and by creating working groups.

In 1991 the Foundation decided to create a wooded area in memory of the victims of state terrorism. After multiple appeals, the city of Buenos Aires passed Ordinance 47.533 on December 6, 1993, to approve the creation of the Parque Indoamericano, which was to include the Human Rights Walk "to remember those from the political, labor, student and other social movements who were victims of disappearance at the hands of state terrorism in the 1970s."

The Walk has occupied three different locations in Villa Lugano since its creation. It was first inaugurated inside the Parque Indoamericano in

THE MAIN PATH OF THE HUMAN RIGHTS WALK.

SCULPTURE BY SARA BRODSKY.

INSTALLATION HONORING DISAPPEARED WORKERS FROM MERCEDES BENZ.

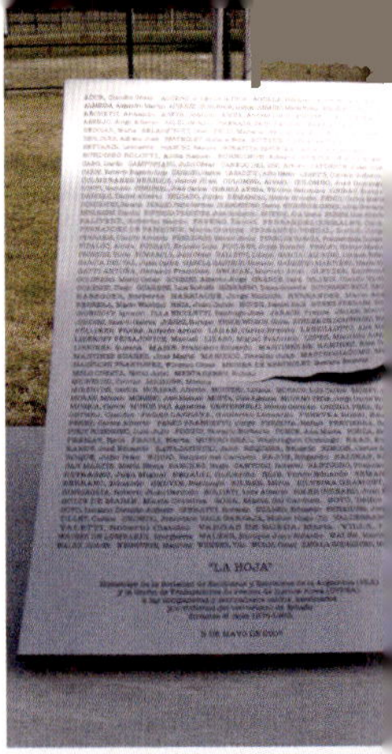

TRIBUTE TO DISAPPEARED WRITERS AND JOURNALISTS.

2002 in a space known as "la Rotonda" (the Roundabout). Yet maintenance difficulties prompted the decision to move it in 2003 to the Parque de la Ciudad. When new obstacles arose relating to the adjudication of the land, yet another location had to be found.

The municipal government of Buenos Aires collaborated with a Work and Consensus Board (Mesa de Trabajo y Consenso) to organize a series of Participatory Design Workshops in 2006. More than sixty organizations took part, and more than 250 residents of the Villa Lugano area attended. The first step in the Plan that emerged from this conference was the designation of seven hectares for the creation of the Human Rights Walk and the construction of a Center for Environmental Information and Training.

The Walk is located in the southern part of the city, an area notoriously lacking in public planning where makeshift housing, neglected public spaces, and inadequate services are the norm.

**The Walk**

The Argentine Foundation for Historical and Social Memory developed the Walk's landscaping in collaboration with Memoria Abierta. It consists of twenty commemorative groves of native trees that will in time grow together to form a fully wooded area. A path runs the length of the wood, branching off to each of the wooded areas honoring different groups of disappeared. A large open area in the center of the Walk is the setting for public functions.

Each grove of trees represents victims of disappearance from a particular union, factory, educational institution, nationality, or neighborhood, to name a few. Each group is assigned its own commemorative space, which it is responsible for maintaining. This convergence of individual spaces makes the Paseo de los Derechos Humanos a space of collective memory that stimulates reflection and fosters a variety of everyday uses by city residents and visitors.

Each group decides on its own way of remembering and naming its disappeared with its own wooded area. For example, maritime workers decided to honor their disappeared workmates by surrounding their space with *ceibo* trees, the national tree of Argentina (known in English as the Cockspur Coral tree). They installed a sculpture representing a boat and bearing the inscription: "Fellow maritime workers, *hasta la victoria siempre* (Ever onward to victory!)."

The group Family Members of Disappeared Persons of European Origin installed a blue plaque with a statement recalling a historic turning-point in their struggle:

PLANTING THE FIRST TREE IN THE GROVE HONORING DISAPPEARED JEWS.

"In commemoration of the European countries' repudiation of the Military Junta's document (06/05/1983) claiming that the disappeared were all dead."

In another grove stands a steel sculpture representing a torn sheet of paper bearing the names of disappeared journalists and writers. Another sculpture dedicated by the Argentine Judicial Federation is entitled *Diálogo* (Dialogue); it resembles a cube-shaped transparent globe containing the photographs of disappeared judicial workers. Its design captures the deep wound and long-term repercussions left by the crime of forced disappearance.

The Walk was inaugurated on April 8, 2006, with the first wooded areas paying tribute to the disappeared from the Buenos Aires National School (Colegio Nacional de Buenos Aires; see p. 43), the Carlos Pellegrini Advanced School of Commerce (Escuela Superior de Comercio Carlos Pellegrini; see p. 61), and the Bolivian community.

Little by little, further tributes were established by the Association of Family Members of Disappeared Jews; the Argentine Maritime Workers; the Association of Former Workers and Family Members of the Disappeared from Mercedes Benz (see p. 31); the Commission for Memory and Justice of Villa Lugano, Villa Soldati and Villa Celina; Journalists and Writers; former students from the Faculties of Engineering, Architecture and Economics of the University of Buenos Aires (see p. 80); Families of Disappeared Persons of European Origin and the Argentine Judicial Federation.

Angel Lepíscopo, a member of the Argentine Foundation for Historical and Social Memory, made the following observations at the inauguration ceremony for the Paseo de los Derechos Humanos: "Memory is the path towards truth, a path we have been following for three decades. We can finally show that our struggle was not only just but necessary. Our only wish is to preserve the identity of the disappeared by planting trees, symbols of life, continuity, and growth, as the disappeared themselves would have wished."

The illegal repression in Argentina touched each and every part of the community. The Paseo reflects the diversity of victims and the desire shared by all the groups to keep collective memory alive.

# 185. **Major Bernardo Alberte Flowerbeds**



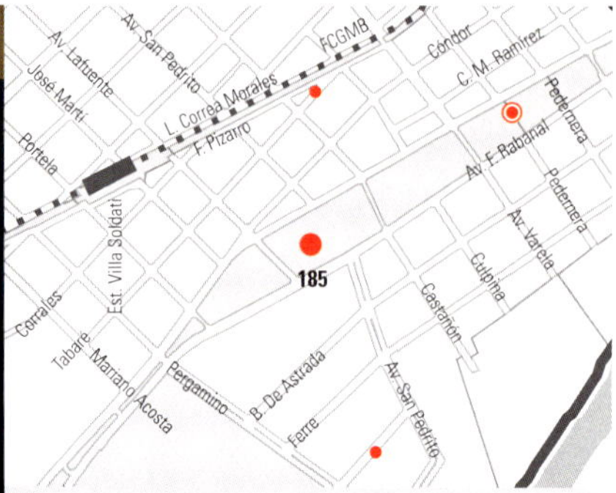


**LOCATION:** AV. FRANCISCO RABANAL BETWEEN LAFUENTE AND CASTANON
**TRANSPORTATION:** BUSES: 6, 76, 91, 115. TRAIN STATION: VILLA SOLDATI (BELGRANO LINE).

Remembered as the first victim of the military coup, Major Alberte was a Peronist political activist for more than thirty years. His son Bernardo remembers how he was murdered: "Just minutes after 2:00 a.m. on March 24, 1976, Federal Police and Army vehicles pulled onto Avenida Libertador between Callao and Ayacucho Streets. The soldiers were dressed in full combat gear. According to terrified neighbors who watched the scene unfold through the windows of their homes, the men swiftly blocked off the area and kept vehicles out of the avenue and the intersection of Schiaffino and Ayacucho Streets. They walked purposefully to the building where my father lived with my mother and my sister Lidia. They broke the lock on the front entrance and climbed the stairs to the sixth floor, accompanied by the building superintendent who, years later, described these events in vivid detail. They broke down the apartment's back door with their bayonets and entered, screaming and hurling insults. My parents were startled and Lidia rushed to them. My father grabbed his gun but never had a chance to use it because, without offering any explanation beyond their verbal assaults, the men grabbed him and threw him out the window. My father's body landed on the first-floor patio." (Gurucharri, 2001).

On December 12, 2006, Buenos Aires city council decided to dedicate the central flowerbeds on Avenida Francisco Rabanal, between Lafuente and Castañon Streets, to Major Bernardo Alberte. On the same day, Alberte's son formally presented Army Chief Lieutenant General Roberto Bendini with a copy of the letter his father had written to General Jorge Rafael Videla denouncing the escalating repression. He was murdered by a Special Task Group* within hours of writing that letter.

Many years earlier, on September 16, 1955, Major Alberte had held out inside the government house (Casa Rosada) against a Naval infantry attack from a position in the port. The Navy was working to overthrow President Juan Domingo Perón during his second term of office, and Major Alberte was one of Perón's military aides. Alberte was taking the first steps in what would become known as the Peronist Resistance* (Resistencia Peronista) while the bombs were falling on the Plaza de Mayo (see p. 3). On September 20, Perón decided to cede control of the government and go into exile. Four captains arrived at Alberte's apartment to arrest him ten days later.

Alberte was released months later when the charges against him were found to be without merit. He sought asylum in the Brazilian embassy when he discovered that the government of General Pedro Eugenio Aramburu planned to arrest him again. He lived in Rio de Janeiro until 1958, where he worked for the newspaper *O Travalhista*.

Alberte set up a dry-cleaning business with another retired Peronist military officer when he returned to Buenos Aires. In the early 1960s he worked with other renowned Peronist activists such as Julio Troxler (see "Julio Troxler Street," p. 240) to build the Peronist Resistance, which confronted the different regimes that outlawed public support for Peronism.

Appointed Secretary General of the Peronist National Coordination Board (Junta Coordinadora Nacional), Alberte served as Peronism's "tactical" leader during Perón's years of exile. He took a stand during the union conflicts that split the General Confederation of Labor (CGT) into two factions, siding with the more combative CGT de los Argentinos*, led by Raimundo Ongaro, against the CGT Azopardo led by Augusto Vandor, which favored dialogue and cooperation with the military government.

Eduardo Gurucharri, Alberte's biographer and editor of his correspondence, maintains that this involvement in internal union conflicts sealed Alberte's removal from the General Secretariat. Juan Perón promoted factionalism within the union movement from exile in Madrid, maintaining an ambiguous political stance in order to use both the Peronist left and the right wing represented by Vandor. In a 1968 interview, Perón declared: "In politics, you always need two reins to maintain control: one group that attacks and another that reflects." (*Revista Extra* 4, no. 41, December 1968).

Soon, a series of popular uprisings including the Cordobazo* (a popular insurrection in the provincial city of Córdoba) gave expression to the growing radicalization and social and cultural conflict affecting broad sectors of the population. These protests would accelerate the return to free elections. Within this context, Alberte helped to found the Peronist wing known as Revolutionary Peronism* (Peronismo Revolucionario) and headed the radical movement known as the "Corriente Peronista 26 de Julio."

He then withdrew from public life until 1975, when he began to denounce the kidnappings and murders carried out by the Triple A* (Argentine Anticommunist Alliance) and the Armed Forces, and to repudiate publicly the imminent military coup. Just a few days before the military took power on March 24, 1976, a paramilitary group burst into the downtown offices of the "Corriente Peronista 26 de Julio" in a failed attempt to kidnap him.

Buenos Aires city council dedicated a bronze plaque in Alberte's memory in front of the building where he was eventually killed. As a gesture of historical reparation, in December 2006 the National Senate approved his posthumous promotion to the rank of Lieutenant Colonel.

## 186. **Julio Troxler Street**

**LOCATION:** BETWEEN AV. SAN PEDRITO AND PERGAMINO
**TRANSPORTATION:** BUSES: 76, 91, 115.

A street in the neighborhood of Villa Soldati was named "Julio Troxler" in memory of this Peronist political activist murdered by the Triple A* (Argentine Anticommunist Alliance). In October 1997, an ordinance passed by what was then the Deliberative Council of the City of Buenos Aires made this tribute possible (see "Coordinación Federal," p. 17).

Troxler's life was shaped by what was known as the Peronist Resistance* (Resistencia Peronista). On June 16, 1955, the Navy bombed the Plaza de Mayo (see p. 3) and the Casa Rosada with the aim of overthrowing president Juan Domingo Perón, who was in his second term of office (see "Major Alberte Gardens," p. 238). Three months later, another military uprising succeeded in removing Perón from power and pushing him into exile. Its leaders called their revolt a "Liberating Revolution" (Revolución Libertadora). The new military government banned Peronism and imprisoned or exiled its leading activists (see "Former Prison Unit 1 in Caseros," p. 134). It became a crime even to mention Juan Domingo Perón's name, and newspapers took to referring to him as "the fugitive tyrant." Yet this repression backfired by making Peronism more cohesive and fostering forms of resistance, including even an attempted insurrection.

The military turned away from state direction of the economy in favor of free market policies, including the privatization of nationalized industries and banks, and the dismantling of regional economies.

The Aramburu dictatorship began to show signs of weakness the following year, as its economic policies promoted both military and civilian reaction. Peronist supporters whose lives had been transformed by the social policies enacted during Perón's two terms in office called on the young to fight and resist the regime.

Troxler dropped out of the Juan Vucetich Police School after the September 1955 coup to join the Peronist Resistance. He worked alongside union leaders Sebastián Borro and Andrés Framini, and also came into contact with the original Peronist Youth Movement* (JP or Juventud Peronista) groups led by figures such as Gustavo Rearte, Envar El Kadri and Felipe Vallese. First arrested in October 1955, he fought alongside his brothers in the failed insurrection of June 1956.

A group of loyal Peronist officers and non-commissioned officers had rejected the new military government as unconstitutional. On June 9, 1956, Generals Valle and Tanco led a failed military and civilian uprising. Though not officially endorsed by Perón, the insurrection drew on popular discontent, the support of Peronist activists, and the participation of military officers displaced by "la Libertadora" (short for the Liberating Revolution).

The military government was aware of the planned insurrection but decided not to act until the plans were in motion. The revolutionary proclamation written by Valle and Tanco was due to be read in public around midnight on June 9, though hundreds of union leaders and Peronist sympathizers were arrested the night before to undermine the uprising's base of support.

The military defeated the insurrection, quickly putting down a series of attempted uprisings in Campo de Mayo, Regiment 2 in Palermo, the Army School of Mechanics, Regiment 7 in the city of La Plata, and in the provincial towns of Santa Rosa (La Pampa), Rosario and Rafaela (Santa Fe), and Viedma (Río Negro). Most of the rebel leaders were captured.

Julio Troxler was arrested along with other members of the insurrection as they listened for the radio broadcast of the proclamation in Florida, a suburb north of Buenos Aires. These arrests took place just before midnight on June 9. The men were transferred to the police station in the Regional Unit of San Martín, another suburban municipality. Aramburu and Rojas signed a martial law* decree that went into effect at 12:32 a.m. on June 10 as Troxler and the others were being held in custody. Another decree passed a few hours later ordered that anyone caught violating the law be shot.

Police Comissioner Rodríguez Moreno, in charge of the San Martín Regional Unit, later received the order to shoot the prisoners detained in the Unit's police station; it came from Colonel Fernández Suárez, chief of the Buenos Aires provincial police. Troxler and the other prisoners were taken to a garbage dump in the provincial municipality of José León Suárez. Following a struggle in the dark, Troxler and six other men managed to escape. Five others were executed.

Rodolfo Walsh later drew on the testimony of one survivor, Juan Carlos Livraga, to reconstruct this crime in his famous work *Operación Masacre* (Operation Massacre; see "Corner of San Juan and Entre Ríos," p. 96). Walsh proved through exhaustive research that the executions were illegal because martial law had been applied retroactively to the detainees; they could not have broken a law that was passed after they were already in custody.

Troxler, like Livraga, was one of the seven men to escape the massacre. Exiled for some time in Bolivia, he remianed active in the Peronist Resistance through the 1960s. In the early 1970s Jorge Cedrón and Rodolfo Walsh invited him to narrate their film version of *Operación Masacre.* The film was screened secretly in a number of locations during the campaign that brought Peronist candidate Hector Cámpora to power in 1973. Troxler also acted in director Pino Solanas's film *Los hijos de Fierro,* which was shot between 1973 and 1975 (see "Plaque in the SICA," p. 72). This film traced Perón's eighteen years in exile, making reference to the Peronist Resistance, the rebellious union movement, and the

Peronist Youth Movement, celebrated as the "Glorious JP" (*jotapé,* the Spanish pronunciation of the group's initials). Three of the actors were murdered by the time Solanas finished the film.

Troxler's experience as a police officer during Perón's first presidency won him an appointment as second-in-command of the Buenos Aires provincial Police when Cámpora won the elections in 1973. He resigned from the position less than three months later. He went on to join the team at the daily newspaper *Noticias* and became Assistant Director of the Institute of Criminology in the University of Buenos Aires Faculty of Law.

Troxler was kidnapped and murdered by the Triple A* paramilitary organization on September 20, 1974, as he headed to work at the Faculty of Law. The Triple A press release read as follows: "The list goes on. Troxler is dead, and the next one, in rhyme, will be Sandler." This death list, which had earlier been made public, contained the names Ortega Peña, Curuchet, López, Troxler, Sandler, Sueldo, Bidegain, Cámpora, Laguzzi, Betanín, Villanueva, Firmenich, Caride, Taiana, Añón, and Arrostito.

In 2007 Troxler's widow, Haydee Leonor von Wernich, became a plaintiff in the legal investigation into crimes committed by the Triple A. In January 2009 a public prosecutor converted this investigation into one of the so-called mega-trials treating crimes against humanity committed during the last dictatorship. This trial that began as an investigation into twelve crimes, may grow to incorporate some 628.

## 187. Norma Scopise Rijo – Santiago Astelarra

On April 14, 2007, the group Neighborhoods for Memory and Justice dedicated commemorative paving stones in front of the home where Norma Scopise Rijo and Santiago Astelarra lived. At the time of his disappearance, Santiago was twenty-five years old and worked at the Center for Medical Education and Clinical Research (CEMIC – Centro de Educación Médica e Investigaciones Clínicas). Norma, also twenty-five years old, was from Uruguay. They were kidnapped together on November 23, 1976.

LOCATION: AV. LARRAZABAL 250, LINIERS

## 188. Jorge Infantino

Jorge Infantino's political activism began in the Union of Secondary School Students* (UES). He worked in the National Telecommunications Company (ENTEL) and was a union delegate. A paving stone remembers him in front of his home. He is also honored along with over 100 disappeared telephone workers in an annual tribute by the Federation of Telephone Workers and Employees (FOETRA). He is named on the memorial in Plaza Martín de Yrigoyen, and survivor Norberto Urso dedicated his *Mansión Seré, un vuelo hacia el horror* (Mansión Seré, a flight to horror) to him.

LOCATION: PILAR 1033, LINIERS.

## 189. Irma Laciar de Carrica

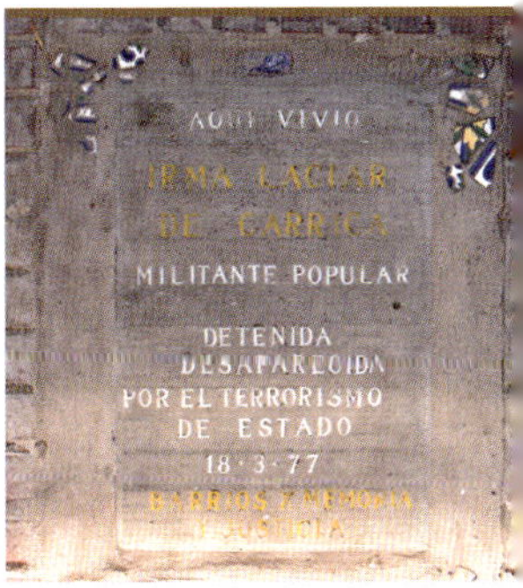


Irma Laciar de Carrica began her career as a nurse in the Rivadavia Hospital in 1953. She also taught at the University of Buenos Aires and was a member of the medical unit at the Faculty of Medicine. She directed the first School of Nursing Assistants. At the time of her disappearance, she was helping family members of the disappeared and trying to determine where prisoners were being held. She was kidnapped along with her brother Carlos, who was later released.

LOCATION: PALMAR 6658, LINIERS.

## 190. Pedro Varas

Pedro Varas was kidnapped on October 17, 1976, at the age of thirty-seven. He was a craftsman and one of the first to participate in the "parallel" craft fair in Plaza Francia. In 1973 he helped to found the Association of Peronist Craft Workers (Agrupación de Artesanos Peronistas), which worked toward the establishment of other fairs such as the one in Plaza San Martín, and the Union of Craft Workers (Asociación Gremial de Artesanos).

LOCATION: VENTURA BOSCH 6408, LINIERS

## 191. **Students from School No. 13**

The Student Union from School No. 13 joined with the Commission for Remembrance, Truth and Justice of the neighborhoods of Liniers, Mataderos and Villa Luro to organize a ceremony dedicating a plaque with the names of disappeared students from the school. Local residents also took part in the event, where they shared anecdotes and recalled the collective political aspirations that had motivated people in those years.

LOCATION: GALLARD 149, LINIERS

## 192. **Marcelo Castello**

Marcelo Castello studied Sociology and Law before abandoning university to begin work at ENTEL, the national telecommunications company. He and his wife Delia had a son Felipe and a daughter María Eva, though he never met her. His mother Isidora became active in the Madres de Plaza de Mayo (see p. 3) after his disappearance. She later helped to found the Commission for Remembrance, Truth and Justice (Comisión por la Memoria, la Verdad y la Justicia) of Liniers, Villa Luro, and Mataderos, who had this paving stone laid.

LOCATION: AV. LISANDRO DE LA TORRE 336, LINIERS

## 193. **Mural in Tribute to the Disappeared of Liniers, Villa Luro, and Mataderos**

A mural by artist Otto Passenheim pays tribute to the disappeared in the plaza in Liniers named for Isidora: mother of Marcelo Castello, member of the Madres de Plaza de Mayo, and co-founder of the Commission for Remembrance, Truth and Justice of the Neighborhoods of Liniers, Villa Luro, and Mataderos. It contains a large map of these neighborhoods showing the homes and the names of victims of state terrorism.

LOCATION: CORNER OF CAAGUAZU AND LARRAZABAL, LINIERS

## 194. **Carlos Quieto – Nora Marx – Ana María Gago – Mónica Pites**

On August 11, 2007, the Commission for Remembrance, Truth and Justice of Liniers, Mataderos and Villa Luro joined with family members and friends of these four victims of disappearance and honored them with a paving stone dedicated in front of the house where they used to meet. At the time of their kidnapping, Carlos was thirty-two years old, Nora was twenty-eight, Ana María was twenty and Mónica was twenty-four.

LOCATION: FONROUGE 2175, MATADEROS

## 195. **Luis Steimberg**

In August 1976, Luis Steimberg was on leave from his mandatory military service. He was kidnapped on August 10. His parents' requests for information from the Military School went unanswered, and the military began to search for him as a deserter soon after. Years later, former sergeant Víctor Ibáñez admitted in a radio interview that he had thrown Luis to his death in the ocean.

LOCATION: PIZARRO 7360, MATADEROS

## 196. **Elena María Ungar**

Elena María Ungar was twenty-one years old at the time of her kidnapping on October 21, 1977. Her family and friends joined with the Commission for Remembrance, Truth, and Justice of the neighborhoods of Liniers, Mataderos and Villa Luro to dedicate a paving stone in her memory on April 12, 2008.

LOCATION: GUARDIA NACIONAL 1270, MATADEROS

## 197. **Nuestra Señora del Carmen Parish Church**

One wall of the Parish church honors three church figures who were victims of state terrorism: Carlos Bustos, a Capuchin priest disappeared on April 8, 1977; father Carlos Mugica (see p. 26), a member of the Movement of Priests for the Third World who was murdered on May 11, 1974; and Bishop and pastor Enrique Angelelli (see p. 138), murdered on August 4, 1976. A community library in front of the church is named for Carlos Mugica.

**LOCATION:** JOSÉ I. RUCCI 3140, VILLA LUGANO.

## 198. **Maestro Eduardo Luis Vicente School No. 2**

Buenos Aires city council officially named School No. 2 after Eduardo Luis Vicente on September 12, 2002. The inscription reads: "Teacher, wherever you may be, your name is here." Eduardo Luis Vicente was a teacher and student of Sociology. He published a children's book collection with Daniel Feldman titled "Los minilibros del Tío Enrique" (The tiny books of Uncle Enrique) that taught children not to discriminate and to show solidarity.

LOCATION: AV. LARRAZABAL 5440, VILLA LUGANO

## 199. **Armando Prieto**

Armando was twenty-seven years old at the time of his kidnapping on July 21, 1976. The Commission for Remembrance, Truth and Justice of the Neighborhoods of Liniers, Mataderos, and Villa Luro joined with his family members and friends to dedicate a paving stone to him in front of the house where he lived.

LOCATION: AV. RIVADAVIA 10270, VILLA LURO

## 200. **Horacio Sosa**

On November 24, 2007, the Commission for Remembrance, Truth and Justice of the neighborhoods of Liniers, Mataderos, and Villa Luro dedicated a paving stone to Horacio Sosa at the house where he lived. He was murdered on April 4, 1975.

LOCATION: AV. LOPE DE VEGA 289, VILLA LURO

## 201. **Maestro Carlos Alberto Carranza School No. 20**

Buenos Aires city council voted to approve the name of this school on September 12, 2002. A plaque was dedicated to teacher Carlos Alberto Carranza in May 2003. "To teacher Carlos Alberto Carranza. I bore witness. I was happy because I took part actively in the unfolding of history. Southern Cooperative Association (Asociación Cooperativa Sur)." Carlos was twenty-six years old when he was kidnapped on August 19, 1976.

LOCATION: MARTINEZ CASTRO 3061, VILLA SOLDATI

## 202. **Osvaldo Sposaro – Juan Carlos Daroqui**

A paving stone was dedicated on November 12, 2006, at the doorway of the home where Osvaldo Sposaro lived. Fellow political activist Juan Carlos Daroqui hid out for some time in this house. Both men were kidnapped from here on September 12, 1977. Neighbors who participated in the ceremony shared stories and memories of life in the neighborhood.

LOCATION: TABARE 2774, VILLA SOLDATI

## 203. **Maestro Guillermo José Barros School No. 21**

A ceremony on October 5, 2007, named this school in memory of disappeared teacher Guillermo José Barros. This initiative, approved by Buenos Aires city council, began with a signature campaign involving teachers in the neighborhoods of Lugano, Soldati, and Pompeya. A plaque and photo of Barros were also dedicated at the same site.

LOCATION: MARIANO ACOSTA 2976, VILLA SOLDATI

# Epilogue: Via Dolorosa

ILAN STAVANS

I'm ambivalent about memorials, such as the one in New York City dedicated to the victims of September 11, 2001. I recognize the psychological role they play. And I'm aware of the societal duty to remember a cathartic event of the past. The question for me is how to use that past. That it is usable I have no doubt. But what kinds of uses should one draw from it?

My duality has to do with what looks to me like a misguided effort of trivialization. Memorials, no matter how sober they are in recounting the atrocious events they pay tribute to (think of Yad Vashem in Jerusalem, the Vietnam Wall in Washington) are, inevitably, trivialization. For any effort to package the past engages in a game of trivia: which facts matter and which don't.

The September 11 memorial is no exception. The suffering that resulted from the terrorist attacks on the World Trade Center and the Pentagon is insurmountable, its echoes infinite. Yet a memorial turns that suffering into tourist kitsch. In making people relive the past, it becomes fake experience.

Years ago I spoke with the Israeli writer David Grossman about the ambivalence I feel toward fake experience. He told me about something he had said to the British playwright David Hare, who at one point was working on a theatrical monologue called *Via Dolorosa,* with him as the solo actor on stage. The monologue was about the Palestinian–Israeli conflict. Grossman told Hare that in the aftermath of the Yom Kippur War in October 1973 Israel went from being a nation looking into the future, devoted to building a new era for the Jewish people, to a nation obsessed with memorializing the soldiers who had died in the war.

Grossman said that before the Yom Kippur War stones were just stones. After it, they became shrines, sites through which to honor those who had fallen. In a landscape reconfigured by a secular ideology such as Zionism, suddenly the soil became sacred. He wondered if memorials might curtail one's capacity to live the present at its fullest.

I too wonder about the impact memorials have on us. Isn't it dangerous when collective memory is institutionalized? Who is in charge of that institutionalization? Why are certain events turned into shrines while others are not? Other than a bunch of ruins, there are no memorials for the Crusades. Neither is there a memorial for the fall of the USSR. And other than makeshift wooden crosses marking the place where an undocumented migrant crossed the U.S.–Mexico border, there is no memorial site commemorating the painful northbound journey millions of people make while crossing the Rio Grande.

I also wonder how sites are chosen. I find it puzzling that the September 11 memorial is in New York, where most of the deaths occurred, but the U.S. Holocaust Museum is in the nation's capital, far away from any place where the Nazis executed their unspeakable acts.

Interestingly, these thoughts were not in my mind on a recent visit to Buenos Aires. I was there to join forces with the documentary photographer Marcelo Brodsky on a project about the terrorist attack in 1994 on the AMIA, the Jewish

Community Center, in the neighborhood of El Once. The project was a *fotonovela* called *Once@9:53am*. Widely popular in the Hispanic world, the genre of the fotonovela uses images to build a narrative that is roughly the equivalent of a graphic novel in the English-speaking world.

The narrative Brodsky and I shaped was about a freelance photojournalist who accidentally finds himself near the AMIA on the fateful morning of July 18. He is attempting to capture for *Playboy* magazine the daily life of this multiethnic enclave, the equivalent of the Lower East Side in New York, where immigrants from around the globe settle as they enter the melting pot that is Argentina. The photojournalist stumbles upon a series of suspicious individuals who, unbeknown to him and the inhabitants of El Once, are plotting to undermine that very melting pot.

I was hypnotized by how photogenic Buenos Aires is. I was also mesmerized by how it carries itself along joyfully, no matter how tangible the ghosts of the past are. What else can it do? I remembered the memorable opening of Jorge Luis Borges's story "The Aleph," in which the protagonist, Borges himself, mourns the death of his beloved Beatriz Viterbo. His personal plight isn't in tune with the outside: "On the burning February morning Beatriz Viterbo died, after braving an agony that never for a single moment gave way to self-pity or fear, I noticed that the sidewalk billboards around Constitution Plaza were advertising some new brand or other of American cigarettes. The fact pained me, for I realized that the wide and ceaseless universe was already slipping away from her and that this slight change was the first of an endless series. The universe may change but not me, I thought with a certain sad vanity."

As I ventured around El Once and beyond, I couldn't help noticing the markers embedded in the sidewalks, known as *baldosas,* memorializing a kidnapping during the "Guerra Sucia," or "Dirty War," the plaques on the facades of important buildings such as the Escuela de Mecánica de la Armada, which was used as a torture site, the Plaza the Mayo, where for years the mothers of *desaparecidos* have staged vigils, and the Parque de la Memoria, a monument Brodsky took me to, built specifically to commemorate the victims of Argentine state terrorism, his brother among them. And while I admired the way Buenos Aires makes its soil sacred in the act of remembrance, I was far less conflicted than I usually am. The fact that the city as a whole was a conglomerate of memorials, none of them serving as epicenter, made me pause at first, then helped me truly understand the vastness of the tragedy.

Everyone in Buenos Aires had been affected. Thus, everyone was involved in the salvaging of the past. It didn't feel as if a corporation or the government was behind the effort. On the contrary, there was spontaneity to the remembrance. That was in part because some of the memorials felt somewhat improvised: graffiti on a wall, impromptu murals in a graveyard, the defacing of a monument that wasn't properly cleaned up, the names of prisoners engraved on a door. These weren't sightings planned for tourists. They felt down to earth, genuine. Clearly some of them were ephemeral, their plasticity appealing yet temporary, which means they would not survive a generation. But what does in Latin America?

As I roamed from place to place, the events of September 11, the actual airplanes crashing into the Twin Towers, kept popping into my mind. That bright, cloudless Tuesday morning I was scheduled to teach, as usual. Having heard the news on the radio, I turned on the television set in the classroom, and the students and I watched as the second crash occurred in front of our eyes as well as the collapse of the buildings.

A few days later an acquaintance of mine said to me that the attacks were the moment the world had become truly global, since everyone was synchronized to the same time and place. Bizarrely, that synchronicity turned millions of us not only into witnesses but also into participants in a historical incident at which we weren't physically present.

Subsequently, the media became our therapist. As they fed us information, we rode a roller coaster of emotions, from shock to sadness and on to dismay, frustration, anger, and maybe some sort of internal peace. Memorials are incapable of provoking that type of response. They are merely an exhibitionist tombstone designed for us to think precise, teachable thoughts.

I was struck by how little technology the Buenos Aires memorials featured. In that sense, they took an old-fashioned approach to remembrance, which comforted me. The "Guerra Sucia," when it happened, was mostly kept off television screens. News of the desaparecidos circulated haphazardly, in whispers. Photos of torture sessions are unavailable. The bodies of victims were thrown into the River Plate, the perpetrators thus erasing evidence of their crime. In short, rather than a visual tragedy, this one took the shape of a shadow-puppet show.

Today we are infatuated with media. Our daily diet of TV shows, phones, music, Internet is enormous. Memory is intimately linked to the media now. Since we spend hours in front of a screen, we want the past to be digitized as well, betting that media images will live forever. But life happens in real time. And memory is unstable, evasive, insubstantial.

I came back from Buenos Aires humbled by my experience in the city. I hadn't gone there wanting to revisit my ambivalence toward memorials. The purpose of my trip was to produce the fotonovela. Yet that's what ended up happening: as I strolled around in my free time, the city, in a quiet, unsuspected way, had caused me to see the other side of the institutionalization of memory.

The conversation I had with David Grossman about the sacredness of the nation's soil forced itself on my consciousness. Ever since it was established in 1536 Buenos Aires has been painted the color of blood. One of its most famous stories is by Esteban Echeverría, a nineteenth-century romantic writer and political activist. Called "The Slaughterhouse," the story was written in 1839 and takes place during Lent as the tyrannical regime of the *caudillo* Juan Manuel de Rosas butchers the opposition. Echeverría's tale is gruesome but certainly not exceptional when one considers the city's record of historical massacres. There is no nation that isn't built on corpses.

Insidiously, those corpses never wash away in Latin America, a continent where, to borrow a famous line from William Faulkner's *Requiem for a Nun,* "the past is never dead. It's not even past." By conservative estimates, approximately one hundred thousand people were killed during the various repressive regimes in power in the twentieth century. In Chile, General Augusto Pinochet ruled with an iron fist from 1973 to 1990. In Argentina, the "Guerra Sucia" brought the population to its knees between 1969, when state repression targeted guerrillas, and 1983, when the freely elected civilian president Raúl Alfonsín took office.

Other countries, including Brazil, Uruguay, Colombia, Venezuela, Peru, and Paraguay, went through similar dark periods. Depending on when democracy was reinstated and how stable that form of government is, an effort to reclaim the memory of the desaparecidos and the murdered has been a recent nation-building project, one which includes memorials, political speeches, official holidays, books, academic symposia, movies, plays, photographic exhibits, and so on.

These cultural events aren't exclusively about expiation and reconciliation, no matter how difficult that reconciliation might be. Their existence also transforms the collective past. Victims whose identity was previously erased now have a place in the present. In some cases, the victims aren't only those who once opposed the government. There has been an evenhanded effort to explore the dilemma of soldiers and policemen who were pushed to perform torture and other acts of aggression and who appear to have been themselves the target of coercion by the authorities.

Whenever I'm in Buenos Aires, a place I'm deeply in love with, I take long walks. I learned to do that from reading Borges. Speaking of Borges, I remember the exact day I first visited the city: June 15, 1986. I had come, like so many other literary fans before me, tracing Borges's footsteps, looking for him, hoping the admired sage would welcome me to his apartment, where I would read him an ode by Pindar, a segment of *Paradise Lost* by John Milton, or a passage from *The Arabian Nights*.

It was not to be. I had been in Brazil the weeks prior and wasn't keeping up with world events. I felt disconnected, so the first thing I did early that morning as I left my hotel in Palermo was go to a newsstand. Surprisingly, Borges was on the front cover: he had died the day before in Geneva. The news had an unforeseen effect. Rather than focusing solely on Borges, I spent the next couple of weeks wandering around Buenos Aires, talking to its residents, looking for old books in antique bookstores, discovering secret alleyways. . . . I was hypnotized.

While I've seen the place grow until it has become overwhelming, just like my native Mexico City, I still spend hours walking through El Once, Recoleta, San Telmo, Belgrano, and Palermo. Most cities in the Southern Cone developed in haphazard fashion, one vision superimposed on another as regime after regime established itself by negating those that proceeded.

As a walker in the city (I sometimes dream I am a reincarnation of Alfred Kazin preparing to write *A Walker in the City*), I'm exposed to a dumpster of modernism. Parks, buildings, streets are constantly being revamped, their original architects' view of the future reimagined to suit a less inspired, more utilitarian reality. In fact, one gets the impression that the future in Buenos Aires is always dead; it was never the future in the first place.

During my fotonovela visit I had been uniquely attuned to an aspect of Buenos Aires I had not been able to register before, at least not as dramatically: the way it addresses pain. So I talked to people endlessly about my experience. I kept looking for ways to go back in order to understand the way Argentines handle pain collectively, to see how that understanding leaves an imprint on the landscape.

Fortunately, there was a sequel, an even more meaningful one. Max Page, a close friend who had spent a year with his family there on a Fulbright scholarship, handed me a copy of a booklet called *Memorias en la Ciudad*. At first I thought it was yet another book about memorials, another product of an industry than runs the risk of becoming overabundant, to the degree that its very mission risks being negated. That's what happened to the Holocaust: such has been the production of material related to it that the public, especially younger generations, feels saturated. Needless to say, saturation leads to numbness, numbness fosters disinterest, and disinterest is the mother of ignorance.

However, as I delved into the small, efficiently organized, handsomely illustrated volume, I realized how innovative its concept was: a guidebook to all the forty-eight neighborhoods in the city where state terrorism occurred during the

"Guerra Sucia." The contradiction at its heart was immediately apparent to me: tourism and memorials need not be incompatible if the term *tourism* is taken to mean authentic experience.

So the next time I departed for Buenos Aires, I took a copy of *Memorias en la Ciudad* with me, browsing as I once again progressed from place to place, revisiting sites I had already seen and stopping at new ones. Having the volume with me changed my perception profoundly. For one thing, the chaos of memory now had order. Someone had taken the time to map out the city, meticulously cataloging each tragic site, offering information about who was kidnapped or died there, name, age, profession, and when the act of state terrorism happened. Such was the history being offered that for the first time I was able to understand the implications: one faction of society was against another, except that it had an asymmetrical balance of power. It was state terrorism, plain and simple.

Then it dawned on me: the booklet was, in and of itself, a memorial—portable, open-ended, encouraging visitors to hopscotch (the word brings to mind Julio Cortázar's metaphysical games with time, space, and human emotion) through the past while making that past an essential, unavoidable part of the present, granting Buenos Aires a humane depth it might not otherwise display to the naked eye.

Looking back now at the effect *Memorias en la Ciudad* had on me, I'm still of two minds about memorials. But the book and the suffering undergone by the city it charts serve as a lesson in humility. History in Latin America is indeed an open wound. It need not bleed in vain, though. No doubt the act of remembering is a duty we all share, no matter where we live. The question is how to remember, what role that remembrance ought to have in our lives, what tools we use to bring it about, and how we channel the insights it fosters.

## Police stations as sites of illegal detention

Twenty-five of the fifty-two police stations in Buenos Aires have been identified as sites of illegal detention during the last dictatorship. According to testimonials, many victims of political persecution were taken directly to one of these police stations after their kidnapping. Police facilities functioned as sites of illegal detention and torture while continuing their normal activities, which included legal detentions. In most cases prisoners were held temporarily in police stations before being transferred to a Clandestine Detention Center or prison.

Agents reporting to the Argentine Army kidnapped Alberto Pites on August 19, 1976. According to his own testimony, he was taken from the home of a fellow activist, Juan Carlos Mazzaglia, in the neighborhood of Mataderos (see the judicial decision to charge Olivera Rovere in the human rights trials relating to the actions of the First Army Corps).

A group of plainclothes men entered the house, beat Pites, and blindfolded him. Someone they called "Colonel" interrogated him on the spot. Roughly twelve hours later they took Pites from the house with his eyes blindfolded and hands tied and moved him to Police Station 42. There he remained blindfolded for five days in an isolation cell and several times was taken to a small room, where he was tortured with an electric cattle prod (*picana**). He encountered Nora Marx and Carlos Alberto Quieto (see p. 244) in this police station; both remain disappeared.

Pites's mother petitioned for a writ of habeas corpus* on his behalf and received a response that "he [had been] arrested by personnel from Police Station 42 under orders from the First Army Corps."

After ten or twelve days in Police Station 42, Pites was moved to Police Station 34 in the neighborhood of Pompeya. Ten days later he was transferred again to Villa Devoto Prison (see p. 199), charged with possession of arms and explosives and with committing acts of violence. Pites declared that those items had never entered either his home or Mazzaglia's, where he was arrested.

A plaque on the door of Police Station 34 denounces more recent events, from 2002. It reads as follows: "Ezequiel Demonty, five years after your torture, disappearance, and murder. Nine police officers from this station took part in the events that ended your life. Because it is our duty to keep memory alive for a *nunca más* [never again]. Your son, mother, brothers and sisters, family members, friends, and neighbors." Ezequiel Demonty was tortured and murdered by police officers from this station on September 14, 2002, at the age of nineteen. The police shoved him at gunpoint and forced him to throw himself into the Riachuelo River. Two of his friends, aged sixteen and fourteen at the time, managed to survive after being thrown in as well. Thanks to their testimony,

PLAQUE INSTALLED IN FRONT OF POLICE STATION 34 TO REMEMBER EZEQUIEL DEMONTY.

two officers and a noncommissioned officer received life sentences for "torture leading to death." Six other officers received lesser sentences.

According to the 2009 report of the Centro de Estudios Legales y Sociales (CELS, Center for Legal and Social Studies), "Policies of remembrance and the prosecution of crimes committed under state terrorism are not enough if we do not examine the 'ESMAs' of today and do not reaffirm the principles and guarantees that limit the state's punitive power.

"The persistence of such violent practices twenty-five years after the return to democracy deserves special attention. Added to the challenge of trying to reform the behavior of bureaucracies permeated by the teachings of the dictatorship, one must also consider the ways in which increasing crime and insecurity have legitimized brutal actions by the police and armed forces" (CELS, 2009).

The following is a list of the police stations that have been identified as sites of illegal detention during the dictatorship:

**204. Police Station 1**
Lavalle 451, San Nicolás
Sector 1

**216. Police Station 2**
Perú 1050, San Telmo
Sector 4

**206. Police Station 4**
Tacuarí 770, Montserrat
Sector 1

**212. Police Station 5**
Venezuela 1931, Balvanera
Sector 3

**213. Police Station 6**
Lavalle 1958, Balvanera
Sector 3

**224. Police Station 11**
Díaz Vélez 5152, Caballito
Sector 8

**209. Police Station 17**
Av. Las Heras 1861, Recoleta
Sector 2

**217. Police Station 18**
Av. San Juan 1757, Constitución
Sector 4

**210. Police Station 19**
Charcas 2844, Recoleta
Sector 2

**214. Police Station 20**
Catamarca 1345, San Cristóbal
Sector 3

**207. Police Station 21.** Julián Alvarez 2373, Palermo. Sector 2.

**205. Police Station 22**
Av. Ing. Huergo 640, Montserrat
Sector 1

**208. Police Station 23**
Av. Santa Fe 4000, Palermo
Sector 2

**215. Police Station 26**
Montes de Oca 861, Barracas
Sector 4

**221. Police Station 29**
Santos Dumont 4350, Chacarita
Sector 6

**219. Police Station 33**
Mendoza 2263, Belgrano
Sector 5

**218. Police Station 34**
Quilmes 456, Nueva Pompeya
Sector 4

**220. Police Station 35.** Cuba 3145, Núñez. Sector 5

**225. Police Station 36**
Pedernera 3405, Villa Soldati
Sector 9

**226. Police Station 42**
Lisandro de la Torre 2243, Mataderos
Sector 9

**227. Police Station 44**
M. P. de Peralta 726, Versalles
Sector 9

**223. Police Station 45**
Cubas 4154, Villa Devoto
Sector 7

**222. Police Station 50**
Gaona 2738, Villa General Mitre
Sector 7

# Glossary

**Argentine Forensic Anthropology Team / Equipo Argentino de Antropología Forense:** An independent nongovernmental organization that applies the techniques of forensic science, particularly forensic anthropology, to investigations of human rights violations. Its work has been highly important in the process of identifying the remains of those disappeared and murdered by the last military dictatorship.

**Campo de Mayo:** A military base located on Highway 202 in the district of San Miguel, province of Buenos Aires. According to investigations conducted by the National Commission on the Disappearance of Persons (CONADEP), it was one of the largest Clandestine Detention Centers in Argentina between 1976 and 1980.

**CGT de los Argentinos / CGT of the Argentines:** A labor federation created in March 1968 after the labor movement divided over its response to the military coup of 1966 led by Juan Carlos Onganía. The existing General Confederation of Labor (CGT, Confederación General del Trabajo) split into two factions. The CGT Azopardo, led by Augusto T. Vandor, favored negotiations with the military government. The more combative and socialist CGT de los Argentinos, led by Raimundo Ongaro, adopted a confrontational stance toward the dictatorship and sought to integrate the union movement into a broader movement for political and social change. It supported grassroots labor organizations and opposed economic denationalization and the power of foreign monopolies in the Argentine economy. It faced harsh repression from the military dictatorship.

**Communist Vanguard / Vanguardia Comunista:** A Maoist political party founded in the early 1960s as a branch of the Argentine Socialist Vanguard Party.

**Cordobazo:** A popular uprising that took place on May 29, 1969, in the city of Córdoba, in which university students joined with workers after the "combative unions" called for a general strike. When the police were unable to contain the situation, the government called in the Army, which clashed in the streets with workers and students. This event hastened the resignation of Finance Minister Adalbert Krieger Vasena. The Cordobazo is considered a symbol of the heightened political mobilization and cross-sectoral alliances that characterized Argentina in this period.

**death flights:** A method used by the repressive forces to dispose of the bodies of prisoners who had been disappeared. Detainees were sedated with Pentothal and thrown alive into the ocean or the Río de la Plata from Armed Forces airplanes and helicopters.

**El Banco:** A Clandestine Detention Center located near the intersection of the Ricchieri Highway and Camino de Cintura (National Road No. 4) on Bridge 12 in the province of Buenos Aires. It functioned from late 1977 to mid-1978.

**El Vesubio:** A Clandestine Detention Center located roughly two hundred meters from the Ricchieri Highway on Camino de Cintura (National Road No. 4) in the town of Aldo Bonzi, district of La Matanza, province of Buenos Aires. It operated from 1975 until October 1978. Three buildings on the grounds belonging to the provincial Penitentiary Service were demolished in 1978.

***escrache:*** A form of shaming protest usually carried out in front of the homes of repressors and torturers who have avoided prosecution (see **H.I.J.O.S.**).

**Fátima Massacre:** This name was given to a massacre that took place on August 20, 1976, in the town of Fátima in the province of Buenos Aires. The security forces murdered thirty prisoners who had been detained and disappeared; they then blew up their bodies with explosives to prevent their identification. In July 2008 the former Federal Police precinct chiefs Carlos Gallone and Juan Carlos Lapuyole were sentenced to life in prison for their participation in the massacre.

**Full Stop Law / Ley de Punto Final (No. 23.492):** A law passed by the government of President Raúl Alfonsín in December 1986. It set a deadline of sixty days for new legal claims relating to human rights violations committed during the dictatorship. It also established a statute of limitations for crimes committed by civilians who had followed military orders. The law did not apply to cases involving the abduction and appropriation of minors.

The Argentine Congress nullified the Full Stop Law in November 2003. In a ruling of June 14, 2005, the Supreme Court found the law invalid and unconstitutional because it contravened international law and did not accord with the guidelines established by the Inter-American Court of Human Rights.

**Grassroots Peronism / Peronismo de Base (PB):** This movement, unofficially linked to the **Peronist Armed Forces** and rooted in the more radical sectors of the **Peronist Resistance**, aimed to build "an independent alternative for the Peronist working class." It fostered grassroots organizing within neighborhoods and unions and maintained a position critical of Peronism and Perón's leadership.

**habeas corpus:** A legal action that requires that a person in detention be brought before a judge. The judge must determine where the prisoner is being held and whether or not the detention is legal, and then has the power to demand his or her release. The vast majority of habeas corpus writs presented during the period of state terrorism were rejected, which meant that the family members of detainees received no response whatsoever from the state regarding the whereabouts of their loved ones.

**H.I.J.O.S. / Children for Identity and Justice Opposed to Forgetting and Silence (Hijos por la Identidad y la Justicia contra el Olvido y el Silencio):** A human rights organization formed in 1996 whose name is a play on the Spanish word for "children." It was founded by young people who sought to reclaim their identities as the children of people who had been disappeared, murdered, exiled, or detained as political prisoners by the military dictatorship. This group has spread the practice of the ***escrache,*** a type of public shaming protest against figures identified with the repression.

**La Cacha:** Clandestine Detention Center also known as El Casco and Arana 2. It operated from 1976 to 1978 in the former offices of Radio Provincia de Buenos Aires, an old run-down building with three stories and a basement that could hold over forty prisoners. It was located between streets 191, 47, 196, and 52 (in the General Belgrano railyard) next to the Olmos Prison in the town of Lisandro Olmos, west of the city of La Plata in the province of Buenos Aires.

**Law of Due Obedience / Ley de Obediencia Debida (No. 23. 521):** This law, passed in June 1987 during the presidency of Raúl Alfonsín, defined grades of legal responsibility for those accused of human rights crimes during the military dictatorship, distinguishing between those who issued orders and those who carried them out. It exempted middle- and low-ranking officers from prosecution for actions undertaken during the so-called antisubversive struggle on the grounds that they were following orders. The human rights movement strongly opposed the law. Legal experts argued that the law presumed that all officers had acted under a state of coercion that gave them no choice but to follow orders, and it prevented judges from investigating the circumstances case by case.

The Argentine Congress nullified the Law of Due Obedience in November 2003. In a ruling of June 14, 2005, the Supreme Court found the law invalid and unconstitutional because it contravened international law and did not accord with the guidelines established by the Inter-American Court of Human Rights.

**martial law:** A law that permits the Armed Forces to exercise control over the national territory in exceptional situations and emergencies with the goal of restoring order. Following this law, the military may order arrests to investigate disruptive activities; hold prisoners in solitary confinement for a set period of time; suspend radio and television broadcasts and the distribution of print media; confiscate, suspend, or censor publications; search private homes; occupy private properties and use them for military purposes; use whatever force is necessary to dissolve seditious groups; and apply the death penalty. Under martial law, military tribunals may be used to prosecute crimes against national and international state security and presumed threats to public order. Any person present during an act deemed a threat to public order could be presumed guilty.

**Montoneros:** A self-identified Peronist armed political movement that emerged out of Catholic nationalist groups in 1970. Its first public act involved the kidnapping and eventual murder of General Pedro E. Aramburu, the officer responsible for the military coup against Juan Domingo Perón in 1955 and the execution of Peronist activists in 1956. The Montoneros won broad support among Peronists and young people as the leading force on the left wing of Peronism. It may be considered the most important armed organization of the period because of its capacity for organization and mobilization of supporters as well as its significant influence on the political scene.

**Montonero Counteroffensive / Contraofensiva Montonera:** In 1979 the **Montonero** leadership in exile decided to launch a counteroffensive against the dictatorship in the belief that popular resistance had significantly weakened the military's power. Many Montonero activists and leaders secretly returned to Argentina to take part in Counteroffensives I and II, which took place in 1979 and 1980. Their activities included jamming television broadcasts to disseminate messages against the dictatorship. Most of these activists were killed or kidnapped by the repressive forces.

**National Commission on the Disappearance of Persons / Comisión Nacional sobre la Desaparición de Personas (CONADEP):** President Raúl Alfonsín decreed the creation of this commission in December 1983. It was made up of ten public figures nominated by the executive office and three representatives of the Argentine Chamber of Deputies. The CONADEP collected testimony about disappearances and investigated human rights violations that occurred between 1976 and 1983. In its first year of operation it received thousands of claims and identified hundreds of Clandestine Detention Centers that had operated throughout the country during the years of state terrorism. In September 1984 the commission members appeared before the Argentine Congress to present their report, which was soon published under the title *Nunca Más* (Never Again).

**National Executive Power / A disposición del Poder Ejecutivo Nacional (PEN):** A situation in which a person may be detained indefinitely without charge during a state of siege under orders issued by the National Executive. The detainee may be someone whose trial has been dismissed, who has been acquitted by the justice system, or who is not facing trial at all. This legal provision was used by the last military dictatorship in most detentions of political prisoners.

**pardon(s):** The presidential power to grant reprieves and commute legal sentences. In 1989 and 1990 President Carlos Saúl Menem signed two decrees pardoning the officers who had been imprisoned or were still awaiting trial for human rights crimes committed during the military dictatorship of 1976 to 1983. The pardons also extended to military officers who had participated in the *carapintada* (literally "painted face") uprisings against the Alfonsín regime, and to members of the armed guerrilla movements whose prosecution had been ordered by President Alfonsín via Decree 157, passed in 1983. The former commanding officers serving out sentences handed down in the **Trial of the Military Juntas** of 1985 were released.

The human rights movement strongly condemned these pardons, and legal experts deemed them unconstitutional on the grounds that pardons cannot be extended to those who have been convicted and are awaiting sentencing. Rodolfo Barra, the minister of justice in Menem's administration, argued that this application of the pardon law was indeed possible. He drew on supposedly ambiguous wording in the Constitution to argue that the relevant article did allow for pardons even when defendants had not yet been sentenced

***patota*:** This was the name given to the **Special Task Groups** that carried out the kidnappings and disappearances ordered under the last military dictatorship.

**People's Revolutionary Army / Ejército Revolucionario del Pueblo:**
See **PRT-ERP**

**Peronist Armed Forces / Fuerzas Armadas Peronistas (FAP):** A revolutionary Peronist group that emerged in 1967 and focused on grassroots organizing in neighborhoods and factories to build support for its armed operations. Some of its leaders were arrested that year in Taco Ralo, in the province of Tucumán, as they attempted to form a guerrilla cell.

**Peronist Resistance / Resistencia Peronista:** The name given to the neighborhood, union, and youth resistance movements that formed after the overthrow of General Juan Domingo Perón in 1955 and that lasted, in one form or other, until his return to power in 1973. The main objectives were to resist the prohibition of Peronism and to achieve Perón's return from exile.

**Peronist Revolutionary Tendency / Tendencia Revolucionaria del Peronismo:** The name given to the civilian political groups and leaders who supported the armed Peronist movement known as the **Montoneros**. It was also known as La Tendencia (The Tendency).

**Peronist Shantytown Movement / Movimiento Villero Peronista:** A political organization based in the shantytowns and allied with the revolutionary movement within Peronism. Its aim has been to raise the political consciousness of shantytown dwellers and promote their political activism.

**Peronist University Youth Movement / Juventud Universitaria Peronista (JUP):** The university wing of the **Peronist Youth Movement**, linked to the **Montoneros**.

**Peronist Workers Youth Movement / Juventud Trabajadora Peronista (JTP):** A union group allied with the **Montoneros** that presented itself as an alternative to the unions within the General Confederation of Labor (CGT, Confederación General del Trabajo). While it never gained power in the country's largest unions, it played a significant role at the level of shop floor organizing in a number of workplaces.

**Peronist Youth Movement / Juventud Peronista (JP):** The youth wing of Peronism, which played a major political role in the 1970s. It is important to distinguish between the original JP, organized in 1958, and later groups using the same initials, many of them allied with the **Montoneros**. These later groups were the main support for the mass demonstrations of 1972 to 1975.

***picana* / cattle prod:** An instrument of torture used to give prisoners electric shocks. In the jargon used in the Clandestine Detention Centers it was also called the machine (*máquina*).

***pinza*:** A road-blocking maneuver designed to stop traffic in order to check identification and vehicle registrations.

**Police Station 5 in La Plata:** Located on Diagonal 74 between 23rd and 24th Streets, it functioned as a site of illegal detention between 1976 and 1978.

**Police Station 8 in La Plata:** Located at the corner of 7th and 74th Streets, it functioned as a site of illegal detention between 1976 and 1978.

**Pozo de Arana / Arana Pit:** Known also as Arana, Puesto Zorzal, and El Campito, this Clandestine Detention Center operated on the grounds of the Anti-Rustling Office of Arana, located at the corner of 137th and 640th Streets in Estación Arana, in the province of Buenos Aires. The testimony of survivors has established that more than one Clandestine Detention Center operated in Arana, but it has not yet been possible to establish exactly how many.

**Pozo de Banfield / Banfield Pit:** A Clandestine Detention Center located in the suburban municipality of Lomas de Zamora, at the corner of Siciliano and Vernet Streets, two blocks from Avenida 10 de Septiembre de 1861, also known as Camino Negro (the Black Way).

**PRT-ERP:** The People's Revolutionary Army (ERP, Ejército Revolucionario del Pueblo) emerged in 1970 as the armed wing of the Workers' Revolutionary Party (PRT, Partido Revolucionario de los Trabajadores), a Trotskyist party founded in 1965 that favored seizing political power through armed struggle. With Mario Roberto Santucho as its leader, the PRT-ERP led a guerrilla cell in the province of Tucumán that was wiped out by the Army. Its failed attack on the Monte Chingolo Barracks in December 1975 brought about its decline, and after July 1976 most of its leading members had been killed, disappeared, imprisoned, or forced into exile.

**Revolutionary Armed Forces / Fuerzas Armadas Revolucionarias (FAR):** A Marxist guerrilla group that emerged on the public scene in the early 1970s. It merged with the **Montoneros** in the latter part of 1973.

**Revolutionary Peronism / Peronismo Revolucionario:** The name given to a coalition of activists from a broad range of social groups (workers, students, professionals, and so on) and from different political tendencies, including the Peronist Resistance, left-wing nationalism, progressive Christian movements, nationalists, and various branches of Marxism. The group's first meeting took place in August 1968 in the offices of the Buenos Aires Pharmacy Union. Its second meeting, in January 1969 in the town of Pajas Blancas, province of Córdoba, attracted a greater number of participants who collectively declared their support for armed struggle. The name Revolutionary Peronism quickly came to be applied to all left-wing tendencies within Peronism.

**Seré Mansion / Mansión Seré:** The former estate of the Seré family located at No. 48 Blas Pereira Street on the border between the suburban municipalities of Castelar and Ituzaingó in the province of Buenos Aires. It functioned as a Clandestine Detention Center in the early years of the dictatorship, under the command of the VII Air Brigade of Morón and the Palomar Air Base. In early 1978 the repressive forces abandoned the site and burned it down. It was demolished in 1985, and excavation work began in 2002 with the goal of recovering it as a site of social memory.

**Sheraton:** This Clandestine Detention Center, also known as the Embudo (Funnel), functioned inside the police detachment of Villa Insuperable. It was located at the corner of Quintana and Tapalqué Streets in the suburban municipality of La Matanza, in the province of Buenos Aires, four blocks from the Avenida General Paz.

**Special Task Group / Grupo de Tareas:** The name given to the squads of unidentified men who carried out the kidnappings and disappearances ordered through the military's plan of repression. The size and structure of these groups varied over time and was dependent upon the Clandestine Detention Centers to which they were assigned and the repressive forces overseeing them.

**state of siege:** A state of emergency involving the temporary suspension of constitutional guarantees whose terms are described in Article 23 of the National Constitution. Every military dictatorship and several elected governments in Argentina have decreed a state of siege. In its second communiqué of March 25, 1976, the last military dictatorship ratified the state of siege established by the government of María Estela Martínez de Perón in November 1974. It remained in effect until October 29, 1983.

**Trelew Massacre:** The name given to a massacre of nineteen political prisoners that occurred on August 22, 1972, under the military government led by General Alejandro A. Lanusse. The prisoners, all militants from the armed guerrilla movements (**Montoneros**, **Revolutionary Armed Forces [FAR]**, and **PRT-ERP**), were shot dead in the Almirante Zar naval base in Trelew, in Patagonia. They had all been part of a failed escape by a group of twenty-five prisoners from Rawson Prison that had taken place a week earlier, on August 15. Only six of the prisoners managed to cross the border into Chile. The remaining nineteen turned themselves in to Federal Judge Alejandro Godoy at the Trelew Airport, in front of a large group of journalists. They were transferred to the naval base, where the massacre occurred. The testimony of three prisoners who had survived the shooting but who were soon "transferred" to another facility brought news of these events to the public and prompted widespread condemnation. The brutal violence exercised by the state was followed by censorship and persecution of the journalists who reported on this event.

**Trial of the Military Juntas:** The public trial of the members of the first three military juntas that governed Argentina from 1976 to 1982. The Criminal and Correctional Court of the City of Buenos Aires conducted this trial between April and December 1985 and allowed full public access to the proceedings, a measure that broke with established judicial practice at the time. The former commanding officers Jorge Rafael Videla, Emilio Eduardo Massera, Orlando Ramón

Agosti, Armando Lambruschini, Roberto Eduardo Viola, Omar Domingo Rubens Graffigna, Leopoldo Fortunato Galtieri, Jorge Isaac Anaya, and Basilio Arturo Ignacio Lami Dozo were all tried for crimes established by the Penal Code: unlawful deprivation of liberty, the application of torture, homicide, and theft. Judge León Carlos Arslanián delivered the court's ruling on December 9, 1985. The sentences were as follows: life imprisonment for Jorge Rafael Videla and Emilio Massera; seventeen years imprisonment for Roberto Viola; eight years imprisonment for Roberto Lambruschini; and four years for Orlando Agosti. The other defendants were acquitted. The Trial of the Military Juntas marked a historic achievement both for Argentina and for the international community. It was the first time that a country's legitimate civilian institutions had been used to try its own repressors following a period of state terrorism. At the same time, the trial forced Argentine society to face up to the unimaginable violence that had been perpetrated by the state but that had involved the entire society to some extent. The revelation and investigation of those horrific crimes became, in those years, the most important steps taken toward a democratic future governed by the rule of law. The former commanding officers sentenced in the Trial of the Military Juntas were released in 1990 following the **pardon** issued by President Carlos Menem.

**Triple A:** The Argentine Anticommunist Alliance, also known by its initials as AAA. It was an extreme right-wing paramilitary organization founded and led by José López Rega, minister of social welfare during Perón's third presidency. The Triple A employed political murders, death threats, bombings, and black lists to achieve its goals. It first came onto the public scene in early 1974 with an assassination attempt against a renowned defense lawyer who had represented political prisoners. The group committed hundreds of murders that year, and the figure increased dramatically the following year. Its most well known victims included Father Carlos Mugica, an influential figure in the Movement of Priests for the Third World, and Rodolfo Ortega Peña, a famous lawyer who defended political prisoners and was highly influential within the Peronist left.

**Truth Trials / Juicios por la Verdad:** Judicial proceedings conducted since 1999 in federal courts throughout the country to investigate the circumstances surrounding the disappearance of persons. The purpose of these trials is to provide family members of the disappeared with the truth about what happened to their loved ones. They do not have the power to establish criminal responsibility or establish sentences, and they operate without defendants. However, those accused of participating in the repression must appear before the courts as witnesses and can be prosecuted for perjury if they lie. The most important examples are the Truth Trials conducted by the Federal Courts of Appeal in La Plata, Buenos Aires, Bahía Blanca, Mar del Plata, Córdoba, and Rosario. The trials restore the family members' right to the truth while also respecting civil society's right to information.

**Tupamaro National Liberation Movement / Movimiento de Liberación Nacional Tupamaros:** An Uruguayan guerrilla movement that emerged in the 1960s, led by Raúl Sendic.

**underground:** Activists "went underground," usually living under false identities, to avoid persecution and arrest.

**Union of Secondary School Students / Unión de Estudiantes Secundarios (UES):** Association of secondary school students created in the early 1950s during the presidency of Juan Domingo Perón. Linked to the **Montoneros** in the 1970s, it was a powerful mobilizing force within the student movement.

**Workers' Politics / Política Obrera:** A Trotskyist political group founded in 1964 when a group of young people split with the group Reagrupar with the goal of forming a working-class political party.

**Workers' Revolutionary Party / Partido Revolucionario de los Traba-jadores:** see **PRT-ERP**.

# Abbreviations

**AFIP:** Administración Federal de Ingresos Públicos / Federal Administration of Public Revenue

**AMIA:** Asociación Mutual Israelita Argentina / Jewish–Argentine Mutual Association

**ATE:** Asociación de Trabajadores del Estado / Government Employees Association

**CCD:** Centro Clandestino de Detención / Clandestine Detention Center

**CGT:** Confederación General del Trabajo / General Confederation of Labor

**CONICET:** Consejo Nacional de Investigaciones Científicas y Técnicas / National Scientific and Technical Research Council

**CTA:** Central de Trabajadores Argentinos / Argentine Workers' Federation

**CTERA:** Confederación Trabajadores de la Educación de la República Argentina / Confederation of Education Workers of the Argentine Republic

**DINA:** Dirección de Inteligencia Nacional (Chile) / National Intelligence Directorate of Chile

**ENTEL:** Empresa Nacional de Telecomunicaciones / National Telecommunications Company

**FOETRA:** Federación de Obreros y Empleados Telefónicos de la República Argentina / Federation of Telephone Workers and Employees of the Argentine Republic

**INDEC:** Instituto Nacional de Estadística y Censos / National Institute of Statistics and Censuses

**SEDRONAR:** Secretaría de Programación para la Prevención de la Drogadicción y la Lucha contra el Narcotráfico / Secretariat for the Prevention of Drug Addiction and the Fight against Drug Trafficking

**SeTCIP:** Secretaría para la Tecnología, la Ciencia y la Innovación Productiva / Secretariat for Technology, Science, and Productive Innovation

**TELAM:** Agencia Nacional de Noticias / National News Agency

**UBA:** Universidad de Buenos Aires / University of Buenos Aires

**UES:** Unión de Estudiantes Secundarios / Union of Secondary School Students

**UTE:** Unión de Trabajadores de la Educación / Education Workers Union

# Works Cited

## BOOKS AND ARTICLES


Arrosagaray, E. 2006. *Biografía de Azucena Villaflor: creadora del Movimiento Madres de Plaza de Mayo* ([repr.]). Buenos Aires: Ministerio de Justicia y Derechos Humanos de la Nación Argentina Secretaría de Derechos Humanos Área de Comunicación y Prensa.

Basualdo, Victoria. 2005. "Cine documental e historia reciente." *Lucha Armada en la Argentina*, no. 4 (October–November), 68–75.

Blaustein, Eduardo, and Martin Zubieta. 2006. *Decíamos ayer: La prensa argentina bajo el proceso.* Buenos Aires: Colihue.

Calveiro, Pilar. 1998. *Poder y desaparición: Los campos de concentración en la Argentina.* Buenos Aires: Colihue.

Caparrós, Martín. 1986. *No velas a tus muertos.* Buenos Aires: De la Flor.

CELS (Centro de Estudios Legales y Sociales). 1986. *Terrorismo de Estado. 692 Responsables.* Buenos Aires: CELS.

———. 2009. *Derechos Humanos en Argentina Informe 2009.* Buenos Aires: Siglo XXI.

CONADEP (Comisión Nacional sobre la Desaparición de Personas). 1984. *Nunca más.* Buenos Aires: Eudeba.

Crenzel, Emilio. 2008. *La historia política del Nunca más: La memoria de las desapariciones en la argentina.* Buenos Aires: Siglo XXI.

D'Andrea Mohr, José Luis. 1998. *El escuadrón perdido.* Buenos Aires: Planeta.

Déotte, Martine. 2000. "Desaparición y ausencia de duelo." In Nelly Richard, ed., *Políticas y estéticas de la memoria,* 93–97. Santiago de Chile: Cuarto Propio.

Garaño, Santiago, and Werner Pertot. 2003. *La otra juvenilia: Militancia y represión en el Colegio Nacional de Buenos Aires, 1971–1986.* Buenos Aires: Biblos.

Gorini, Ulises. 2006. *La rebelión de las madres: Historia de las Madres de Plaza de Mayo. Tomo I (1976–1983).* Buenos Aires: Norma.

Gurucharri, Eduardo. 2001. *Un militar entre obreros y guerrilleros.* Buenos Aires: Colihue.

Jelin, Elizabeth, and Victoria Langland, comps. 2003. *Monumentos, memoriales y marcas territoriales.* Buenos Aires: Siglo XXI.

Kimel, Eduardo. 1986. *La Masacre de San Patricio.* Buenos Aires: Lohlé-Lumen.

Longoni, Ana, and Gustavo Bruzzone. 2008. *El Siluetazo.* Buenos Aires: Adriana Hidalgo.

Obra Colectiva de 112 prisioneras políticas entre 1974 y 1983. 2006. *Nosotras, presas políticas.* Buenos Aires: Nuestra América.

Paleo, Natalia. 2004. "Una historia familiar." Manuscript.

Peregrino Fernández, Rodolfo. 1983. *Autocrítica policial.* Cuadernos para la democracia, no. 10. Buenos Aires. El Cid Editor.

Rice, Patricio, and Luis Torres. 2007. *En Medio de la Tempestad: Los Hermanitos del Evangelio en la Argentina (1959–1977).* Montevideo: Dobleclic.

San Cristóbal Residents Against Impunity (Vecinos de San Cristóbal contra la impunidad). 2008. *Compañeros Detenidos–Desaparecidos del barrio de San Cristóbal.* Buenos Aires: Edición de los autores.

Schmucler, Héctor. 2007a. "¿Para qué recordar?" In *Seminario 2006. Entre el pasado y el futuro: Los jóvenes y la transmisión de la experiencia argentina reciente.* Eudeba: Ministerio de Educación.

———. 2007b. "La inquietante relación entre espacios y memorias." Available at www.memoriaabierta.org.ar/materiales/pdf/hector_schmucler.pdf.

Seisdedos, Gabriel. 1996. *El honor de Dios: Mártires Palotinos, la historia silenciada de un crimen impune.* Buenos Aires: Lohlé-Lumen.

Sigal, Silvia. 2006. *La Plaza de Mayo.* Buenos Aires: Siglo XXI.

Urso, Norberto Pedro. 2002. *Mansión Seré: Un vuelo hacia el horror.* Buenos Aires: Ediciones de la Memoria.

Verbitsky, Horacio. 1986. "La investigación inconclusa de Rodolfo J. Walsh: López Rega, la CIA y la Triple A." *El periodista de Buenos Aires,* no. 80 (March 21–27).

Walsh, Rodolfo. 2006 [1957]. *Operación Masacre.* Buenos Aires: De la Flor.

———. 2006 [1977]. "Carta abierta de un escritor a la Junta Militar." In Walsh, *Operación Masacre.*

## DOCUMENTS AND ARCHIVES

Archivo de Memoria Abierta, Fondo "Fiscalía Luis Moreno Ocampo."

FMA. Fondo Memoria Abierta.

Buenos Aires Forum for the Enforcement of Human Rights. 1973. *Proceso a la explotación y a la represión en la Argentina.* Buenos Aires, n.p.

CTA. 2007. "La Germán presentó un mural en homenaje a las Madres." By Mariano Vázquez. October 11. Online at http://archivo.cta.org.ar/La-German-presento-un-mural-en.html.

H.I.J.O.S. 2009. *H.I.J.O.S. Hijos por la identidad y la justicia contra el olvido y el silencio.* Section "Hermanos/Preguntas frecuentes." Online at http://hijos-capital.org.ar.

Ministry of Culture and Education. 1977. *Subversión en el ámbito educativo (conozcamos a nuestro enemigo)*. Buenos Aires: McyE.

National Executive Branch. 1979. *El terrorismo en la Argentina: Evolución de la delincuencia terrorista en la Argentina*. Buenos Aires: Gobierno Nacional.

Permanent Assembly for Human Rights. 2001. Press release on the Truth Trials issued by the La Plata office, May 23.

Poder Judicial de la Nación, "Causa Primer Cuerpo de Ejército." Subzona Capital Federal: Procesamiento Olivera Róvere (27 de abril de 2004), available online at Centro de Información Judicial, http://www.cij.gov.ar/causa-primer-cuerpo-del-ejercito.html.

*Populorum Progressio*. 1967. Papal encyclical.

San Patricio Parish Church and Human Rights Office of the City of Buenos Aires (2001). *4 de Julio de 1976 – 4 de Julio de 2001. 25 años de la Masacre de San Patricio*. Buenos Aires.

Santoro, Roberto. 1976. "Letter of Denunciation" [Carta de denuncia]. Presented to the Confederation of Latin American Writers, June 1976.

## NEWSPAPERS AND MAGAZINES

*Clarín*. "Murió Cipriano Reyes, testigo de casi un siglo de historia argentina." August 2, 2001.

*Clarín*. "Fueron hallados 30 cadáveres en Pilar. Repudio del gobierno." August 21, 1976.

*Clarín*. "El albañil que construyó el pozo donde estuvo detenido." September 23, 2006.

*Clarín*. August 5, 1976.

*El Descamisado* no. 10. July 24, 1973.

*El País* (Spain). "Noruega vende por razones éticas títulos de Freeport y de Wal-Mart." June 7, 2006.

*La Causa Peronista* 1, no. 1. July 1974.

*La Nación*. "Recuerdo de Mario Abel Amaya." Sepetember 30, 2001.

*La Nación*. "Halláronse 30 cadáveres en la localidad de Fátima." August 21, 1976.

*La Nación*. November 3, 1977.

*La Nación*. July 5, 1976.

*Página/12*. "La hora de la indignación." September 4, 2004.

*Página/12*. "Me torturaron en Coordinación Federal durante 15 días sin descanso." August 12, 2007.

*Página/12*. December 1, 2008.

*Página/12*. June 29, 2003.

*Página/12*. "En esta carrera, gana la memoria." March 30, 2003.

*Radar: Suplemento cultural de Página/12*. "Operación Ja Ja." October 1, 2006.

*Revista Cuestionario* no. 1. May 1973.

*Revista Extra* 4, no. 41. December 1968.

## FILMS

*Actualización Doctrinaria*. 1971. Octavio Getino and Fernando Solanas.

*Argentina, mayo de 1969: los caminos de la liberación*. 1969. Enrique José Juárez.

*Flores de septiembre*. 2003. Pablo Osores, Roberto Testa, and Nicolás Wainszelbaum.

*Informes y Testimonios*. 1973. Diego Eijo Jr., Eduardo Giorello, Ricardo Moretti, Alfredo O. Oroz, Carlos Vallina, and Silvia Vega.

*La hora de los hornos*. 1969. Fernando Solanas.

*La mirada de los otros*. 1980. Fernando Solanas.

*La revolución peronista*. 1971. Octavio Getino and Fernando Solanas.

*Los traidores*. 1973. Raymundo Gleyzer.

*Milagros no hay, los desaparecidos de Mercedes Benz*. 2003. Gabriela Weber.

*Operación Masacre*. 1972. Jorge Cederrón.

*Raymundo*. 2002. Ernesto Ardito and Virna Molina.

*Ya es tiempo de violencia*. 1969. Enrique José Juárez.

## Acknowledgments

Jorge Auat

Valeria Barbuto

David Blaustein

Daniel Bustamante

Fátima Cabrera

Juan Carlos Cena

Emilio Crenzel

Daniel Divinsky

Isabel Fernández Blanco

Fernando García

Adrián Gorelik

Elizabeth Jelin

Ana Longoni

Diego Martínez

María José Méndez

Julieta Parellada

Patrick Ricc

Mariana Satrángelo

Jimena Valdez

Carolina Varsky

Miguel Vitagliano

Centro de Estudios Legales y Sociales – CELS

Equipo Argentino de Antropología Forense – EAAF